CW01084356

CALTON HILL

CALTON HILL

AND THE PLANS FOR EDINBURGH'S THIRD NEW TOWN

Kirsten Carter McKee

First published in Great Britain in 2018 by
John Donald, an imprint of Birlinn Ltd

West Newington House
10 Newington Road
Edinburgh
EH9 1QS

www.birlinn.co.uk

ISBN: 978 1 910900 17 8

The publishers gratefully acknowledge the support of
The Edinburgh World Heritage Trust,
The Strathmartine Trust

and The Marc Fitch Fund

towards the publication of this book

British Library Cataloguing-in-Publication Data
A catalogue record for this book is available on request from the British Library

Designed and typeset by Jules Akel
Printed and bound in Latvia by PNB Print

Contents

To
Paul, Holly and Sandy
for their infinite patience
and love

Acknowledgements

Many people should be particularly thanked for their help with the research, collation and production of this book. The following list is by no means exhaustive: John Lowrey, Dr Jim Lawson, Dr Ruxandra-Iulia Stoica, Dr Alex Bremner, Professor Iain Boyd Whyte, Margaret Stewart, Dr Dimitris Theodossopoulos and Dr Viccy Coltman at the University of Edinburgh; Fiona MacDonald, Adam Wilkinson and the staff and board at Edinburgh World Heritage; Mairi Sutherland, Neville Moir, Hugh Andrew and the staff at Birlinn who helped bring this publication together, including indexer Roger Smith, designer Jules Akel and copy-editor Nicola Wood. Thanks also go to the late Professor Charles McKean, Professor Johnny Rodger, Dr James Simpson OBE and Dr Allen Simpson. Jane Brettle, Diane Watters, Dr Anthony Lewis and Dr Joe Rock have also been generous with their support, time and advice.

This work has been largely archive-based, and assistance from the staff at Edinburgh City Archives, Edinburgh City Library, the National Library of Scotland, the Royal Scottish Academy, the National Gallery of Scotland, the University of Edinburgh Library (in particular, those based in the Art and Architecture library and the Centre for Research Collections), Historic Environment Scotland Archives, the Burns Archive in Ayrshire, the RIBA Archives at the Victoria and Albert Museum, the British Library, the Bodleian Library at the University of Oxford and the National Archives at Kew have been extremely important in putting together this work.

Funding for this publication was generously provided by the Marc Fitch Fund, the Strathmartine Trust, and Edinburgh World Heritage.

Kirsten Carter McKee

Plate 1—Aerial view of Calton Hill taken from the east.
© Edinburgh World Heritage Trust Library

Introduction

At the eastern end of the Edinburgh World Heritage Site, a protrusion of volcanic rock known as Calton Hill is situated on the northern side of the Waverley Valley (Plate 1). This area sits approximately 100m above sea level at its highest point—around 20m higher than Princes Street in the First 'New Town' and at roughly the same height as the Castle Esplanade in the 'Old Town' of Edinburgh.[1] During the early nineteenth century, the hill and its land to the north were developed, to extend the city of Edinburgh towards the Port of Leith, in order to open up new routes of access and communications between the port, the city and the surrounding lands to the south and east. The resulting development provoked debates on the best approach to the development of the urban landscape, the suitability of certain architectural styles within that, and the use of public funds for large-scale urban development projects. In addition, the visual prominence of the hill presented a stage for massive changes to the understanding of the city's boundaries, the relationship between the Old and New Towns, and Edinburgh's relationship with its surrounding countryside. This blurring of the rural and the urban alongside new interpretations of the classical and the gothic further emphasised the discordance between societal classes, initially marked out by the mid-eighteenth-century expansion of the first New Town and further emphasised during the city's industrial expansion in the latter half of the nineteenth century.

The clarity of the argument that defined the hill's architectural character as an allegorical commentary on Scotland's role within the constitutional development of the United Kingdom became muddied throughout the nineteenth century, as shifts in both societal perceptions and government constructs resulted in an evolution of the hill and its structures within the mindset of the Scottish populus. Although the structural evolution of the site during the later nineteenth and twentieth centuries had less visual impact on the city, as Scottish national identity swayed from a political to a culturally led discussion in architectural terms, perceptions of the structures on Calton Hill were considered to be representative of Scottish support for the construct of the British state during the nineteenth century. This was further confirmed by the development of the Scottish Office in the 1930s on the southern side of the hill, and the failed establishment of a Scottish parliament in 1979, which was to be sited in the vacant Royal High School building. This culminated in the site becoming the focus for grassroots led campaigns for Scottish independence and home rule by the later twentieth century.

This book therefore focuses on the changing relationship between the perception of the hill and its structures over time, by exploring the architectural evolution of the site within broader aesthetic, social and political dialogues. It looks at how much the site, its structures and its development represent the nuances that define Scotland as a nation, and helps us to understand how Scots viewed their identity, within both a British and Scottish context, from the late eighteenth to the early twentieth centuries.

GEOGRAPHICAL LIMITATIONS

Due to the wide variety of themes that this book explores, and the extended timeframe that it covers, the geographical limitations of the study area are mercurial in their extent, change focus with the issues being discussed throughout the text. However, for clarity and for ease of reading, the physical study area has been defined as that of the external limits of Playfair's 1819 plan for the Third New Town (see Plate 3.1b), which today is defined through the following locations: the southern limit is the North Back of Canongate; the northern limit is the bottom of Leith Walk, at the intersection with Great Junction Street; the western limit is where Waterloo Place meets Princes Street, and follows Leith Street to the top of Broughton Street; and the eastern boundary is at the junction of Easter Road, Regent Road and Abbeymount, running down Easter Road to meet Leith Walk at its northernmost point.

HISTORY OF THE SITE BEFORE ITS DEVELOPMENT

The visual prominence of Calton Hill on the periphery of Edinburgh created a special relationship between this site and its surrounding landscape in the eighteenth century, which existed well before its development into a suburb of the city. Calton Hill's use before the 1770s is discussed in detail in Malcolm Irvine's nineteenth-century publication,[2] and Henry Paton's articles from the 1930s on the Barony of Calton, in *The Book of the Old Edinburgh Club*.[3] These, alongside late twentieth-century archival

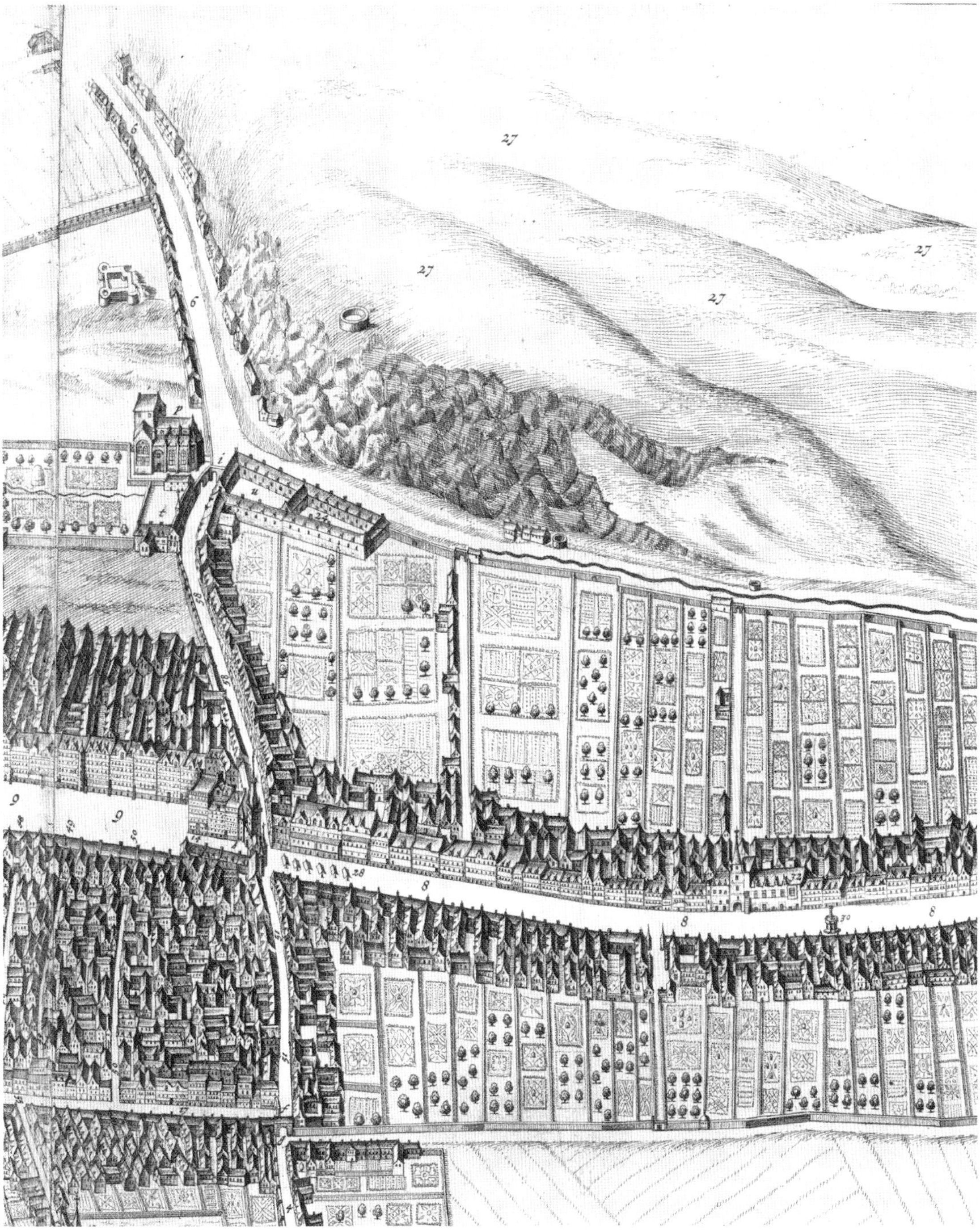

Plate 2—James Gordon, *Edinodunensis Tabulam*, 1647. Detail of Calton Hill and the associated hamlets on the north side of Edinburgh. © Courtesy of National Library of Scotland

analysis by Bill McQueen, mostly carried out using the City of Edinburgh Council Archives,[4] and the archaeological analysis carried out by AOC Archaeology Group,[5] note the main activities on the hill from the prehistoric period to the eighteenth century. These include the area being a possible prehistoric hill fort,[6] an area for quarrying, a jousting ground[7] and an area for pastoral[8] and arable farming.[9] In addition, its open landscape, and its elevation and proximity to Edinburgh were considered a useful viewing point to the city and its environs to the west and east from the north side of Edinburgh.[10]

Much of the development in the vicinity of Calton Hill before the 1800s was of residences that made up small hamlets surrounding the hill. These were located at the southwest foot of the hill, in the hamlet of Calton, which is depicted on Gordon's map of 1647[11] (Plate 2) and at the western side, near Greenside, in the hamlet of Craigengelt, which was later renamed 'Mud Island'.[12] Being outside the boundaries of the royal burgh, the ownership and management of the land was in the superiority of the Balmerino family of Restalrig, who, under John Elphinstone, 2nd Lord Balmerino[13] granted a deed of gift in favour of Calton in 1631 to bring the inhabitants around Calton Hill together into a society that would provide exclusive rights over trade and taxation within the barony.[14] In 1718, this society, by then known as the Incorporated Trades of Calton, opened a burial ground halfway up the summit of Calton Hill. During the early seventeenth century, the legal rights of the kirk and parish of Restalrig—the kirk associated with the hamlet of Calton—had been conferred upon the parish of South Leith, as the destruction of the collegiate church of St Triduana in Restalrig during the Reformation

in the mid sixteenth century had removed the traditional burial ground and place of worship for those living on Lord Balmerino's lands.[15] As a result, residents of Calton began using South Leith Kirk and Kirkyard for both religious worship and the interment of the dead.[16] This became problematic not only because it was a mile and a half to the north of the hamlet, but also because the high volume of burials that occurred at this site resulted in residents of Calton only gaining use of South Leith burial ground on specific times and days of the week. In the early eighteenth century therefore, permission was granted to the inhabitants of Calton by Lord Balmerino to form a burial ground on an area of land on Calton Hill.[17]

Due to the nature of the establishment of the burial ground, the management of 'Old' Calton has never been under the control of a parish kirk,[18] but instead was run as a business by the Incorporated Trades of Calton.[19] This society used the money collected from trade dues (the annual payment for the privilege of being freemen of Calton), the renting of burial plots, the provision of mortcloths for the dead and the interment of the recently-departed within the Old Calton burial ground to help freemen of Calton and their families who were poor, infirm or widowed. Further information on this group and how they functioned can be found in two volumes of the *Book of the Old Edinburgh Club* from the 1930s,[20] and in M. S. Irvine's *The Caldtoun of Calton of Edinburgh*.[21] In addition, many of the meeting minutes and account transactions survive in the Edinburgh City Archives. These hold a record of everyone buried within the Old Calton burial ground, and who paid for a burial plot.[22]

The remaining land on the western side of the summit of the hill, described as the 'North

Craigs' or 'Neils Craigs' in Gordon's 1647 map, but given the name Calton Crags by Edgar's 1765 edition,[23] was sold by Lord Balmerino to Edinburgh Town Council between 1722 and 1725.[24] The ownership of the eastern side of Calton Hill was held by Heriot's Hospital, and the lands to the north, leading down to Leith, were split almost in half between the large institutions of Trinity and Heriot's Hospitals, with a few smaller individual farmsteads located at specific sites in between (Plate 4). The area of Greenside to the north of the hill does not appear to be in private ownership. It had housed a chapel of the Holy Cross before being gifted to the Carmelite monks in the early sixteenth century for the erection of a monastery.[25] However, according to Hugo Arnot, in a *History of Edinburgh*, it was disbanded shortly after the Reformation, and by 1591, the area housed a Leper Hospital by John Robertson, a merchant in Edinburgh.[26] By the early nineteenth century, this area is depicted in maps as developed land, with numerous residences and commercial premises.

BROADER CONTEXT

Previous studies of Calton Hill and its surrounding area (known together as the Third 'New Town') have concentrated on understanding this site mainly through architectural or historical analysis, often with a focus on individual buildings on or close to the hill's summit, or of specific persons or groups of people who have been associated with the site. This has resulted in a plethora of research on specific buildings, architectural genres and events relating to the area and its development within the city. For example, studies such as Malcolm Irvine's nineteenth-century publication on the Calton communities,[27]

Henry Paton's articles on the Barony of Calton[28] and Ann Mitchell's study of the communities living in Regent, Royal and Carlton Terraces[29] provide detail on the events and use of this site by its residents before and after its development in the nineteenth century. Particular focus on the site's architecture and landscape can be found in A. J. Youngson's *The Making of Classical Edinburgh*,[30] Connie Byrom's *Edinburgh's New Town Gardens*[31] and Peter Reed's chapter on the proposals for the urban layout of the grounds to the north of Calton Hill.[32] Concerning specific structures on Calton Hill, Marcus Fehlmann's research on the unfinished National Monument and John Gifford's 2014 article provide a fairly thorough outline of the events surrounding the development of this structure,[33] and texts by both David Gavine and D. J. Bryden provide a good general history of the observatory complex on the site.[34] Joe Rock and Ian Fisher's work on Thomas Hamilton have looked at the development of both the Royal High School and the Burns monument in the context of the architect's career,[35] whereas other buildings and monuments on the hill have been considered as part of wider studies on Napoleonic commemorative structures,[36] institutional representation, or reactions to, state and municipal control.[37] Finally, the burial grounds of Old and New Calton have been considered both in terms of the architectural significance of their memorials,[38] and for their genealogical interest.[39] Recent studies carried out for the purpose of the site's management and conservation have involved detailed explorations of its history and evolution alongside other burial grounds within Edinburgh World Heritage Site, in order to contextualise and evaluate their significance and importance.[40]

Many of the seminal texts on Calton Hill

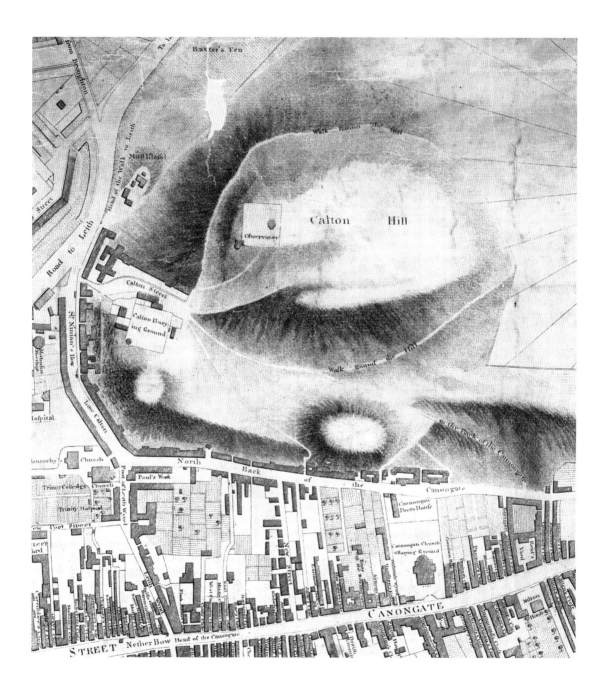

Plate 3—Alexander Kincaid, *A Plan of the City and Suburbs of Edinburgh*, 1784. Detail of Calton Hill.
© Courtesy of National Library of Scotland

Opposite: Plate 4—John Ainslie, *Old and New Town of Edinburgh and Leith with the proposed docks*, 1804.
© Courtesy of National Library of Scotland

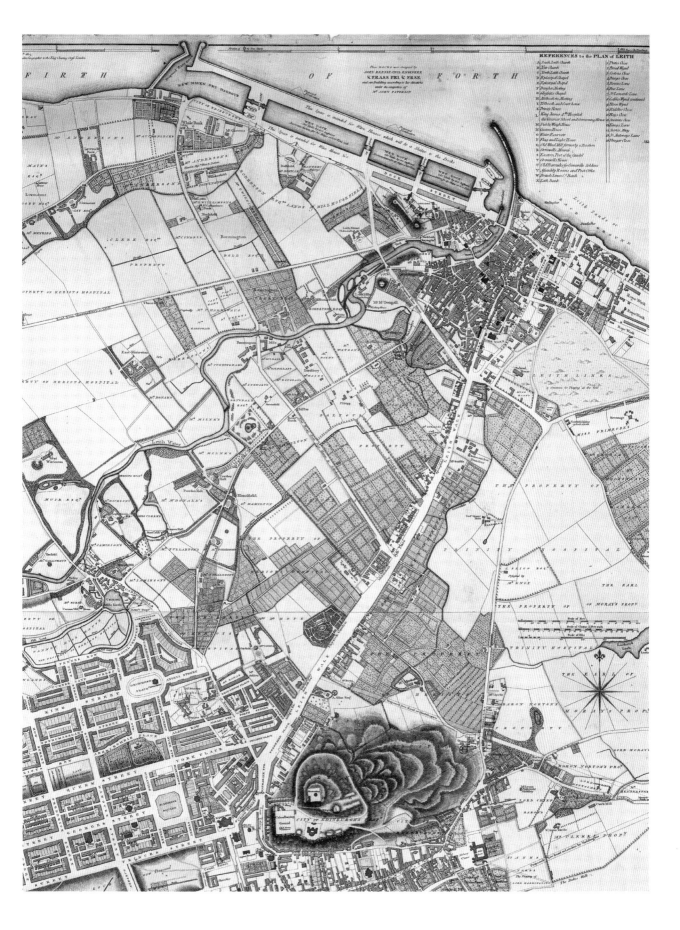

to date have tended to focus on the design, idioms and layout of the site, discussing Calton Hill and the development of its monuments either as a chronological chapter in the history of the development of Edinburgh, or with regard to its architectural or typological rhetoric. Those texts that have considered the site as a singular whole are fewer in number and include both published and unpublished papers[41] and conference proceedings.[42] These show that a more in-depth understanding of the area of Calton Hill has been of interest to both academics and local government for at least the last forty years. Much of the interest in the present day has focused on the management and conservation of the site and its structures, and is gathered together in the production of the 1999 Calton Hill Conservation Plan by LDN Architects[43]—the most comprehensive survey of the site to date. The survey included architectural, archaeological and historical analysis of the summit of Calton Hill, researched through primary archival sources and on-site analysis. However, the geographical remit of the plan, which limited its focus to the upper part of the hill, and the intellectual scope for its output, which was to consider current management issues and the hill's cultural significance, brought only a partial understanding of the site. Its conclusions therefore related mainly to the hill's situation with regard to a range of themes bearing upon the cultural significance of the World Heritage Site. There remained the need for further analysis of Calton Hill within a wider cultural, political and social context, in order to fully understand its evolution, and explain why its cultural significance is considered to be of international importance.

Up until now, analysis of Edinburgh and Calton Hill within the context of nineteenth-century British urban design has been limited to brief research papers and footnotes discussing the monuments of Calton Hill within the broader discussion of Scottish national identity in the nineteenth century.[44] These have demonstrated that consideration of the broader constructs that define Scottish identity alongside the development of Calton Hill help to further understand the architectural rhetoric used in the structures on the site. Studies of Edinburgh and other Scottish towns from the post-modern period going back to the mid eighteenth century have also included the effects of contemporaneous societal events on the aesthetic of the urban townscape in their analysis.[45] The anglification of the city during the development of the first New Town in the 1760s, for example, was a deliberate attempt to create a visual homogeny with other British cities, such as Bath and London, in order to establish British government control after the second Jacobite uprising.[46] The early nineteenth century society in which the urban landscape of Calton Hill developed, however, evolved from an entirely different political outlook, as urban development not only sought to tighten control over British society but to promote its governing constructs—particularly on an imperial stage.

Conscious efforts to promote the monarchy and the British state after the events of the French Revolution (1789–99) and during the Napoleonic wars (1803–15) were made through a plethora of commemorative structures to public heroes and the enhancement of the urban landscape throughout Britain, and the British Empire,[47] and it is in this context that Calton Hill was developed. In addition, the hill's landscape evolved at a time when Scottish society, in the throes of its Enlightenment period, was much more confident in its sense of self and the outputs of its Golden Age. The role of Edinburgh's urban layout during the Scottish Enlightenment in the eighteenth century is often considered as the stage and backdrop to the broader philosophical,[48] cultural and scientific ideas that were developed during this period, and that have evolved into modern society. The opportunities provided for many learned and inquisitive minds living in close proximity to the university, law courts and the kirk—as well as to each other in the claustrophobic closes and wynds of the Old Town—allowed for the illuminati to engage in cross-disciplinary discussion. It has previously been noted that this opportunity to meet other like-minded scholars facilitated the further pursuit of knowledge within their own discipline, and allowed for the emergence of new studies and theories that became the backbone of Enlightenment thought.[49] However, the effect that this discourse had on the development of the city is often only discussed in connection

with specific aesthetic considerations, such as rationalism within the urban design of the New Town[50] or the honouring of antiquity in the architectural form.[51] It has not previously been considered how the shaping of cultural and social theories of the eighteenth century, and their evolution through scholarly and political dialogue of the nineteenth century, can also be identified in the developing urban landscape in the city—despite recognition of the necessity of including both aesthetic and social analysis in studying architectural history. As a result, the cultural and scientific remnants now found on Calton Hill are argued to have been as influential on the development of this area as the accompanying political discourse. This has already been recognised by both architectural historians and more mainstream texts relating to the social history of late eighteenth- and early nineteenth-century Edinburgh and the Enlightenment.[52]

PART 1

Rural Urbanism to Urban Arcadia: the Evolution of Calton Hill

The evolution of Calton Hill from a rural hilly nub into an urban hub reflecting the city's grandiose imperial ambitions occurred mainly during the Enlightenment and post-Enlightenment period in Edinburgh. Both the layout of the hill and the structures built upon it are recognised as demonstrating a rationality and restraint in execution, which resulted in a synthesis between urban design and picturesque theory at the pinnacle of antiquarian interest in Greek architecture. Yet, how this interpretation of the surviving urban landscape can be understood within the broader social, cultural and political context of eighteenth-, nineteenth- and twentieth-century thought is less widely known. Much is a consequence of the previous research on Calton Hill, which has mainly focused on the site within the parameters of the history of urban development in Edinburgh and Scotland, or—with regard to the current surviving landscape—its comparison to the neoclassical aesthetic found in Bath or Regency London. It has, to date, tended to disregard the wider zeitgeist of the emerging British Empire, and the effects of political policies and social trends that were influenced by this on the aesthetic discourse that surrounded the development of the urban fabric of the British city during the late eighteenth and early nineteenth century.[1]

Previous study on the expansion of London and Britain during the early 1800s has engaged with this connection between government policy and the urban form.[2] This has recognised the importance of the contribution of localised schemes in reflecting and maintaining a sense of national equilibrium through the promotion of the British state and the glorification of British campaigns during the early years of the Empire.[3] It therefore seems appropriate that a similar analysis be applied to the development of Calton Hill as this area is both a reactive response to the needs of late eighteenth- and nineteenth-century society, and an output of national government policy through local civic interpretation.

Calton Hill's changing relationship with the city of Edinburgh from the eighteenth-century onwards must also be considered within a broader aesthetic discourse. Theories of the picturesque and its application to urban landscape design are relevant to the site. In addition, other responses to the hill, both before and after the development of the urban layout in the early nineteenth century correlate with emerging dialogues on the aesthetic that evolved throughout this period. Calton Hill's setting and topography provoked unique responses to aesthetic dialogues that emerged in Britain during the late eighteenth and early nineteenth centuries. The chronological development of the site's cityscape therefore requires contextualisation alongside the contemporaneous aesthetic discourse in order to better understand individual responses to the hill's development as specific points in time.

Plate 1.1—Old Observatory House, c. 1776.
© Kirsten Carter McKee

The Sentient Gaze: Observatories, Panopticons and the Panorama

Apart from some of the monuments in the burial ground established by the Incorporated Trades of Calton in 1717 (discussed in Part 2), the oldest structure that survives on Calton Hill[1] is a small circular gothic building, located on the western edge of the hill's summit (Plate 1.1).[2] This building is the remnants of a late eighteenth-century development, when Thomas Short, a mathematical instrument maker, applied to the town council to place a popular observatory[3] on the summit of the hill. This was to house a large reflecting telescope that he had inherited upon the death of his brother James.[4]

Accounts of the history of Thomas Short's involvement in the development of the Edinburgh Observatory have been published in two different scholarly articles by D. J. Bryden[5] and in the 1982 doctoral thesis by D. M. Gavine.[6] The latter considers the historical implications of the development of the discipline of astronomy in Edinburgh in relation to the rest of Scotland, and the former explores the complex relationship between Thomas Short, the town council and the University of Edinburgh in the establishment of an observatory for the city.[7] To date, however, no more consideration has been given to the unusual character of the design.

After Short's application for the land feu on Calton Hill was granted,[8] it came to light that some monies to build this structure would be available from the University of Edinburgh, if the university were permitted to house their astronomical instruments within the proposed building and have access to the observatory.[9] The funds far exceeded the money required to build what was initially mooted by Short, which, according to the *Scots Magazine* was to be a simple stone and wood building:

> Mr Short had confined his ideas to what was truly necessary towards the purpose in view, and no great sum would have been requisite for carrying them into execution; for it is in furnishing it with instruments and not in masonry or wright work, that the expence [sic] of an useful Observatory chiefly consists.[10]

Both Short's and the city magistrate's ambitions for the structure grew with the availability of the additional monies and it was soon suggested that 'an Observatory . . . much more magnificent and ornamental . . . could be built'.[11] By June 1776 therefore Short was advertising in the *Caledonian Gazetteer*, *Edinburgh Evening Courant* and the *Caledonian Mercury* for further subscriptions 'as many Gentlemen seem to be desirous that a building should be erected on a more elegant plan'.[12]

The magistrates of the city assumed greater control of the scheme during this additional fundraising stage. It is likely that it was at this point that James Craig was commissioned to design the new observatory, as the town magistrates had favoured Craig for a number of its projects during this period.[13] His original design was double the height of the previous wood and stone structure (48ft/14.5m), and consisted of a central octagon 30 feet (9m) across, topped with a dome.[14] A sketch of the elevation (Plate

1.2) depicts a two-storeyed, octagonal building[15] with rough-hewn stonework on the ground floor, and rectangular doors and windows. It is topped by a domed roof, which can be opened to undertake astronomical observations. The whole effect is rather plain,[16] but it is clear that it was influenced by James Stuart's design for the Tower of the Winds, a belvedere built in 1764 for the Shugborough Estate, Staffordshire, which he had based on his own drawings in 'Antiquities of Athens'.[17]

An early plan dating to April 1776, completed by John Laurie,[18] of the proposed layout[19] (Plate 1.3a) details not one, but two buildings for this site. The first is a regular octagon, which is assumed to be the octagonal observatory noted above, and the second, situated to the northwest, is an eight-sided lozenge-shaped structure with two elongated parallel sides. There are no surviving elevations for this structure and its use is conjectured to house the astronomical instruments owned by the University of Edinburgh.[20] However, comparing this plan with a second drawing of identical date (Plate 1.3b) it is clear that further discussion on the development of this site continued after Craig's proposals. This second plan is similar in layout and presentation and displays the same two buildings found in Plate 1.3a, but within a curtilage delineated by circular towers at diagonally opposing corners.[21] In addition, the two central buildings in Plate 1.3b are oriented differently to one another than in Plate 1.3a, implying that these two drawings are alternative proposals for the same site.

Considering these two drawings together, it is therefore questionable whether they were the original plans proposed for the observatory alongside Short's application for the land. Although both plans are dated April 1776, it is likely that Plate 1.3b was drawn later and was backdated to the original proposal, once more ambitious plans for the observatory had been mooted and Craig had been brought in as architect. The quality of the paper used, and the more considered execution of Plate 1.3b compared with Plate 1.3a supports this theory, as does the inclusion of the two towers inside a more defined curtilage wall in Plate 1.3b. These additions to the design become particularly relevant when considered alongside comments made on the observatory by Hugo Arnot in his 1779 History of Edinburgh:

> Mr Robert Adam architect, happened to come to Edinburgh. Upon seeing the intended observatory, founded upon the top of an high and abrupt hill, which terminates in a precipice, he conceived the idea of giving the whole the appearance of a fortification, to which it was excellently adapted.[22]

This 'fortification' suggested by Adam is often attributed to survive as a circular tower which forms part of the gothic structure that now stands as part of Old Observatory House on the hill (Plate 1.1).[23] This is a three-storeyed circular structure, supported by buttresses, which merge into part of a curtilage wall.[24] The arched fenestration found on the first storey and the use of random rubble construction[25] give the impression of a fortified structure. It is evident from Plate 1.4 that, in the early nineteenth century, this tower stood alone with only a small supporting wall on either side. This was added to in the mid nineteenth century by Charles Piazzi Smyth, who extended the structure to the east in order to create more living space. It is likely that this remaining building on Calton Hill is the southernmost circular tower depicted on Laurie's second plan (Plate 1.3b), and that it was executed

in a gothic manner as a result of Adam's suggestions for the site.

In order to understand why Robert Adam, according to Arnot, suggested a fortified style for the site, it is necessary to ascertain Adam's perspective on landscapes such as Calton Hill. Until this point, Calton Hill had been mainly considered as somewhere to view the city from rather than somewhere for the city to view towards. John Slezer's seventeenth-century view of the city (Plate 1.5), for example, exploited the hill's pastoral character to artistically frame the central focus of the built-up burgh at the centre of the image, and the 6th Earl of Mar's proposals for the city in 1728 (Plate 1.6) proposed avenues of trees on the hill to provide controlled vistas to key points in the medieval town and within Mar's own planned baroque New Town.[26]

However, with the adoption of the picturesque theory of landscape, particularly in contrast to the 'beautiful' and 'sublime' as discussed in Edmund Burke's mid eighteenth-century publication,[27] new perspective was brought to the consideration of the real-life open landscape as an artistic entity in its own right. Adam's understanding of this discourse with regard to the relationship between the hill and the city were key to the changing role of Calton Hill in the latter part of the eighteenth century. His involvement in the hill's development during the 1770s can be understood as a rudimentary attempt to give a 'sublime' character to the landscape through the introduction of antiquarian structures at key points on the hill that would cause maximum dramatic impact. This can be particularly understood in light of Adam's interest in the sublime nature of the Scottish landscape, which was rooted in his ambitions as a landscape painter in his formative years. These

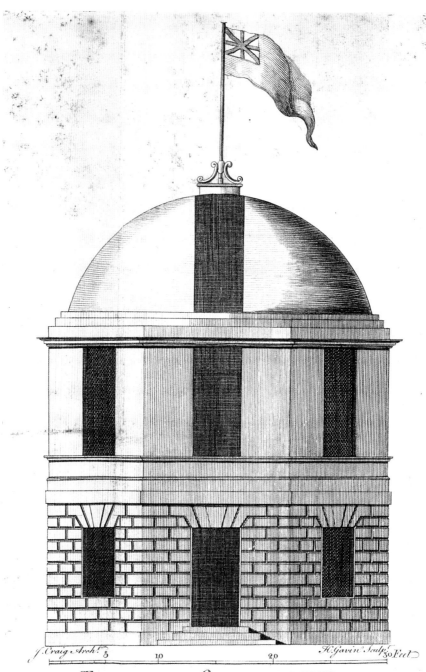

EDINBURGH OBSERVATORY.

Plate 1.2—James Craig, *Proposal for the Edinburgh Observatory*, c. 1776.
Courtesy of the Bodleian Library

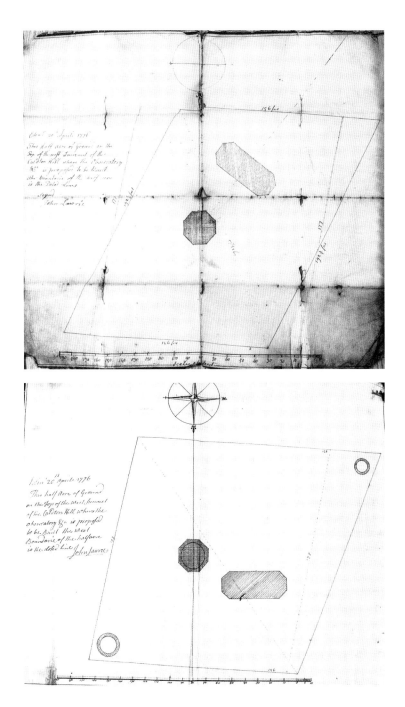

Plate 1.3a—John Laurie, *Plan of Half the Acre of Ground at the Top of Calton Hill—Site of the Observatory*, 1776.
© Edinburgh City Archives
Plate 1.3b—John Laurie, *Plan of Half the Acre of Ground at the Top of Calton Hill—Site of the Observatory*, 1776.
© Edinburgh City Archives.

Plate 1.4—J. and H. S. Storer, *The Old Observatory (Calton Hill)*, 1820.
© Courtesy of Historic Environment Scotland. (Taken from 'Views in Scotland')

had been cut short at his father's death in 1748 when he became more heavily involved in the family business.[28] But his interest in sketching structures within rural landscapes continued during the European travels of his Grand Tour in 1754. Set within the Italian Campagna, many of the images he produced reveal a fascination not only with Roman domestic fortification, but also with how these buildings related to the romanticism of the landscape within which they were set. In his later years, when much of his time was spent in Scotland, he began to revisit this relationship between architecture and the rural landscape, by painting numerous watercolours of castellated and fortified structures within hilly and pastoral landscapes. These were for the most part imaginary, but are thought to have been inspired by real scenes of the Scottish countryside, as their rugged aspect and foreboding atmosphere simulated the harsh Scottish climate and the landscape found in much of the Scottish countryside north of the central belt.

Whether Adam's watercolours were executed

for pleasure or as serious artistic studies, many of his imaginary Scottish landscapes depicted scenes that were considered to have had 'a direct, rather than a parallel relationship with his buildings'.[29] This can be particularly recognised in his country estate designs at Culzean, Barnbougle, Kirkdale and Seton Castle, where romantic and ruinous structures were placed within designed landscapes of an irregular and dramatic nature.

Adam's proposal for a gothic-style curtilage around Craig's Palladian building would have therefore been consistent with his aesthetic vision as represented through his watercolours of similar views.[30] By the building of the curtilage wall and moving the larger building depicted on Laurie's plans onto the slope of the hill to the south of the octagonal observatory as opposed to the summit, Adam's idea of Calton Hill as a sublime rural landscape would have prevailed, since Craig's designs would have been completely hidden by the gothic fortifications.

However, as it is unclear how much input Adam really had in the final executed project, it is difficult to confirm whether this was definitively the reason behind the sudden abandonment of Craig's half-finished octagonal observatory in favour of the construction of a gothic curtilage. Building accounts for the observatory and the gothic tower at the southwestern corner[31] do not mention Adam being involved with the scheme, or receiving any official credit for his input through payment of monies. Neither is his name mentioned in the lengthy litigation process that occurred in the 1780s and 1790s after the failure of the project.[32] It is therefore only through our understanding of Adam's acute interest in the relationship between architecture and landscape and through reference to other work by Adam

and Craig that we can further consider their relationship on this project.

Craig's final accounts, held in the Edinburgh City Archives, claim payment for a 'tower with wings.'[33] This may be his proposal for the octagonal observatory,[34] but could also easily match the description of the southwest tower. However, as the detail in the southwest tower is so far removed from Craig's original Palladian vision, it could be that Craig had some outside assistance with the final design. Gothic, castellated buildings are not often associated with Craig. In fact, the few pieces of gothic architecture that Craig is known to have proposed or executed during his career were all renovations of earlier gothic structures—i.e. no 'new' designs appear to have been built by him in this mode.[35] It is, then, possible that Adam's influence may have not only been responsible for the outer curtilage wall and the circular towers shown in Laurie's second plan (Plate 1.3b), but also for the gothic design of the structure. This is supported by Arnot's writings, which noted that Adam had recommended that the structure should have 'Gothick towers on the angles'.[36] The surviving structure also incorporates other recommendations by Adam, such as the suggestion that the observatory should have the 'appearance of a fortification . . . with buttresses and embrasures'.[37]

Collaboration between Adam and Craig to romanticise the view of Calton Hill is possible. Scholars of the development of eighteenth-century Edinburgh are of the opinion that the Adam brothers were often extremely influential in the design of many of the buildings of the city during this period: 'Robert Adam influenced many of the new town builders who can be called the Adam Group . . . Even local Edinburgh

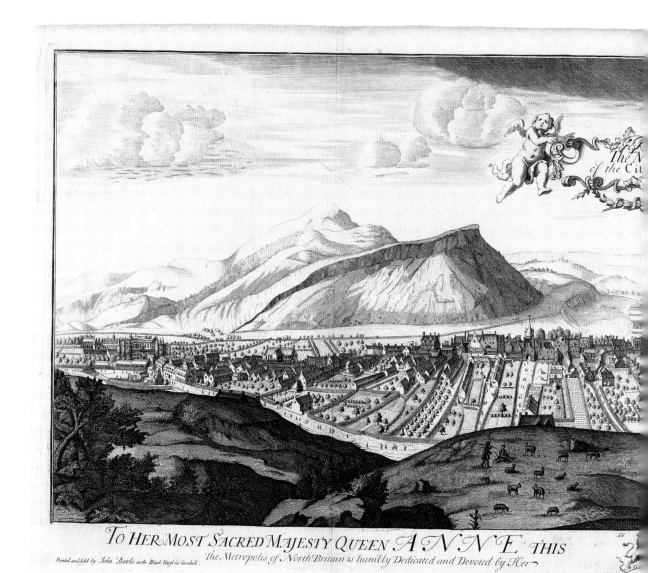

Plate 1.5—John Slezer, *The North Prospect of
the City of Edinburgh*, 1693.
© Courtesy of National Library of Scotland

architects like James Craig . . . [were] dependent
on John and Robert Adam at times.'[38]

Other structures in Edinburgh now known

to be a product of Adam/Craig collaboration
further strengthen the likelihood of this alliance.
Examples include Botanic Cottage—previously
attributed to James Craig, but now known to
have been designed by John Adam,[39] and the
monument to Linnaeus in the Botanic Garden
in Edinburgh,[40] which was designed by Robert

PROSPECT OF HER ANCIENT CITY OF EDENBURGH
Majesties most Dutifull and most Obedient Subject and Servant

Adam and executed by James Craig. Both of these structures are dated within two or three years of the observatory development, which would place the timing of the collaboration at a similar juncture in their careers.

The above information and Arnot's account of the development of the gothic tower suggest that Adam had more involvement in the execution of this structure than has been previously acknowledged. Of course, it is possible that Adam's influence was in more of an unofficial manner, in a conversation between colleagues, rather than a direct working partnership on the observatory development.[41] Adam's appreciation

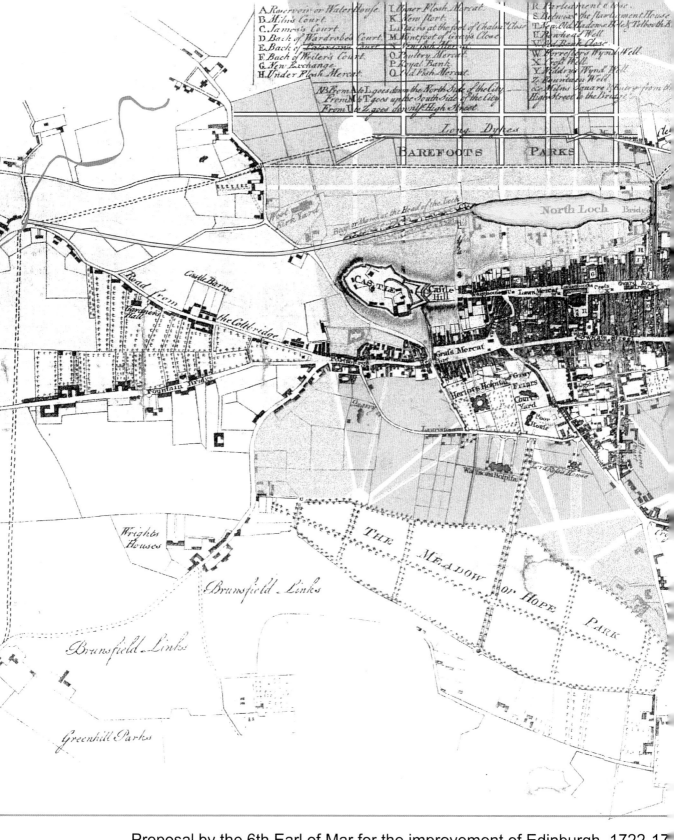

A. *Reservoir or Waterhouse.*
B. *Milns Court.*
C. *James's Court.*
D. *Back of Wardrobe Court.*
E. *Back of .... Court.*
F. *Back of Writer's Court.*
G. *New Exchange.*
H. *Under Flesh Mercat.*

I. *Upper Flesh Mercat.*
K. *New Port.*
L. *Lawns at the foot of Chalm Close.*
M. *Minefoot of Grays Close.*
S. *............*
O. *Poultry Mercat.*
P. *Royal Bank.*
Q. *Old Fish Mercat.*

R. *Parliament & .....*
S. *Gateway the Parliament House.*
U. *........ Old Meadow Pots & Tolbooth &.*
U. *Penhead Well.*
......*Old Back Close.*
W. *Forresters Wynd Well.*
X. *..... Well.*
Y. *Fleshers Wynd Well.*
Z. *Fountain Well.*
&c. Milns Square & ....
......*High Street to the Bridge.*

N.B. From No. L goes down the North Side of the City ——
From M to T goes up the South Side of the City
From U to Z goes down High Street.

Long Dykes

BAREFOOTS PARKS

North Loch *Bridge*

West Kirk Yard

Bog or Marsh at the Head of the Loch

CASTLE *Castle Hill*

Castle Barns

Road from the Coltbridge

Gardners Hall

Lawn Mercat

Grass Mercat

Heriots Hospital *Gray Friars Church Yard*

Poor House

Fountain Bridge

Laurieston

Watson and Hospital

Old Royal House

Wrights Houses

THE MEADOW OF HOPE PARK

Brunsfield Links

Brunsfield Links

Greenhill Parks

Proposal by the 6th Earl of Mar for the improvement of Edinburgh, 1722-17

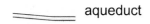 aqueduct    streets    residential

Plate 1.6—
Margaret Stewart
and Pete Mullin,
*Interpretation of
the Proposal by
the 6th Earl of Mar
for the improvement
of Edinburgh*,
1722–1727.
© Interpretation by
Margaret Stewart
and Pete Mullin,
2004

Interpretation by Margaret Stewart and Pete Mullin, 2004

bridges   plantation

Plate 1.7—Robert Adam, *David Hume Monument
in Old Calton Burial Ground*, 1777.
© Kirsten Carter McKee

of the similarities between Calton Hill and the rural hilly landscapes represented in his watercolour paintings can be further considered through his early proposals for the memorial to the philosopher and historian David Hume (1711–1776), which was constructed around the same time as the octagonal observatory. The monument sits within the graveyard of the (Old) Calton burial ground (Plate 1.7) and is a neoclassical interpretation of a Roman circular mausoleum, with a fluted frieze, Doric entablature and classical funerary urn.[42] Despite its neoclassical components, the six proposals created by Adam during the design phase of the mausoleum are not reminiscent of the typical Adam style practised in London.[43] Instead, it is argued by Iain Gordon Brown that these are more closely

associated with the ruinous circular temples of the Roman Campagna, which were converted into fortified buildings in the Middle Ages.[44]

This 'blurring' of the traditional antique-style memorial with rusticated gothicised forti-fortifications suggests that Adam may have been trying to create two simultaneous effects. Firstly, through the idea of architectural decline, he is incorporating the antique symbolism of death and mourning in this structure. Secondly, he is exploiting the dramatic nature of the site to create a romanticised landscape, akin to the ruined medieval fortifications that he often painted. This approach to the design would therefore not only provide a sense of decay and the passage of time through the allegory of classical antiquity, but would also exploit the memorial's placement on a precipice of Calton Hill, as had also been suggested for the 'gothic fortifications' that would surround the observatory. The hill's relationship with the broader landscape was

therefore key to Adam's early architectural vision for this site, and in fact, when looking towards the Hume Monument from the North Bridge (Plate 1.8), it is possible to conceive that Adam's suggestions to Craig on the design for the walling around the observatory may have been to avoid compromising the view towards the carefully planned rhetoric of his design for that monument. The addition of structures in this landscape had been intended, in Adam's mind at least, to focus the eye and augment the scene as a whole, rather than be stand-alone architectural entities.[45] The use of classical architecture reminiscent of the Roman Campagna alongside medieval gothic fortifications would have added to the air of decline and ruin, befitting the memento mori of a public figure, and would also enhance and augment the romantic nature of this site.[46]

In both Gordon Brown's paper on the Hume Monument[47] and John Lowrey's article on Robert Adam and Edinburgh,[48] it is argued that defining the relationship between Calton Hill and the city was a focus of Adam's designs for the city as a whole. The development of the hill would cause Adam's first building in the city, the National Repository or 'Register House' (1774–89) at the foot of the North Bridge to become a centre point of the New Town development. In addition, the dramatic topography of the Waverley Valley would extend the significant views visible from the northernmost point of his South Bridge that linked the Old Town to the New Town. This connecting route, or 'Via Triumphalis', approached the New Town from the south leading from Adam's College for the University of Edinburgh (commenced in 1789—now known as 'Old College') down to Register House. This was

Plate 1.8—
View of David Hume Monument from North Bridge.
The Hume Monument is the circular tower located to the left of the Martyrs' Monument obelisk.
© Kirsten Carter McKee

to be created using an enclosed route of grandiose neoclassical regularity, which passed over (and blocked the near view of) the Old Town, while at the same time providing an enclosed vista that terminated at Register House. This route led directly into the New Town by linking up with William Mylne's North Bridge of 1765–9, and opened out into the drama of the emerging view of the Waverley Valley, which would be perfectly exploited by the romantic views to Calton Hill and in particular, the towering drama of Hume's mausoleum on its precipice.

However, Calton Hill's connection to the city had become more prominent by the end of the eighteenth century, and Adam's later proposals show that his understanding of the hill's relationship to the city had evolved to acknowledge the 'picturesque'—a concept established through the cultural debates surrounding William Gilpin's 1782 publication of 'Observations on the River Wye'.[49] In particular, as Adam further considered the site's relationship with the urban townscape of both the neoclassical New Town and the adjacent medieval Old Town, his choice of architectural rhetoric swayed from neoclassical proposals to monolithic castellated gothic, as he struggled to determine to what extent the hill should become a picturesque part of the New Town, or remain as a romantic backdrop.[50] Eventually, Adam settled in favour of bringing the hill into the existing cityscape as a semi-rural periphery, rather than emphasising it as a sublime and wild entity.[51] He did this by suggesting both the medieval and the classical in his design, by combining a regulated Palladian façade with castellated parapets and corner turrets. This creates the impression of a medieval-style fortification, which is controlled in its overall presence. This later interpretation of the hill was influential

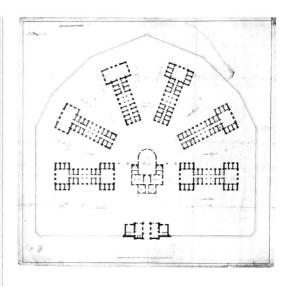

Plate 1.9—James Wardrup,
Calton Jail, Bridewell. General Plan, 1791.
© Historic Environment Scotland

enough to provide something of a blueprint for two key structures built on Calton Hill at least ten years after Robert Adam's death—the Calton Jail and the Nelson Monument. In addition, his ideas and overall vision for the site and how it should be a part of the city can be recognised in the incorporation of the site into the urban landscape during the nineteenth century.

Despite both the Hume Monument and the observatory development bringing focus to Calton Hill as a backdrop for the city, it took a further ten years before Edinburgh magistrates considered it as a potential site for any further development. This was a Bridewell (poorhouse and prison) for the county. The story of the development of a Bridewell for Edinburgh is told in detail by Thomas Markus.[52] He outlines part of the early proposals, championed by the Lord Provost David Steuart in the early 1780s,[53] and the subsequent proposals of the three architects who submitted designs for the competition in

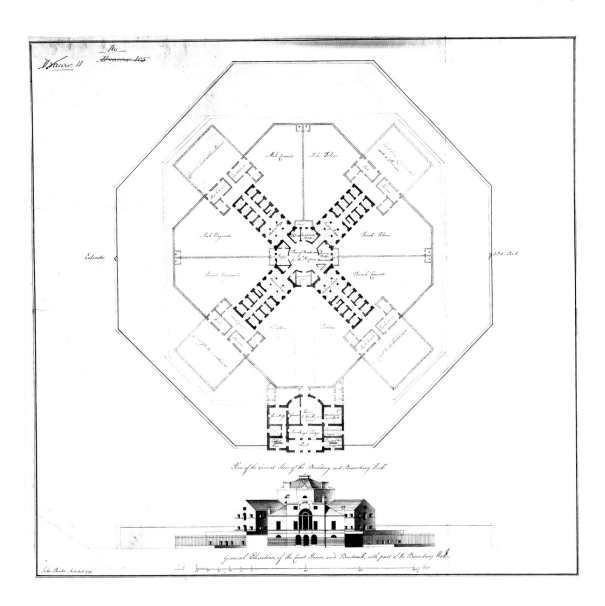

Plate 1.10—John Baxter, *General Elevation of Court House and Bridewell and Plan of the General Form of the Building*, 1791.
© Historic Environment Scotland

the early 1790s—James Wardrup, John Baxter and Robert Adam. Adam won the commission and offered eight proposals in total,[54] two in the classical style and six in the castle style, the final one of which was adopted for the building.[55] These design proposals not only demonstrate the application of emerging theories in prison design during the late eighteenth century, but also show Adam's exploration of the relationship between the hill and the city.

The form of the prison was determined in the original proposal for the 1782 building,[56] which

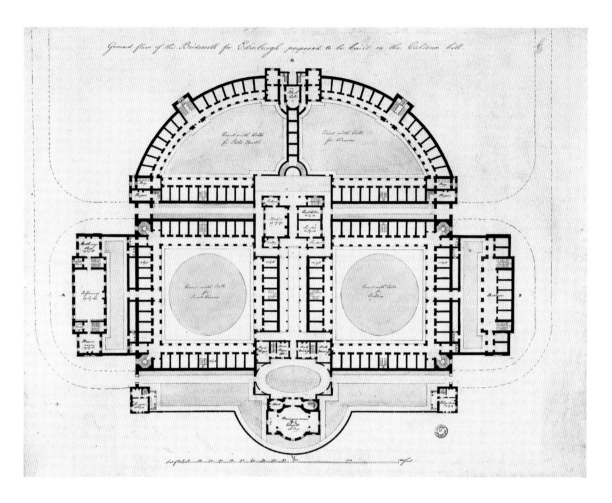

Plate 1.11a—Robert Adam, *Bridewell Design*: Classical Style 2—Plan, 1791.
© Sir John Soane's Museum, London. Photograph: Ardon Bar-Hama

had taken inspiration from prison buildings developed by John Howard and William Blackburn after Howard's report on 'The State of Prisons in 1777'.[57] Lack of ventilation and hygiene had been amongst the reasons behind the spread of disease found in penitentiaries examined by Howard. His commentary on the conditions of prisons that he visited throughout the country, and his suggestions on appropriate design, were influential in the construction of many prisons in Britain. In particular, Howard's work with the

architect William Blackburn, who implemented many of Howard's theories, 'helped to establish a reformed prison system . . . [as they] were . . . involved with many reconstruction programmes until their deaths in 1790'.[58]

Much of Howard's study of the prison system centred around the provision of separate cloisters or 'yards' for different gradations of prisoner, and the activities that they would undertake on a daily basis, from sleeping, to eating, and to work defined by the penitentiary.[59]

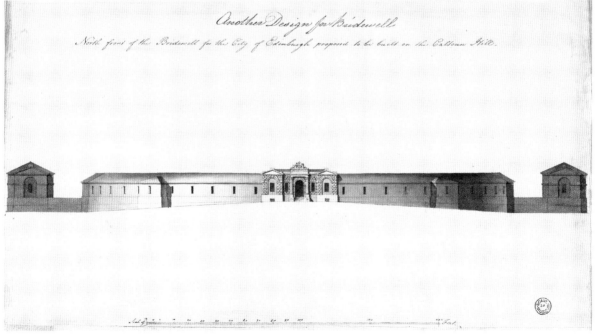

Plate 1.11b—Robert Adam, *Bridewell Design*: Classical Style 2 – South Elevation, 1791.
© Sir John Soane's Museum, London. Photograph: Ardon Bar-Hama
Plate 1.11c—Robert Adam, *Bridewell Design*: Classical Style 2—North Elevation, 1791.
© Sir John Soane's Museum, London. Photograph: Ardon Bar-Hama

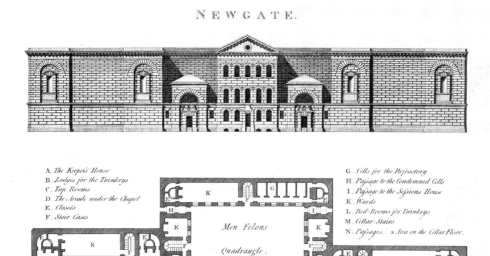

Plate 1.12 George Dance, *A Plan of Newgate Prison in London*, 1800.
© Courtesy of the British Library

Early competition proposals by Adam, Wardrup and Baxter all followed these courtyard-plan designs[60] (Plates 1.9–1.11a), and in Adam's and Baxter's cases in particular, were directly influenced by Blackburn's New Bailey prison in Manchester.[61] The elevations that survive for the 1791 competition entries by Adam and Baxter also present an exterior style found in many other contemporaneous prison designs during this period, such as London's Newgate Prison (Plate 1.12). This was fortified Palladianism, with heavily rusticated high walls and limited openings, that created an impenetrable air. Adam's second proposal (Plates 1.11b, c) includes references to this prison style, with dentilled decoration (small square block mouldings that are repeated to form a long horizontal set) on the cornices on the south side of the building, and an imposing near-impenetrable exterior wall on the the north side, with a rusticated central block defining the only access to the Bridewell through a porticoed entranceway flanked by Doric columns.

As Adam moves onto a more castellated style for the Bridewell, the layout for the building changes as dramatically as the the external style (Plates 1.13a–c and Plates 1.14a–f). Rustication

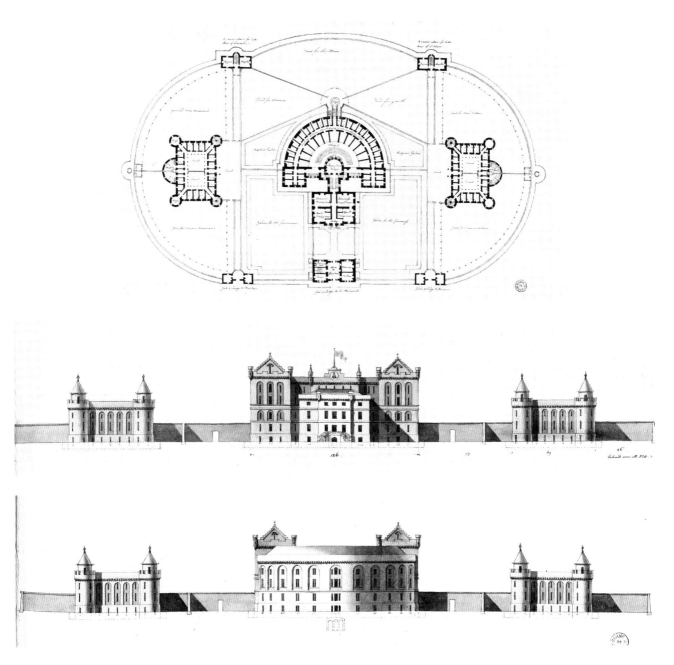

Plate 1.13a—Robert Adam, *Bridewell Design*: Castle Style 2—Plan, 1791.
© Sir John Soane's Museum, London. Photograph: Ardon Bar-Hama
Plate 1.13b—Robert Adam, *Bridewell Design*: Castle Style 2—North Elevation, 1791.
© Sir John Soane's Museum, London. Photograph: Ardon Bar-Hama
Plate 1.13c—Robert Adam, *Bridewell Design*: Castle Style 2—South Elevation, 1791.
© Sir John Soane's Museum, London. Photograph: Ardon Bar-Hama

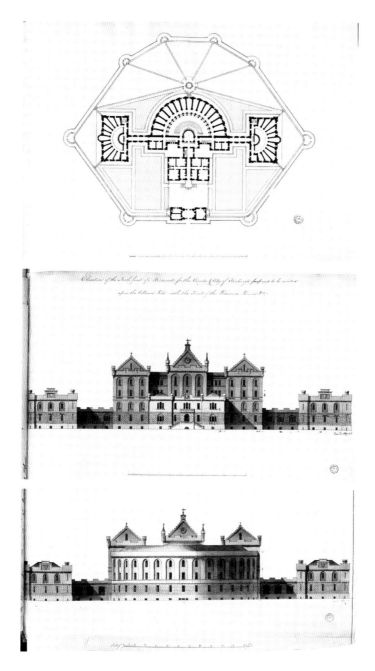

Plate 1.14a—Robert Adam, *Bridewell Design*: Castle Style 3 – Plan, 1791.
© Sir John Soane's Museum, London. Photograph: Ardon Bar-Hama
Plate 1.14b—Robert Adam, *Bridewell Design*: Castle Style 3—North Elevation, 1791.
© Sir John Soane's Museum, London. Photograph: Ardon Bar-Hama
Plate 1.14c—Robert Adam, *Bridewell Design*: Castle Style 3—South Elevation, 1791.
© Sir John Soane's Museum, London. Photograph: Ardon Bar-Hama

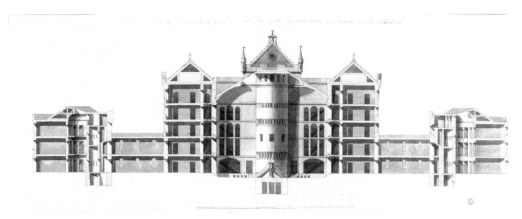

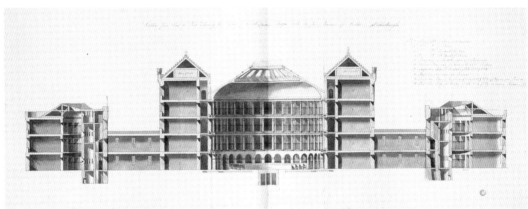

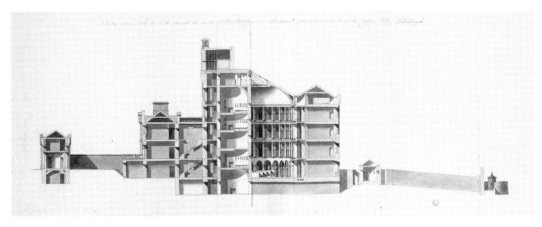

Plate 1.14d—Robert Adam, *Bridewell Design*. Castle Style 3—East–West Section looking North with detail of inspection lodge, 1791.
© Sir John Soane's Museum, London. Photograph: Ardon Bar-Hama
Plate 1.14e—Robert Adam, *Bridewell Design*. Castle Style 3—East–West Section looking South, 1791.
© Sir John Soane's Museum, London. Photograph: Ardon Bar-Hama
Plate 1.14 f—Robert Adam, *Bridewell Design*. Castle Style 3—North–South Section looking East, 1791.
© Sir John Soane's Museum, London. Photograph: Ardon Bar-Hama

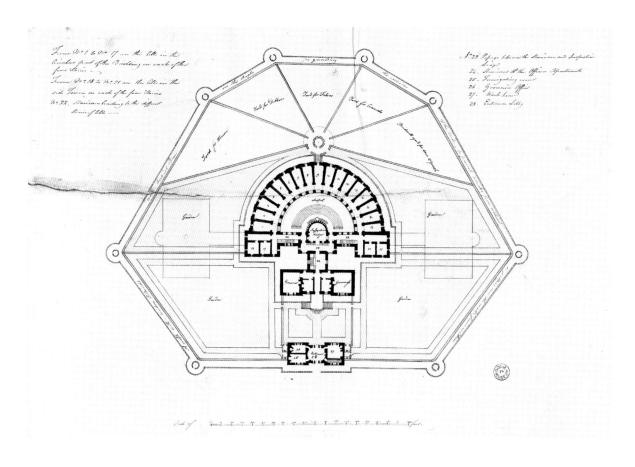

Plate 1.15—Robert Adam, *Bridewell Design*: Castle Style 4—Plan, 1791.
© Courtesy of Sir John Soane's Museum

covers the lower storey and arched recesses are still included in the external facades, but the crow-stepped gables, turrets and slit windows give the building the air of a fortification, much more in keeping with Scottish castellated architecture.[62] The plan is also quite notably different. Rather than following the standard convention for penitentiary design in the late eighteenth century, Adam chose an alternative prison design by a relative unknown, Jeremy Bentham, whose work had never yet been put into practice for a penitentiary. Instead of segregated blocks surrounding internal courtyards, a main central

semi-circular structure is proposed, with two radiating wings to the east and west and a small gatehouse to the north. These wings are removed in the subsequent proposals for the building, leaving only a central semi-circular block and gatehouse in the final design (Plate 1.15).

Bentham's idea for a single structure that would provide constant surveillance of its inmates—the Panopticon (Plate 1.16)—had originally been created to supervise a large workforce and had been built by Bentham's brother, Samuel, in Russia, with some success. Yet, Bentham's publication of his letters on the Panopticon in

1787[63] suggested that his design could be adapted to a much greater number of potential uses, ranging from prisons and houses of correction, to factories and even schools. The benefits of using a panoptic structure lay in the ability to create solitary confinement for the inmates, yet still provide constant surveillance through a series of lenses and pipes. Bentham also claimed that his design had the benefit of being much more cost-efficient than many other designs for this purpose, as it required only one central building, which kept material and construction costs down and a smaller area upon which to site it.[64]

As limited ground size was not a consideration for Adam (he had already demonstrated that a Bridewell in the Howard/Blackburn style could easily be accommodated on the site), it is likely that Bentham's ideas appealed to Adam on a visual level. Bentham's proposal was that the exterior of the structure should give the impression of a 'fortress'[65] or a military citadel, as he believed this would strike those who looked upon it as a secure and impenetrable institution.[66] This would—according to Adam's clerk of works, John Paterson—have suited how the structure was to be run, which was '[T]o be guarded by military . . . the guard house to be placed on the highest ground within the walls that the officer on guard might see every post where the sentinels stood and the courts for the felons'.[67] In addition, it appears that the design of a prison in the style of a fortress may have put to use the unfinished gothic structure on the summit.

> [B]uilding the Bridewell on the top of the Hill would give full room for finishing a plan partly designed,[68] & what might be designed by you, if the Provost & Town honoured you with that employment, it would not only be highly ornamental but add very much to the

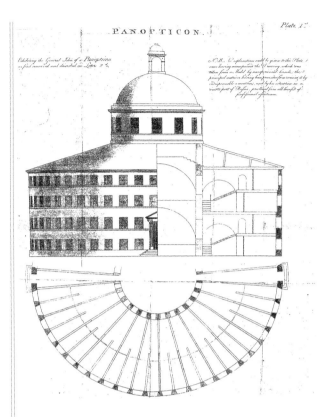

Plate 1.16—Jeremy Bentham, Panopticon, 1787. Taken from J. Bentham, *Panopticon: Or, the Inspection-House. Containing the Idea of a New Principle of Construction Applicable to Any Sort of Establishment, in which Persons . . . Are to Be Kept . . . and in Particular to Penitentiary-Houses, Prisons . . . in a Series of Letters, Written in . . . 1787, 1791*

> *Towns revenues. Mr Elder was present . . . & both he & the provost thought that what I had said ought to be well considered before any further opinion was given of your plans, as most certainly said the provost they would both ornament & enrich the Town.*[69]

The introduction of a new style of prison layout so dramatically different from the standard courtyard prison plans of Howard/Blackburn contrasted with other contemporaneous prisons

and houses of correction that were being con-structed throughout the country. Its panoptical layout allowed constant surveillance of inmates Plates 1.14d–f), while its exterior design also cre-ated a constant imposing presence overlooking the Old Town—from where most of its inmates would be. The duality of a structure that would both overlook the most insalubrious parts of the city and be particularly visible to those insalubri-ous characters that currently resided in them must have appealed to Adam. This establishment of an institutional sentinel would have also further vin-dicated the use of a castellated vernacular on the exterior aesthetic,[70] rather than the 'impenetra-ble Palladianism' of Dance's Newgate Prison in London (which was considered a more likely style envisioned for this structure by Jeremy Bentham).

Calton Hill had been considered as the ideal place for the new penitentiary by the city magistrates, as the hill's airy setting would provide health benefits to the inmates.[71] In Markus' paper on this structure, he argues that this choice of site was considered 'central' to the city, as it was placed in a visible location overlooking the inhabitants of Edinburgh.[72] However, it is clear from Adam's choice of architectural rhetoric that he did not consider this building central to the city, but rather as part of a semi-rural periphery. This ties in with contemporaneous practices of siting municipal buildings that performed more basic or potentially dangerous functions to the outskirts of urban settlements.[73]

Adam's struggle to find an appropriate exterior aesthetic to define the Bridewell's—

and Calton Hill's—relationship with the city can also be identified through his proposals for a connecting bridge between Calton Hill and the New Town. Although this bridge was never constructed during Adam's involvement with the project,[74] the ideas behind its conception can be identified as a continuum of Adam's development of prominent sight lines and vistas for the gateways into the New Town.[75] Adam's understanding of the relationship between architectural style and the city determined his proposals, as he and Paterson envisioned this access as a further opportunity to create a grand approach into the urban centre, as was already under way from the south:

> *I mentioned to the Provost that I thought*
> *if they made any purchases of houses*

Plate 1.17—Robert Adam, *Bridge over (?) from Princes Street at (?) Calton Hill Edinburgh*, c. 1791. © Sir John Soane's Museum, London. Photograph: Ardon Bar-Hama.

> *on the Calton Hill it would be throwing*
> *away money on property that could not be*
> *improven if he thought of bringing the road*
> *from Haddington over the Calton Hill. He*
> *ought to think seriously of it before he gave*
> *his consent to a plan that would bring a*
> *reflection on himself and the city. I said they*
> *had it in their power to make one of the finest*
> *approaches into Princes Street in the world 'tis*
> *true there is better property in the way if they*
> *convey'd the road by a bridge over the Calton*
> *Street in a straight line with Princes Street*

Plate 1.18—Robert Adam, *Sketch of a Bridge of Communication between the New Town & Buildings on the Calton Hill, Forming an Entrance to the Old Town by the Calton Street & Leith Wynd to the High Street of Edinburgh*, c. 1791.
© Sir John Soane's Museum, London. Photograph: Ardon Bar-Hama

but then he got a double return by improving there property on each side of the bridge and gave a grand entry into the town. . .[76]

The survey drawings of the options for an approach to the Bridewell survive in the form of two ink sketches for the bridge, and a faint pencil sketch over an inked landscape of the city.[77] These are attributed to Robert Adam,[78] and most probably date to around the time of the above correspondence between Paterson and Adam, at the early stages of the Bridewell competition and before Adam developed his own designs for the Bridewell, as an undated sketch[79] (Plate 1.17) includes a Bridewell design that is similar to the 1782 proposals. This suggests that Adam may not have initially considered the Bridewell to be a key development in this part of the city, rather that the development of the prison on Calton Hill was a way to facilitate the establishment of

an additional access route into the New Town.[79] Adam's focus on the stylistic relationship between the proposed bridge and the classical New Town is further emphasised by the prominence of his neo-classical structures within the sketch which include the dome of the university building in the Old Town and a classical version of the (unexecuted) monument to David Hume.[80] A further structure with classical features running off the left hand side of the page can also be identified, providing further contextualisation to the proposed colossal bridge with its pedimented, classical character. This link between the urban landscape and Adam's bridge designs is also identified in Adam's second proposal (Plate 1.18) inscribed *Sketch of a Bridge of Communication between the New Town & Buildings on the Calton Hill, Forming an Entrance to the Old Town by the Calton Street & Leith Wynd to the High Street of Edinburgh*.

Plate 1.19—W. Tombleton after Thomas Shepherd, *View from Calton Hill, looking towards Salisbury Crags and the Bridewell*. Taken from Thomas Shepherd and John Britton, *Modern Athens! Displayed in a Series of Views: or Edinburgh in the Nineteenth Century: Exhibiting the Whole of the New Buildings, Modern Improvements, Antiquities, and Picturesque Scenery, of the Scottish Metropolis and its Environs*, 1829

This is of a castellated design and provides no indication of its location in relation to the hill. However, the inscription and its emphasis on it being an 'entrance to the Old Town' makes clear that the relationship between this bridge and the Old Town was pertinent to its design, as does its 'Court Revival' style execution.[81]

Both of the inked bridge sketches of Calton Hill appear to have advanced no further than these conceptual designs. Progress was delayed perhaps as the city magistrates were clear from the outset in their reluctance to consider additional development that might detract from the development of the Bridewell.[82] This further demonstrates Adam's understanding of the relationship between architecture and landscape which has been explored through both the David Hume monument and the Bridewell designs. Both of his sketches for the bridges provided access into the city, through the form of grand entranceways, but in their differing architectural style, emphasised a different relationship with different parts of the city. In Adam's classically designed bridge sketch, for example, this included stylistic linkages with other classical structures by Adam within the city—even ones that were not yet executed, or that were designed in a slightly different manner in their final execution. The castellated bridge design, despite still providing east-west access from the

Plate 1.20—Robert Barker,
Edinburgh From the Calton Hill, 1792.
© Centre for Research Collections,
University of Edinburgh

New Town to Calton Hill, also emphasised its structural purpose as an entrance into the Old Town at a lower level, under the bridge.

The city magistrates' refusal to include an access bridge in the Bridewell project was therefore more than likely to have been influential on Adam's final design decisions for the prison (Plate 1.19). Rather than the site becoming integrated into the New Town through the construction of a new access route, the hill's continued access from the Old Town through Calton Street maintained the physical link with the medieval burghs of Edinburgh and Canongate, which had already been metaphorically explored through the use of the Bridewell and its considered necessity within the county. Adam's use of a castellated design, therefore, was one that connected with the surrounding landscape within which it was set, as well as providing a prominent narrative regarding the use of the building and its purpose within society.

Adam's understanding of the relationship between the hill and the city had proposed structures which had turned what had been a rural periphery into a romantic rural landscape. However, the hill had also been somewhere to view landscape from, and this focus on the hill brought about through the introduction of prominent structures led to other opportunities to understand the surrounding landscape. The gothic observatory provided the first chance of further understanding of Calton Hill's placement within its surrounding landscape. This was not through astronomical observations during hours of darkness, but in its use during the day and the views that the gothic tower provided of its environs. This was first brought to attention by Robert Barker (1739–1806), an art teacher and portrait painter, who painted six scenes from a single fixed spot on the roof of the gothic tower (Plate 1.20),[83] and placed them together in a single continuous view.[84] By doing this, Barker created what was to become the first ever 'panorama'.[85] The popularity of this scene, and of the idea of the 'panoramic view', became a method considered 'capable of representing nature in a manner far superior to the limited scale of pictures in general'.[86] This was soon applied to a number of different cityscapes, countryside views, and even re-enactments of both historical and concurrent events.[87] Its popularity as a sightseeing tool for the tourist and the local visitor became so great that purpose-built structures purely

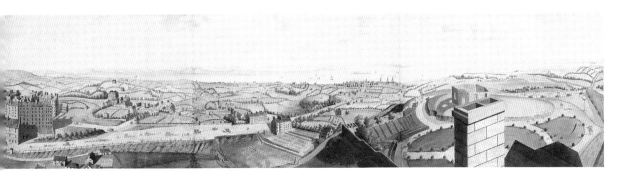

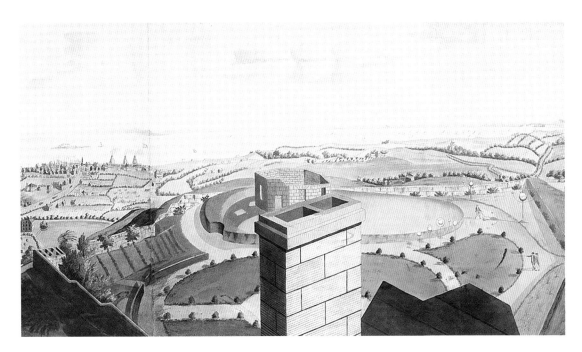

Detail showing unfinished Octagonal Observatory

for viewing panoramic landscapes were being erected by 1793.[88]

In Edinburgh, the popularity of the panorama not only provided a new method by which to view the Lothian landscape, it also contextualised the city's situation within it. Scholars of nineteenth-century art have considered this manner of displaying landscape painting crucial to the understanding and reception of urban landscapes by the public.[89] Although considered a frivolous form of popular entertainment as well as edification by some, it was expected to be an accurate rendition of actual views and was, on occasion, created by 'surveyors' rather than artists.[90] In particular, the panorama created a means by which to experience views of cities within the British Isles from a different perspective. The opportunity to view the seemingly endless wonder

Plate 1.21—Alexander Nasmyth,
Proposal for Nelson Obelisk, 1806.
Taken from J. Nasmyth, S. Smiles.
James Nasmyth, An Engineer, 1897.
© Courtesy of National Library of Scotland

also emphasised the scale of a city and the effect of topography on the urban landscape. In particular, the contrast of city and countryside was an important factor, and it was common for viewpoints to depict countryside on one side, and cityscape on the (Wilcox) other.[91]

Rather than viewing Edinburgh within the limited confines of the Old Town ridge, as had been depicted in Slezer's 1693 perspective of the city (Plate 1.5), or focusing on the Old Town as a central point with suburbs radiating to the north and south,[92] the panorama on Calton Hill opened up the landscape to include the Lothian countryside to the east and the Firth of Forth to the north. The view, taken from the summit of the gothic tower, depicts limited activity on the hill through the half-finished structure of Craig's octagonal observatory, and a number of paths leading around the hill in a pleasure walk (detail from Plate 1.20). Many of the paths within the curtilage of the lands laid out for the observatory (as shown in Plate 1.3b) have dioramas placed at intervals, of planets to represent the solar system, no doubt to educate and inform those on a walk around the grounds, and to maintain the presence of astronomical science on the site. Apart from a small kitchen garden within the grounds of the observatory, the rest of the hill's summit blends into a rural landscape that continues to the east and north of the hill, which on both sides extends into the distance, eventually ending at the Firth of Forth. On the western side, some more defined semi-rural settlements are identified, as is the encroaching urban development of the first New Town. The southern view, dominated by the cramped urban hub of the Old Town in the foreground, extends out towards Arthur's Seat and the Lammermuir Hills in the distance.

of Man's 'improvement' on God's creation from a birds-eye perspective not only brought awareness of the layout of streets, building masses, parks and farmland into a new perspective, it

Plate 1.22—W. Tombleton after Thomas Shepherd, *Nelson's Monument, Calton Hill, Edinburgh.*
Taken from Thomas Shepherd and John Britton, *Modern Athens! Displayed in a Series of Views*, 1829

This image of the city within its broader landscape presented a much greater visual connection between the city and its surrounding environs than had previously been considered. It opened up the confines of the city's layout beyond the city limits and popularised the hill as a famous viewpoint in Edinburgh.

The land to the north of the Calton Hill as a viewpoint was further popularised with a monument to commemorate the great naval captain, Lord Nelson, in the early nineteenth century. This structure, which was to 'be placed on the Calton Hill—a situation grandest perhaps in Europe', [93] included a viewing platform that would provide a view of the landscape almost as depicted in

Barker's panorama. However, it also further tied the hill to the land beyond the city by providing a visual connection with the port at Leith. This was emphasised through the placement of a telegraph pole[94] on the top of the building, and later, through the installation of the 'time ball' on the roof, both of which were methods of communication with the ships at Leith.[95]

The design chosen for the Nelson Monument was a stylistic relationship to other structures placed on the hill. During the competition phase in 1806, two designs were shortlisted. The first, by Alexander Nasmyth (Plate 1.21), consisted of an obelisk with three string courses recalling Nelson's significant battles at the

Plate 1.23—Robert Adam, *Brizlee Tower, Alnwick*, 1781.
© Courtesy of Northumberland Estates

Nile, Copenhagen and Trafalgar. The viewing platform was in the form of a neoclassical temple, with Corinthian columns, a domed roof and topped by a finial supporting a flagpole. The second proposal, by Robert Burn (Plate 1.22), was the chosen design.[96] This consisted of an octagonal base supporting a circular stone tower, decorated with three string courses and topped by a viewing platform with a recessed tower above. Its likeness to an 'upside-down spy-glass' or telescope has been remarked upon ever since.[97]

Historians who have commented on the surviving edifice have not only voiced a dislike for the structure but have also considered it much inferior to Nasmyth's design for the site.[98] This may well stem from criticism of the structure in the autobiography of James Nasmyth, engineer,[99] who was the son of Alexander Nasmyth:

> My father supplied a design, which was laid before the monument committee. It was so much approved that the required sum was rapidly subscribed. But as the estimated cost of this erection was found slightly to exceed the amount subscribed, a nominally cheaper design was privately adopted. It was literally a job. The vulgar, churn-like monument was thus thrust on the public and actually erected and there it stands to this day, a piteous sight to beholders.[100]

The minutes of the committee formed for the erection of this structure concur that Burn's proposal was the cheaper by around £700 and was likely to have been chosen because of this.[101] However, Burn's design was not wholly unsuited to the site, and its place within the shortlist suggests that it may have not only been picked for its lower price, but also its design. Its composition took a similar form to Brizlee Tower, an observation tower constructed between 1777 and 1781 by Robert and James Adam in Hulne Park, Alnwick, for the Duke of Northumberland (Plate 1.23). Brizlee's gothic windows and doorways have been substituted in the Nelson Monument for castellated, 'Court Revival' detailing complementing Robert Adam's Bridewell—the only other structure of significance on the hill at the time.

Alison Yarrington's study of monuments erected to Lord Nelson in the nineteenth century[102] notes that the thinking behind many of these was 'guided by economic rather than aesthetic considerations'.[103] The Edinburgh monument was, therefore, no different. However, in continuing Adam's stylistic influence on the hill alongside the exploitation of Barker's (now famous) view, the monument provided a draw as a tourist attraction,[104] which honoured a 'highly illustrious hero', providing positive images of Edinburgh as a city of the Empire which venerated its heroes and forged strong connections with its naval port from the summit of Calton Hill. This centring of the hill within the landscape provided a visual and social consciousness of Calton Hill, which further opened up the possibility for expansion of the city onto the hill and beyond, to the north and east as the nineteenth century progressed.

Plate 2.1—W. Tombleton after Thomas Shepherd, *The New Jail from Calton Hill.*
Taken from Thomas Shepherd and John Britton, *Modern Athens! Displayed in a Series of Views*, 1829

Linking Calton Hill to Edinburgh and Leith

D espite the integration of Calton Hill into the broader Lothian landscape in visual terms by the early nineteenth century, and its stylistic relationship with the architectural rhetoric of the Old Town through the development of Adam's Bridewell, a physical connection between the city and the hill did not exist until 1817. This came in the form of a bridge linking Calton Hill to the eastern end of Princes Street in the New Town, and spanning Low Calton, just as Adam had proposed for his classical bridge design in the 1790s. This bridge, according to 'Cockburn's memorials', 'would never have been where it is except for

the [city] gaol'[1] which suggests that its original purpose was purely to provide access to the prison, rather than extending the New Town to the east, or providing an alternative route to and from the city, as it quickly became by the time it was developed.

Proposals for the city jail (Plate 2.1) (to replace the Tolbooth Jail situated on the High Street, to the west of St Giles' Kirk) had been the subject of an Act of Parliament in 1813.[2] It was first intended that this new prison would be relocated in the Old Town.[3] But in December 1813, a report by the Sheriff William Rae was published in the *Scots Magazine*, which discussed its needs in terms of layout and space, in comparison to a number of other similar institutions around the country.[4] It concluded that a much greater area was required than the small patch of land allocated and that the only place large enough to accommodate it was on the southern side of Princes Street (where the Scott Monument in east Princes Street Gardens is currently situated).

Calton Hill was considered in Rae's 1813 report for this building, and was dismissed as unsuitable due to the greater distance between the court and the jail—increasing opportunities for escape. A response to this article, published in the following edition of the *Scots Magazine* in January 1814, argued the case for Calton Hill as the most appropriate site for the prison and supplied plans in support.

This response argued that the jail would benefit from fresher air and better drainage than would be achievable at the proposed Princes Street site. It also considered the matter of ownership of the land, which would have to be purchased by the magistrates if the jail were to be sited on Princes Street.[5] Perhaps most significantly, the article provided a solution to Rae's concerns about access, which could easily be dealt with by building a bridge over Low Calton. This would provide better access to and from court and could replace a road planned to the north of Calton Hill, intended as the new grand access route from London into the city, instead exploiting the views made famous by Barker's panorama. This road would sit on the south side of Calton Hill, and would provide an eastern access route to and from the city.

> *I propose that it should be the great approach to the city of Edinburgh from the London Road; and truly, I think, that a more striking and magnificent entrance cannot be figured—to gain the level of the Bridewell by gradual ascent—to overlook the Town*

> *and environs from that most striking of all points—to descend gently and arrive upon a great thoroughfare of Prince's Street [sic], the great point of divergence at Register Office—having commanded the Town in its most striking aspect . . .*[6]

By March 1814, the council magistrates had petitioned the House of Commons to add the development of an access route to the 1813 Act.[7] A large amount of funding would be needed to construct a bridge to connect Calton Hill with the city. The engineer Robert Stevenson was commissioned to design the bridge and the new access road to the city jail. He concluded that the most direct and practical solution to connect Calton Hill to the east end of the New Town would be a bridge and road running from the eastern end of Princes Street, that would lead around the hill and away from the city to the east, which would also become the main approach from the south.[8]

He took into account the benefits of easier access to Calton Hill as a pleasure ground, and in opening up the potential of the area for feuing,[9] as well as the practicalities of building the bridge and routing the road. It was no small task, as it required the removal of old buildings blocking the eastern end of Princes Street, bridging a fifty-foot deep ravine, blasting a passage through solid rock, and the relocation of part of the (Old) Calton burial ground (more about this in Part 2). These proposals were complicated and disruptive, but Stevenson also explained how the nature of the hill, its perceived assets, and the development both surrounding the site and on the hill could be utilised to enhance his design.[10]

> *[T]his line [of road] . . . seems best suited to the peculiar situation of the ground, being calculated to show to much advantage the*

rugged rocks on which Nelson's Monument is erected, which beautifully terminates the view in looking eastward; and in entering the Town from the opposite directions, it exhibits at one view, from a somewhat elevated situation, the striking and extensive line of Princes Street.[11]

In addition, Stevenson recognised the aesthetic asset of the views from the Old Town towards the hill and took great pains to retain and enhance these in his proposals. This sensitivity can be particularly identified in the treatment of the road in front of what was later to become Hamilton's Royal High School building. Stevenson needed to build a substantial retaining wall at this point to ensure that the road, which curved around the hill, would not begin to slip. By covering the retaining wall with rustic stonework facing to look like the outcropping rock found at other points on the craggy hillside, he ensured that this new intervention blended into the hill and became a part of the overall aesthetic enhancement of the site.[12]

The specifications for the layout of the roadway included another consideration. In 1813, the year before the Act permitting the construction of the new road was passed, a competition was held to design a third New Town that would stretch from the north side of Calton Hill to Leith.[13] The competition did not have a successful winning design, but the impact of this proposed development on the north side of the hill was significant, as by the time that Stevenson designed his plan of 1814, he understood that his road on the south side of the hill must tie in with it. He therefore had to consider its context within the third New Town development as a whole, which included both the aesthetic impact and practicality of the road design, as well as its

hierarchical placement as a thoroughfare within the New Town development.[14]

[T]his road is not only to be the great approach from the eastward, but likewise to become the chief thoroughfare to the extensive lands of Heriot's and Trinity Hospitals, and to the lands of other conterminous proprietors, henceforth likely to become the principal building grounds for this great city, which is always increasing towards its port of Leith, it becomes desirable for these purposes, and particularly to preserve the interesting view of the Calton Hill . . . two elegant buildings in the form of pavilions or wings to the bridge, would have an effect similar to what is strikingly observable in looking from the western end of George Street towards the Excise Office.[15]

Archibald Elliot's[16] designs for Waterloo Place, built on top of Stevenson's bridge spanning Low Calton, provided the 'elegant and striking effect' envisioned by Stevenson for the entrance to Calton Hill from Princes Street. He was also commissioned to design the new prison and governor's house.[17] This streetscape had an entirely different feel in its execution from the buildings that already stood on the hill, as Elliot used a restrained Georgian classicism for this access, more in keeping with the rhetoric of the adjacent New Town. For example, he had screens designed as triumphal arches[18] on either side of the bridge (Plate 2.2), which complemented and showed off Stevenson's engineering by affording views through the screen to Calton Road below.

The inception of Waterloo Place was influenced by the proposals for the Crown's London estate of Marylebone Farm, and its linking to Portland Place and St James' Park, by John Nash.[19] Where Nash et al.[20] had used surprise

Plate 2.2—Archibald Elliot's 'Triumphal Arch' Screens over R. Stevenson's Regent Bridge, as seen from Waterloo Place. © Kirsten Carter McKee.

and movement in the processional route up to Regent's Park to hint at the picturesque nature of the street's destination, Elliot had hinted at the semi-rural nature of Calton Hill by providing a visual connection with the outlying landscape to the north and south of the city through the screens of Regent's Bridge. In particular, the key viewpoint into Waterloo Place in London from the Prince Regent's residence at Carlton House (Plate 2.3) was copied almost exactly for Elliot's key view from Princes Street for the entrance into Waterloo Place in Edinburgh (Plate 2.4).[21] Elliot designed an access that connected to the landscape, replicating the most fashionable and *urbane* project of its period. By making a direct connection between the Prince Regent, the triumphs of the Napoleonic wars, and the development of the classical urban streetscape, Nash and Elliot encapsulated the prevailing mood and exploited the notion of nationhood and loyalty to the Crown that was to become a prominent factor in early nineteenth-century thinking.[22]

The Regent Street development in London has been described as 'a wish on the part of

George IV and his ministers to reinforce the position of the Crown and enhance the authority of State'.[23] Keeping these aims in mind, further similarities can be seen in the development of both these great cities from the eighteenth century onwards. After this point, Edinburgh adopted a homogeneous British architectural style in order to legitimise itself as a city of significance within Britain, rather than as an unsophisticated backwater. Edinburgh's struggle to be regarded as a city of comparison to its English counterparts during this period is often viewed as the impetus for much of its planning.[24] The development of regulated and rational townscapes had sought to instil a message of uniformity and togetherness throughout Britain by building in an 'English Manner', after a period of nearly fifty years of unrest during the Jacobite rebellions. For example, in a 1752 pamphlet[25] it is clearly stated that works were considered to be beneficial not only to the city in which they were carried out, but to the British nation as a whole:

[B]uilding bridges, repairing high-roads, establishing manufactures, forming commercial companies and opening new veins of trade, are employments which have already thrown a lustre upon some of the first names of this country . . . the leading men of a country ought to exert their power and influence . . . what greater object can be presented to their view, than that of enlarging, beautifying an improving the capital of their native country? . . . [and] prove more beneficial to Scotland and by consequence to United Britain.[26]

The implementation of this plan had been advanced through the development of James Craig's first New Town of 1766[27] (Plate 2.5), and its access, with the building of 'North Bridge'

Plate 2.3 (top)—W. Tombleton after Thomas Shepherd, *Waterloo Place, London* (n.d.) © Courtesy of www.alamy.com
Plate 2.4—W. Tombleton after Thomas Shepherd, *Waterloo Place, The National & Nelson's Monument, Calton Hill &c. Edinburgh*.
Taken from Thomas Shepherd and John Britton, *Modern Athens! Displayed in a Series of Views*, 1829

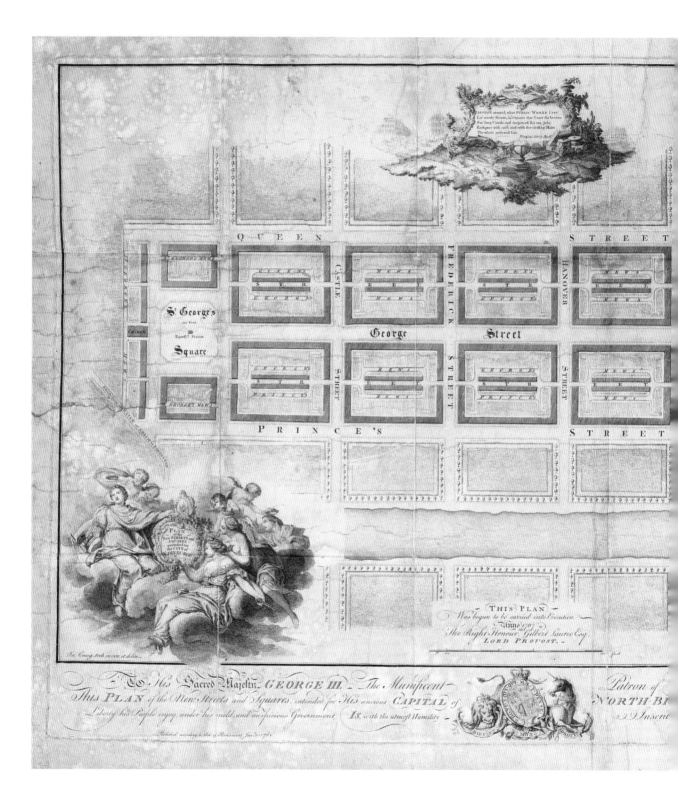

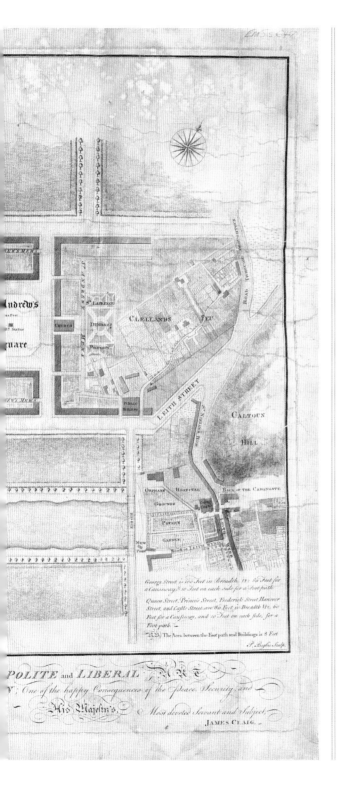

(1769).[28] However, the city's attempts to compete with its English counterparts could not consider its development in light of political events only.

Its reputation as a picturesque burgh, admired by genteel visitors when viewed as a distant landscape, was not so beautiful close up. Thomas Gray, for example, in his *Journey into Scotland from the 1760s* noted that Edinburgh was 'that most picturesque (at a distance) and nastiest (when near) of all capital cities'.[29]

The building of access routes into the New Town provided some opportunity to address this problem by developing a grand processional route from the south that would conveniently bypass some of the more insalubrious and poorer parts of the Old Town commented on by Gray.[30] Robert Adam's input into this processional route was significant, as much of his focus in the 1770s and 1780s was on the development of major public buildings here and the manipulation of views towards the New Town through axial vistas and dramatic sweeping landscapes. It included plans for a triumphal arch at the entrance to the city.[31] This would be immediately followed by Adam's new university building[32] and classical South Bridge development.[33] His enclosed bridge design created a vista towards Adam's Register House building at the entrance to Craig's New Town. This was further emphasised by the meeting point between the North and South Bridge, which opened out to reveal the view of the Waverley Valley to the west, incorporating the distant view of the castle and the New Town

Plate 2.5—James Craig,
*To His Sacred Majesty, George III,
the Plan of the New Streets and Squares,
Intended for his Ancient Capital of North Britain*, 1768.
© Courtesy of National Library of Scotland

and eastwards towards Hume's monument and the gothic observatory on Calton Hill.

In addition to providing a direct access route to the New Town that would bypass the less attractive parts of the Old Town, North and South Bridge were also part of a larger scheme of infrastructural development to enhance trade and commercial routes to and from the city. These had been part of the larger plans for the city at the early stages of proposals for the development of a New Town, mainly from canals that would have connected the city and Leith docks,[34] or that were to run east–west through the Waverley Valley.[35] However, with the onset of the French Revolution of 1789, and the restriction in European travel, a new focus on the city as a stopping point in the increasingly popular British Grand Tour[36] brought further focus on Edinburgh and its comparison with other cities of the British Isles. The success of small local projects was therefore considered key to displaying Edinburgh's advancement as a city of the Empire and its role in the strengthening of the country as a whole.[37] In particular, a need to improve connections between major British cities and their ports was mooted concerning the relationship between Edinburgh and Leith from as early as 1752.[38]

An increase in sea trade with the colonies in the late eighteenth century had prompted schemes to connect and improve many of the ports of Great Britain. This was not only to increase access to goods and services to and from ports, but also to allow for winter docking of the growing shipping fleet.[39] By the 1800s, modernisation and improvement within both urban and rural areas in Scotland meant that the rate of economic growth in Scotland surpassed that of England,[40] with Leith being second only to Glasgow/Greenock in the tonnage of shipping entering Scotland from abroad,[41] and it struggled to keep up with the demands of this level of shipping industry. As the City of Edinburgh was the (then) port authority for Leith, it was responsible for the development of the docks, but had no means to finance these improvements. At the end of the eighteenth century, therefore, the city gained government authority to raise £80,000 on the security of the rates to construct a series of small docks leading off the west side of the Water of Leith (the river running into the Forth from the south). This work was carried out between 1800 and 1817, alongside improved access from the city enhancing the streetscape between the new docks in Leith and Leith Walk.[42]

Before the development of Leith Walk,[43] access between Edinburgh and Leith was along two routes—either through the Canongate, up through Abbeyhill and onto Easter Road, or through Broughton Village to Leith Mills on the western side. The city appears to have maintained the walk at public expense from at least the late seventeenth century[44] (Plate 2.6) but as a pleasure promenade, rather than a main access route, as all commercial wheeled traffic was banned from using it until the late eighteenth century.[45] By the time that the docks were being developed, the direct access between Edinburgh and the Port at Leith that was afforded by Leith Walk meant that it was considered, alongside Easter Road to the east, as a primary connecting route between the two urban areas.[46] The enhancement of routes of access and communications between cities, ports and surrounding lands could be identified all over the country as part of the strengthening of naval ports during the Napoleonic wars. These were a priority for the Edinburgh town council, and considered a vital part of the city's future

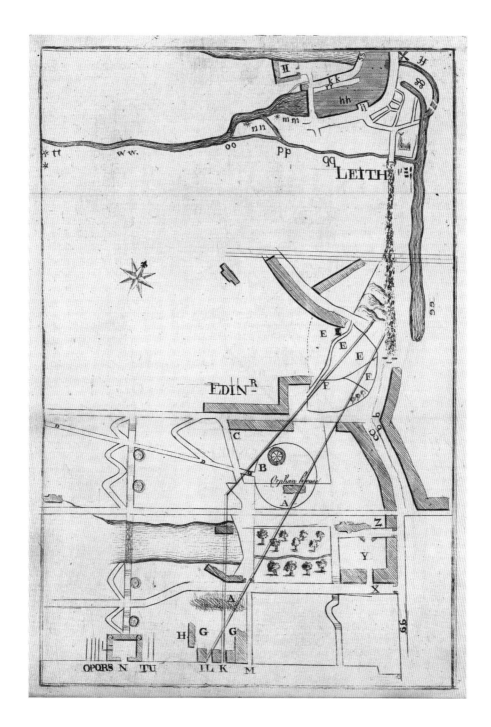

Plate 2.6—Robert Mein, *Plan of Edinburgh showing Leith Walk as a Gravel Track.*
Taken from R. Mein, *The Edinburgh Paradise Regain'd, on the City Set at Liberty, to Propagate and Improve her Trade and Commerce . . .*
By a Merchant-Citizen, . . ., 1764. © Courtesy of National Library of Scotland.

and prosperity. It is therefore unsurprising that while upgrading these two main access routes was taking place, the area between these two streets was considered for development.

During the eighteenth and early nineteenth centuries, the ownership of Calton Hill, Greenside and the land east of Leith Walk and west of Easter Road was split between a number of feus of differing sizes (Plate 4). These ranged from large swathes of land owned by the charitable institutions of Heriot's and Trinity Hospitals in the northern part of the site, to the large area of common ground owned by the city on the summit of the hill, to small individual farmsteads, which were dotted in between the larger estates.[47] The development of this area was proposed at a meeting between Heriot's and Trinity Hospitals, and a key landowner—Mr Allan of Greenside.[48] At the same meeting, the Lord Provost of Edinburgh, William Creech, who sat on the boards of Heriot's Hospital and Trinity Hospital trusts, proposed that there should be a committee, entitled the 'Committee for Feuing Calton Hill Grounds and Co.', set up purely for developing the land. It was therefore agreed at the meeting that:

> the ground belonging to Heriot's Hospital, Trinity Hospital and Mr Allan, situated between the Easter and Wester Roads to Leith, Also a small part of Heriot's Hospital Ground, and a part of Trinity's Hospital Ground lying on the East side of the Easter Road to Leith shall be laid out on Joint plan for building ground.[49]

A letter was sent by the newly formed committee to the City of Edinburgh to invite the council to consider including their common land on the Calton Hill in the plan.

The proposal of the third New Town to be sited to the 'east of Leith Walk' therefore included the open common land of the city, as well as that of private landowners. The proprietors entered 'into a joint contract' and John Bell, a land surveyor, was commissioned by the committee to prepare a measured plan of the area. This was to serve as both a visual guide to the boundaries of ownership and to set the limits of the development for an open competition to find an appropriate design.[50] The competition was advertised to the public in late 1812, and published in both local and national papers, such as the *Edinburgh Courant* and *The Times*.[51] The advertisement stated that an area roughly an oblong square had been surveyed and that 'plans of the land, sections and levels' had been prepared for proposals to be submitted for 'a BUILDING-PLAN or DESIGN . . . for the Lands situated to the East of Leith Walk'. The best plan would 'be entitled to receive the premium of THREE HUNDRED GUINEAS, and the designer of the next best plan, to the other premium of ONE HUNDRED GUINEAS [sic]'. All proposals for the competition were to be submitted (sealed up and anonymous), to Messrs Macritchie and Little, lawyers based in Edinburgh.

By the start of 1813, at least thirty-four proposals had been submitted. Ten competitors submitted two or more designs.[52] Although only the four plans of the successful competition winners survive (Plates 2.7–2.10),[53] the notes relating to all of the submitted proposals to Macritchie and Little can still be viewed, as well as the comments on the designs by the judges for the competition, who were well-known architects of the time.[54] From the descriptions that accompanied the designs, and the assessors' comments on their preferred submissions, the priorities of the development and, to some extent,

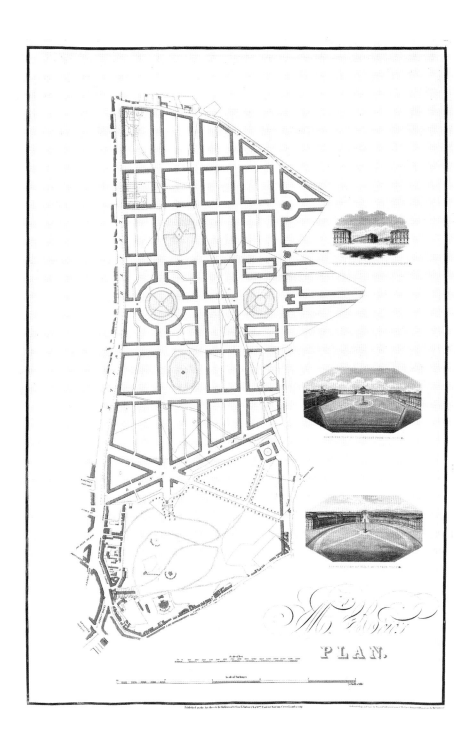

Plate 2.7—William Reid, *Proposal for the Third New Town between Edinburgh and Leith*, 1813.
Copied from Kirkwood's Plans and Illustrations of the City of Edinburgh © Historic Environment Scotland

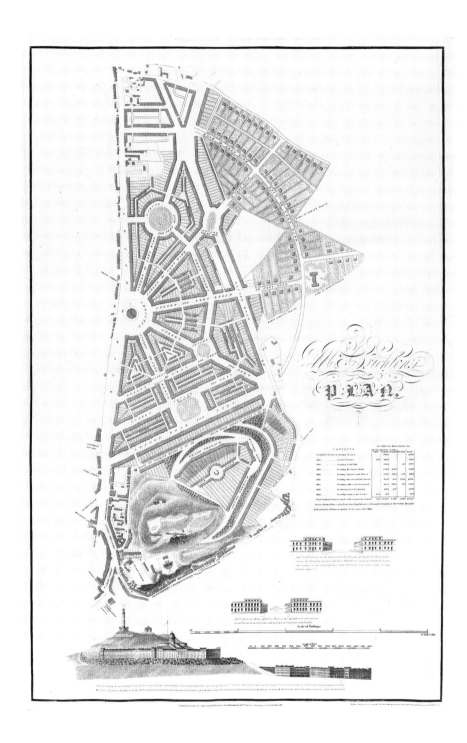

Plate 2.8—Richard Crichton, *Proposal for the Third New Town between Edinburgh and Leith*, 1813.
Copied from Kirkwood's Plans and Illustrations of the City of Edinburgh © Historic Environment Scotland

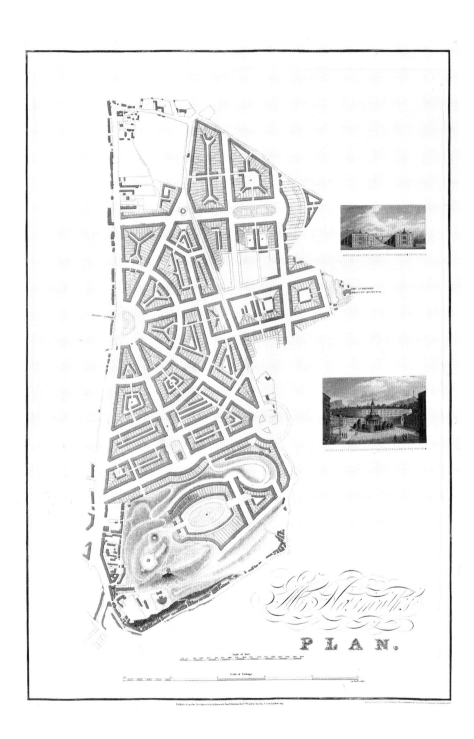

Plate 2.9—Alexander Nasmyth, *Proposal for the Third New Town between Edinburgh and Leith*, 1813.
Copied from Kirkwood's Plans and Illustrations of the City of Edinburgh © Courtesy of Historic Environment Scotland

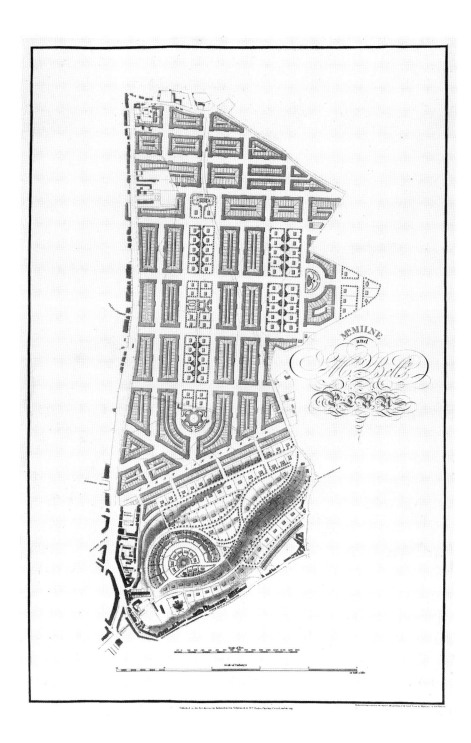

Plate 2.10—James Milne and Benjamin Bell, *Proposal for the Third New Town between Edinburgh and Leith*, 1813.
Copied from Kirkwood's Plans and Illustrations of the City of Edinburgh. © Courtesy of Historic Environment Scotland

the mindset of the entrants and the committee emerge. It is clear from the judges' comments that it was expected that the winning design needed to establish Leith Walk as a main route to the port of Leith, and enhance the link between the city and the newly developed Leith Docks.

In addition, as the comments about the location of the new jail in *Scots Magazine* in January 1813 made clear,[55] much emphasis was placed on the health benefits of the design. The quality of the air was of great concern. This included a combination of features found in other new towns of this period, Bath and Clifton, such as squares, circuses and crescents, believed to be healthful as well as providing aesthetically pleasing terminating views and vistas. A stipulation of the competition was that no alterations could be made in the plans to the observatory, Nelson Monument, flagstaff or Bridewell,[56] and many of the proposals used the Nelson Monument as a key focal point for proposed vistas to the south. A number of them also included additional commemorative and monumental architecture such as statues and public buildings to create more focal points throughout the development. However, despite the incorporation of vistas towards the Nelson Monument in the urban layout of the four competition winners, not one placed a commemorative monument on the summit of the hill. Instead, provision was made for large monumental edifices to be placed within the proposed urban layout to the north of Calton Hill.

Despite the many submissions, no overall winner could be decided upon.[57] Instead, rather than focusing on the entrants' plans, decisions for the development of the site were taken from comments made by one of the judges, William Stark, on how the picturesque nature

of the site should be improved.[58] Unlike the other committee members, it is unclear if Stark had favoured any of the competition designs submitted. Instead, he compiled a report that included general details on the considerations that should be made in any proposals. This report, which was never completed due to his sudden death in 1813, commented mainly on the existing landscape and how it should be developed. Its contents were considered so insightful that it became highly influential for the layout of the site. Stark believed that any new architecture or urban plan must exploit the site's topography and its existing elements.[59] Unlike the first New Town, of which Stark was highly critical, its layout should not follow a regulated grid plan,[60] but instead the contours of the site should be the starting point, enhancing its natural assets through the introduction of new architecture: 'It is of the utmost importance that the plan should be well considered, since the site is so well calculated to display either all its beauty or deformity.'[61]

The elevated situation of Calton Hill was also to be taken into account. As the hill sat above the city, any development there would be prominent within the landscape and therefore should be carefully and thoughtfully executed.

To a community like that of Edinburgh, where a taste for fine scenery is so generally prevalent, it is impossible that such situations should not have high attractions, if adorned with buildings worthy of them and combined so as to retain even a portion of their local beauties and splendid views.[62]

In particular, Stark's insistence that the natural assets of the landscape should be exploited rather than removed was one of his heaviest criticisms of the competition proposals. Not one of them had considered using these natural assets to enhance the layout of the site. Instead, most sought to remove or build over them.

> There are assemblages of trees, besides, which might be well worth preserving, even at some expence [sic] of ground, as they might adorn a square or public walk, or give interest to the picturesque effect to a church . . . as an instance I select the fine double row of elms which stand in a line with the buildings of Baxter's place, and form the northern boundary of Mr Allan's property . . . it would seem impossible for any one to approach them without being struck with the beauty of their forms, or remarking . . . how much indeed they enrich and give interest to the whole surrounding scene.

Stark's premature death in 1813 resulted in 'a friend' posthumously publishing his comments. In this publication, the friend added a postscript of opinions that Stark had—according to the author—'intended' to be part of the completed work.[63] This included further suggestions for the site, specifically: the need to provide access from Princes Street to the south side of Calton Hill; the development of a sweeping grand terrace around the lower and southern parts of the hill; and the retention of the upper part of the hill as public open space. These remarks were also included in the later designs for the hill and became key elements in the development of the site during the 1820s.

Comparison of these proposals for Calton Hill to Nash's plan for London's Regent Park particularly demonstrates the widespread interpretation of the principles of the picturesque and its application in urban design by the early nineteenth century. Although Nash and Stark's proposals both aimed to develop a semi urban/rural area, Stark's focus on giving precedence to existing topographical features of Calton Hill brought a more sensitive approach to the retention of the landscape by designing an urban framework around existing rural features. Conversely, Nash's designs aimed to impose an urban landscape on a rural site, by creating a controlled urban feel within a semi-rural setting through the introduction of formal geometric avenues and circuses. The differences in these two approaches was no doubt due to the visual prominence of Calton Hill, compared to Regent's Park, but it is also relevant that there was a priority for the London development to reflect Crown and state interests. This may also be the reason that a more formalised idea of an urban landscape was implemented in Nash's London development, as topographical concerns did not play such a prevalent part in the design. Instead, as the development was determined by the boundaries of land ownership on the west London site, focus was given to the statement that the landscape would make once it was developed, rather than the landscape that already existed.

Stark's reputation as an architect of particular taste and refinement led to his opinion on Calton Hill and expertise in the understanding the urban picturesque being lauded in influential circles. Sir Walter Scott is said to have commented at Stark's death that 'More genius has died than is left behind among the collected universality of Scottish Architects',[64] and Lord Henry Cockburn considered him to have been 'the best modern architect that Scotland had ever produced'.[65] McKean (2005) exemplifies why this was by stating that '[T]he inspiration to break with precedent, by responding to the landscape rather than dominating it, came from William Stark . . . Stark's recommendations . . . elevated the values of landscape, contour, prospect and trees above the seduction of geometry'.[66] His influence on his contemporaries, the third New Town committee, had a massive impact on the focus for the design of this site, and his localised approach to the application of the aesthetic was key in the development of Calton Hill after his demise.

While Calton Hill was considered as one large development area for the 1813 competition proposals, a number of smaller proposed developments within the site played an essential part in stimulating interest in the development of this area in the early nineteenth century. Firstly, the city's aspiration to be a port town, through the development of Leith Docks and the connections between the city and Leith, brought focus to the adjoining area as a site for development. Secondly, the need for a new city jail, and the suitability of Calton Hill as the location for it, again brought up the discussion that had occurred in the 1790s regarding access between the hill and the New Town. In spite of the consolidation of these proposed developments within the overall 1813 competition, however, it was not until Stark's 1814 report that the proposals for the third extended development of the city were considered within the realms of picturesque design.

Stevenson's reflections behind his 1814 designs for Regent Bridge and Regent Road, for example, incorporated the picturesque, since his proposals for the new road emphasised the importance of views towards the south side of the hill and enhanced the hill's natural features. In addition, his proposals for the layout of housing (Plate 2.11) directly reflected Stark's comments regarding residential development on top of Calton Hill. His three grand terraces planned for the eastern side of the hill emphasised the natural landscape and provided outlooks 'far excelling the views of Clifton, or Bath, or the Terrace at Ramsgate'.[67]

That Elliot's design for Waterloo Place was so different from his contemporaneous design for the prison is also telling. He had continued to use Adam's fortified castellated style as the key influence for the jail, but in Waterloo Place Elliot took influence from the classicism already adopted in the first New Town and applied it in a picturesque urban setting. This choice of design was an attempt literally and figuratively to 'bridge the gap' between the urban New Town and the rural Calton Hill. By taking the lead from the ideas implemented by Nash and his colleagues in the urban picturesque, the new bridge and road was brought into the forefront of fashionable architecture. In addition, it also legitimised the project as one of national consequence—an effect that would continue during the subsequent development of the hill.

Plate 2.11 (overleaf)—Robert Stevenson, *Sketch Plan & Section Shewing how the Lands of Heriots Hospital upon the Eastern Side of the Calton Hill were Proposed to be Laid out for Feuing Agreeably to a Report By Robert Stevenson Civil Engineer of date 12th Feby 1814, 1819.* © Courtesy of Historic Environment Scotland (George Heriot's Trust)

A detail from Plate 3.1b—William H. Playfair, *Design for a New Town between Edinburgh and Leith*, December 1819.
© Courtesy of Historic Environment Scotland (George Heriot's Trust.)

of a direct route to the Port of Leith from the city, which would be beneficial to commerce and provide suitable housing more in keeping with a modern city of the Empire. However, it was in Playfair's understanding of how to ensure the 'Beauty of the Metropolis' that the greatest similarities to the London plan can be identified. Playfair's inclusion of leafy, grand streets lined with villas, splendid circular terraces, squares and crescents embellished and terminated by commemorative monuments and key structures of architectural merit, showed he intended to give 'a magnificence that nothing else could impart'. These elements are all key components of both Regent Street and Regent's Park, where Nash had stated that vistas, grand circuses and monumental architecture would 'add to the beauty of the approach'.[10]

Playfair's plan for his residential development was essentially in two parts: the north end, where the majority of the dwellings were laid out; and the south end, which included Calton Hill, park and garden land and some higher-end housing. The most prominent of these high-end developments consisted of a street that would continue around the hill from Elliot's Waterloo Place, and a crescent to the north facing onto Calton Hill, fronted by public gardens. Playfair's street around Calton Hill followed, as Stevenson's proposals had, Stark's suggestion for terraces to be built following the contours of the hill. This was executed through the development of one continuous curving road around Calton Hill, but split into three different terraces, named Royal Terrace, Regent Terrace and—confusingly—*Carlton* Terrace.[11] This comparison with the contemporaneous developments in London further emphasises Playfair's ambition to connect his design within the general zeitgeist that

surrounded British urban development during this period, and specifically that of Regent Street and Regent's Park.

In his design for the three terraces, Playfair accommodated the sloping street, which hugs a contour around the hill, while designing a uniform classical façade for the streetscape. His aim was to keep the architecture on the streetscape quite simple and 'subordinate' to the hill's natural landscape. Yet he stated that the presence of a small amount of development on the hill would add to the 'charm . . . [of] the surrounding scenery'.

To ensure some form of continuity between the development and the summit of the hill (which was to be left as public pleasure grounds), Playfair proposed that part of the land to the rear of the terraces should be made into private gardens, as this would 'present a pleasing foreground to the enchanting landscape which is to be seen from the public walks above'.[12] Playfair's enthusiasm for these gardens was such that his instructions to the builders digging the foundations of the houses on Regent Terrace (the rubble of which was to be used to lay out the road leading from Leith Walk to the terrace) limited the amount of soil that could be taken from the foundations, in case this compromised the size and quality of the gardens (see Plate 3.2). This attempt at visual continuity on the hill and the blurring of the private and public grounds can still be discovered in the Ha-Ha (Plate 3.3) within the boundaries of the private gardens. It created the illusion of a far-reaching landscape when looking up towards the public area.[13]

Playfair also wanted to retain many of the natural assets that surrounded Calton Hill by easing the transition between the urban

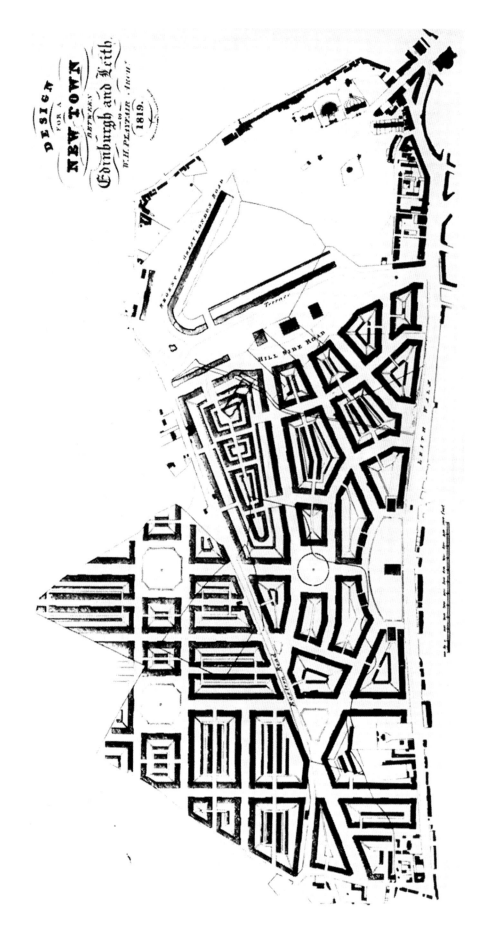

Plate 3.1a—William H. Playfair, *Design for a New Town between Edinburgh and Leith*, April 1819.

Taken from Byrom, C. *The Edinburgh New Town Gardens: 'Blessings as well as Beauties'*, 2005

Plate 3.1b—William H. Playfair, *Design for a New Town between Edinburgh and Leith, December 1819.*
© Courtesy of Historic Environment Scotland (George Heriot's Trust.)

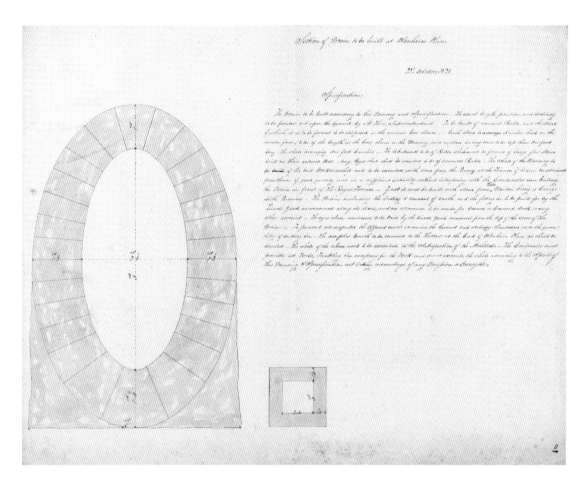

Plate 3.2—William Henry Playfair, *Section of Drain to be built at Blenheim Place*, 1821.
Drawing demonstrates detailed instructions provided for workmen excavating and laying the drain
© Courtesy of Centre for Research Collections, University of Edinburgh

residential development in the north part of the plan, and the rural nature of the hill, through the development of public gardens at the base of the hill.[14] Hillside Terrace, another of Playfair's higher-end streetscapes at the foot of Calton Hill is particularly associated with this transition. At the southern side of the street, two gardens, one on the south side of Hillside Terrace, the other directly behind at the bottom of Calton Hill, provided a glimpse of greenery from the north end of the proposed development that would create a suggestion as to what could be found at the south end of the site.[15] This, Playfair states, was designed in the 'interests of the proprietors', to 'add beauty to the scene . . . [which would] render the adjoining houses much more valuable, beauty of situation being now so much and justly prized in Edinburgh'.[16] This idea can also be identified in Nash's design for the entrance to Regent's Park from the south. His controlled, enclosed vista leading northwards up towards the entrance of the park ensures that a hint of

Plate 3.3 Ha-Ha at Royal Terrace Gardens. © Kirsten Carter McKee

open space is maintained in the distance, yet it is not until you are relatively close to the entrance to Regent's Park that the extent and nature of the open landscape are brought into full view.

The pleasure grounds of Calton Hill had already been established prior to Playfair's plan—pleasure walks on the summit of the hill had been laid out as paths by 1816 as a method of employment for the poor.[17] The area around the gothic and octagonal observatory had also been used as the site for an astronomical diorama from the late eighteenth century,[18] and its summit had been a further point of touristic interest with the building of the Nelson Monument. Playfair's plan, in accordance with Stark's suggestions, leaves this site virtually empty, so that the much-lauded views discussed in guidebooks and made popular through Barker's panorama would continue to be appreciated. Part of the appeal

to Playfair of leaving this area partly rugged may also have been to provide a contrast to the manicured and landscaped private gardens of the adjacent terraces.

The final part of Playfair's proposal is the inclusion of commemorative monuments and architecture. These were to provide terminating focal points for streetscapes throughout the site, as well as to emphasise the importance of specific thoroughfares and the connection between Leith and Edinburgh. Again, there are similarities in Nash's plan to link his Regent's Park scheme to Carlton Place, where numerous monuments, public buildings and statues are included in the landscape masterplan.[19] Recent research has placed much importance on these monuments as celebrating not only the glory of Britain, but also her intellectual achievements, identity and culture.[20] Playfair's design provided a number of opportunities to celebrate Britain and its subjects in a similar manner. However, this was specified at only a few of the site locations.[21] Squares at the centre of the urban layout, for example, were to have 'an obelisk or column, in memory of some remarkable person or event',[22] and the large crescent halfway between Edinburgh and Leith, on Leith Walk was to have 'in the centre . . . the proposed National Monument intended to commemorate the victory at Waterloo'.[23] These were also intended to provide focal points within the landscape, and to add drama and depth to the design. In particular, he singles out the public buildings proposed for the gardens of Hillside Road stating that these are intended to form an 'appropriate termination to each of the principal streets' leading up from Leith towards Calton Hill, which would also focus the eye up towards the backdrop of Calton Hill and Royal Terrace to the rear.[24]

In providing these grand evocative views and landscapes, there is no doubt that Playfair was attempting to create a triumphal route between Leith and Edinburgh, similar to the one that Nash had proposed between Carlton House and Regent's Park. However, unlike Nash's proposals for Regent's Street and Park, which were realised by a team of architects/builders and developed over the ensuing decades, Playfair's plan was never fully executed. Within five years of its implementation, interest in the development of the eastern side of the city began to diminish in favour of the Earl of Moray's development to the West. This resulted in the site being only partially built to around a third of the way down Leith Walk before stopping altogether. This is how it remained until the arrival of the railways in the mid nineteenth century, which cut through the site around halfway down Leith Walk.

The use of Stark's key considerations regarding the visual importance of the hill within the design alongside Nash's approach to urban expansion, is telling of the calibre of Playfair's skills as an architect and urban planner. In his plan, he manages to cover the requirements of his clients through maximising commercial profit, and displays an acute understanding of the site, implementing within his scheme the most up-to-date methods in urban design in the early nineteenth century.

By including public architecture in his urban plan, Playfair synthesised the emotive nature of commemorative architecture with the visual drama of the picturesque, in order to represent the notions of nationhood, identity and civic duty. These had been explored in their individual components through Adam's proposals for the hill, and through the key role that the hill and its environs played in facilitating access to the port, in order to reinforce the city as a British military stronghold. Yet, it was only through Playfair that all of these elements combined, and this was in part due to the understanding of the role the wider landscape played in connecting the city to the port, captured and appreciated in the panoramic views from the rooftops of the structures placed on Calton Hill. ⁓

CONCLUSION

The complicated nature of the development of Calton Hill from an urban periphery to an integral part of the city was influenced by a number of factors that encompassed not only eighteenth- and early nineteenth-century aesthetic thinking regarding landscape design within the urban realm, but also the political aspirations of Great Britain as an imperial power.

Also contributing to the development of the hill during this period were the efforts of the numerous architects, engineers, opticians, artists and all-round visionaries, who developed the landscape and installed buildings which enhanced the hill's relationship with Edinburgh.

The architectural manifestations of Enlightenment through the establishment of an astronomical observatory and a panopticon were joined by experimentations in aesthetic theories, through the development of the panoramic landscape, and consideration of how notions of the romantic and the picturesque could be exploited through architectural design. All this was integral in the evolution of the urban design of Calton Hill in the nineteenth century, as without the dialogue created by Adam on the role of the hill within the cityscape, or a heightened consciousness of how the picturesque nature of the city contributed to the broader Lothian landscape, the hill's potential to enhance these aspects during the expansion of the urban realm may never have been considered.

The contribution of the practical and the cultural within Playfair's design reflected the concerns of the city in developing the third New Town in a manner that would befit Edinburgh's political standing within the British Isles, while also producing maximum economic gain for those involved in the development. In providing large swathes of new housing for the upper and middle classes, Edinburgh would be encouraging higher levels of commerce while strengthening its links to the wider Empire. By exploiting the area's aesthetic potential in terms of the picturesque, and by the placement of commemorative monuments to heroes of the British Empire at key points within the design, the plan would not only create a visually attractive outcome, but would also further affirm Edinburgh's place within the imperial construct.

This dialogue, within which the third New Town was created, reflected the aspirations and outlook of Edinburgh and Scotland as a part of Great Britain at the end of the Napoleonic wars. Although the contemporaneous developments carried out in London were also an outward display of British nationalism and expansion for economic gain, London had much less to prove than Edinburgh. Edinburgh, in assimilating itself to London in terms of its architectural aspirations, as well as in its urban design, did so to prove its legitimacy as a key city in the northern part of Great Britain, as Craig's design had also attempted in the mid eighteenth century. However, by also including good communication links to London, and particularly by providing a key route to the port of Leith, as well as establishing the port as a place of navigation in the North Sea, Edinburgh was also asserting its presence as a city of consequence within the British Isles. The inclusion of commemorative monuments to state and cultural icons within a picturesque urban setting only served to further support this display of state and imperial power, expressing Scottish identity through a newly defined role within the British Empire.

PART 2

Burial, Memorial and Commemorative Monuments

In Lord Henry Cockburn's[1] famous 'Letter to the Lord Provost on the best ways of spoiling the beauty of Edinburgh',[2] Cockburn describes Calton Hill as the 'Glory of Edinburgh . . . adorned by beautiful buildings, dedicated . . . to the memory of distinguished men'.[3] This description of the hill as a commemorative landscape dedicated to the memory of the deceased was one that was deliberately cultivated alongside the development of the urban layout during the early nineteenth century, as part of a civic demonstration of national identity and allegiance to the British state. However, Calton Hill's role as a place for memorial did not start out as one focused on the glorification of state martyrs and national heroes as Cockburn describes it, but instead as a community's control over the right to bury its dead in a proper and timely manner.

Part 2 explores this shift from private to public through an investigation of the development of the commemorative landscape of Calton Hill during the eighteenth and early nineteenth centuries. It looks at the idea of memorial and veneration as both a religious and secular activity and the changing attitudes towards death and mourning in Western Europe that evolved from the late sixteenth century. By focusing on how and why people were commemorated, and where those memorialising the deceased chose to erect their monuments, it will place into context the hill's development from a local place of burial to a proposed national pantheon.

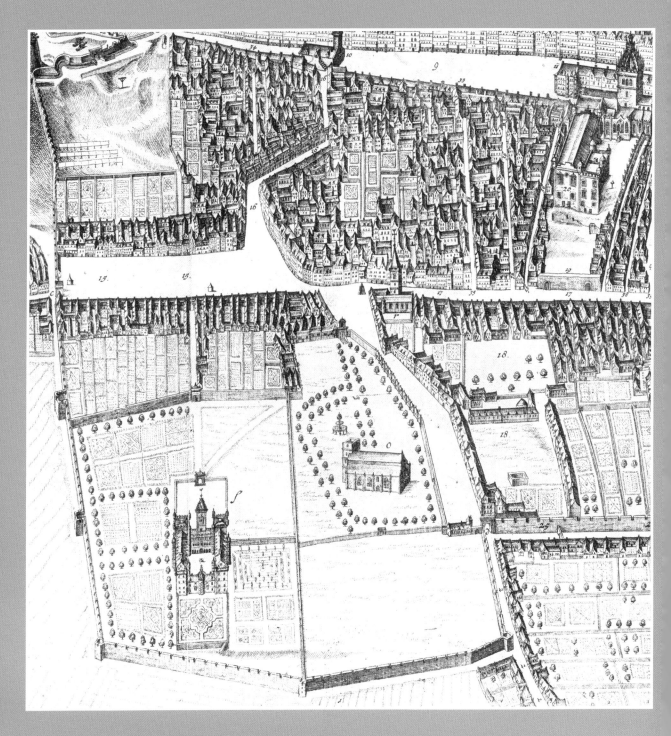

Plate 4.1—James Gordon. *Edinodunensis Tabulam*, 1647. Detail of Greyfriars Kirk and Kirkyard on the south side of Edinburgh.
© Courtesy of National Library of Scotland.

Memorial, Monuments and the 'Athens of the North'

By the end of the sixteenth century, the traditional Christian practice of burying the deceased inside churches had led to the overcrowding of crypts, creating unsanitary conditions that raised public health concerns and questions over the decency of the practice. Although the installation of statuary and memento mori continued within many Christian churches throughout the subsequent centuries, the dominant Protestant faith in seventeenth-century Scotland forbade statuary and imagery inside its ecclesiastical buildings as part of the Church of Scotland's dominant (Calvinist influenced) Protestant practices. This rejection of idolatry inside ecclesiastical establishments and the concerns over the links between disease and the burial of the dead therefore resulted in new large spaces for burials outside churches, or outside of city walls.[1] In Scotland, a good example is Greyfriars burial ground,[2] established outside of the city walls to the south of the Old Town (Plate 4.1) in the late sixteenth century, to give relief to the graveyard of St Giles in the heart of the burgh. This (relatively large) expanse of new burial space resulted in the erection of opulent grave monuments, for those who could afford them, allowing inclusion of both images and text to mourn the deceased's passing and describing their contributions to society.[3] This practice of commemorating status provided

Plate 4.2—Robert Milne, *Monument in Memory of John Milne*, 1667. © Kirsten Carter McKee.

benefit to living family members who associated themselves with the deceased. For example, the monument to John Milne, royal master mason[4] (Plate 4.2), carries a poem in English glorifying John Milne's place within a prestigious lineage of master masons to the Crown while also providing a Latin inscription that names his nephew Robert as his successor:[5]

> To John Milne, who, at the expiry of fifty-five years of this frail life, sleeps softly here, sixth master mason to the King of the family of Milne, of remarkable skill in the building art, frequently deacon convenor of the trades of Edinburgh, the circumspect and faithful representative of the metropolis on several occasions in the public parliament of the

kingdom; a man adorned with gifts of mind above his condition in life, a remarkably handsome person, upright, sagacious, pious, universally respected. Robert, his brother's son, emulous of his virtues, as well as his successor in office, has, out of gratitude, erected this monument, such as it is, to his uncle. He died 24th Dec. 1667, in the fifty sixth year of his age.[6]

This commemoration of the rank, wealth and position of the dead assisting the aspirations of the living is discussed by Nigel Llewellyn in 'The Art of Death'.[7] He explains how the dead are separated from their social level at the point of death'. By memorialising the status that the deceased had attained during their living years,

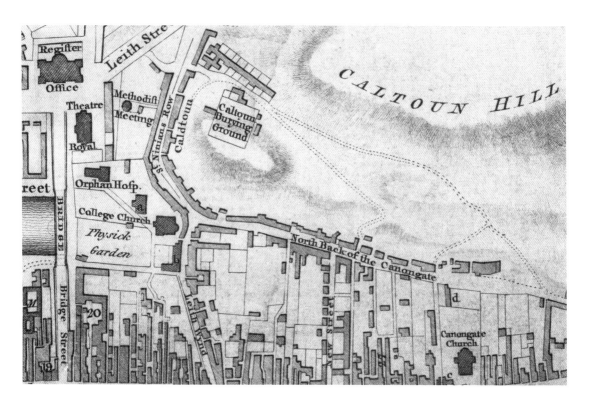

Plate 4.3 Andrew Mostyn Armstrong, *Map of the Three Lothians*, 1773. Detail showing Calton Burial Ground on south side of Calton Hill. © Courtesy of National Library of Scotland.

through effigies or gravestones, continuity of position and connection is retained by the surviving family.[8]

This practice of veneration of the deceased alongside the living also became common in burials outside the landed classes, where money was available to erect permanent memorials. The (Old) Calton burial ground in Edinburgh,[9] on the south side of Calton Hill (Plate 4.3) contains a number of gravestones erected to the memory of tradesmen from the 1700s and into the 1800s that display the deceased's profession alongside familial connections.[10] This burial ground was established in the early eighteenth century by the Incorporated Trades of Calton[11] for the local tradesmen and their families living in the hamlets

that surrounded the hill. The close proximity of this burial ground to local inhabitants and the prominence of its members' burials served as a visual reminder of the families involved in established professions locally, ensuring continuity from father to son, or uncle to nephew that would provide for the family after the death of the paterfamilias.

In addition to memorials emphasising the connection between the recently deceased and living through lineage and inheritance, monuments also played a symbolic role in the veneration of the dead, particularly those who had held offices of state. This is referred to in the opening lines of an early eighteenth-century book on the burials in Greyfriars kirkyard, which warns the bailies of the city that although they may believe themselves to be in powerful positions, death eventually will bring them to the same position as those who held office before them:

> *This treatise may serve as a monitor to whisper you in the ear that you are men; and tho you be called gods, you must die. This sets before you the memoir of those excellent worthies, whose steps you tread and whose vertues you imitate; and whose (following) inscriptions, changing only the names, may be thought of as just delineations and descriptions of your selves, your way and walk. This theatre of mortality may raise in you an assiduous and daily contemplation of Death; which will enable you, through grace, so to number your days, and to wait your change as to apply your hearts to heavenly wisdom.*[12]

Despite the Calvinistic interpretation of the monuments in Greyfriars by the author of *An Theatre of Mortality*, its emphasis on the importance, virtue and sacred responsibility of government office was a focus for many memorials found throughout the British Empire at this time. Barbara Groseclose, in her study of ecclesiastical monuments in colonial India during the eighteenth and early nineteenth centuries, identifies this focus on the importance of status in many of the memorials found throughout Mumbai (Bombay) Kolkata (Calcutta) and Chennai (Madras) during the period:

> *From the Baroque onward, sepulchral art situated allegories within secular as well as religious realms and sometimes even presented the deceased as he or she might have been alive, not only in physical likeness but also biographical narrative . . . the shift in sepulchral imagery after the Baroque was not so much downward, from the transcendental to the secular, but upward, promoting characteristics associated with worldly achievement to pious accomplishment.*[13]

Matthew Craske identified this transition of 'worldly achievement to pious accomplishment' in his study of the monuments within Westminster Abbey.[14] Many of those commemorated in the hallowed grounds of what was considered 'the sole church building that could be classed as national territory',[15] were people recognised for their contribution to the British state. Richard Jenkyns, in his book on Westminster Abbey, claims that the monuments to notable writers, poets and men of science were removed from the act of mourning and were instead purely commemorative, since these men were actually buried elsewhere.[16]

Because of this, Craske describes the abbey's role from the early eighteenth century as being 'the public space in which the notion of the exemplary national citizen was articulated through the erection of monuments'[17]—something that had been recognised as early as the mid eighteenth century by Voltaire.[18] This is in contrast to Christopher Wren's St Paul's Cathedral (1675–1710), which was viewed as the national church for the state mourning of military leaders from the eighteenth century onwards.[19]

As monuments veered further from religious towards secular veneration during the early part of the nineteenth century', the act of commemorating outstanding members of society, either through cultural, or military acclaim, took on a more public form, evolving completely outside of their original ecclesiastical context.

This was enhanced by the funding of a large number of public monuments by government on the pretext of investing in public good.

Between 1802 and 1812, at least £40,000 of public money was spent on national monuments to people deemed important to national and imperial pride. Such was the extent of this that the Treasury appointed a Committee of Taste for National Monuments to act on the government's behalf, who would decide on an appropriate use for and administration of the funds.[20] This can be seen as a form of public relations exercise, a response to the American and French revolutions which had left the government feeling vulnerable to the threat of popular insurrection, as well as invasion from overseas. By recalling the recent success of military battles in the Napoleonic campaigns, these monuments were an attempt to raise patriotism, chivalry and heroism and to encourage civic perception of self sacrifice for the good of the country.[21] In other words, by glorifying the state and its military prowess and commemorating men who had played a role in defending the British state, these monuments reinforced the role of the citizen in strengthening unity at a time of their country's need.[22]

The connection between an increase in the number of monuments erected and urban improvement in the early nineteenth century has also been acknowledged. In London,[23] as well as in other English towns and cities,[24] there appears to have been an attempt to further pursue the idea of 'self sacrifice for the good of the country'[25] by merging commemorative memorials into the urban landscape.[26]

> Public monuments commemorating national heroes of the French Wars were a means of expressing the emerging national and civic pride of the British people, particularly in expanding provincial towns and cities . . . In the case of provincial monuments national pride was closely linked with the desire to improve the physical appearance of new cities and towns, providing central symbols of their civic pride and patriotism.[27]

This increase in the commissioning of public monuments coincided with the boom in urban expansion that occurred throughout the country in the early nineteenth century (see Part 1). Memorials could take the form of buildings, bridges and streets named after notable citizens,[28] as well as the more traditional form of a free-standing monument, set at key points in a town. This allowed the idea of the commemorative landscape to escape from the burial ground and into the everyday fabric of British towns and cities.

The state purse did not stretch to funding commemorative monuments outside London. Instead, memorials to notable members of society were financed through local government schemes, or private ventures—particularly as many citizens of means considered it their public duty to invest in local development. Texts such as William Godwin's *Essay on Sepulchres* (1809)[29] and William Wood's *Essay on National and Sepulchral Monuments* (1808)[30] explain how such a display of civic virtue was also perceived to be of benefit to national endeavours. In these, both Godwin and Wood explain that there are many ways to protect and celebrate a country, and that the erection of public monuments to celebrate achievements is almost as good as carrying out the achievements themselves.[31]

In Alison Yarrington's work on the spread of monuments to commemorate the Napoleonic wars during the early nineteenth century, she concluded that building local monuments was '[i]n no way . . . part of a centrally organised, politically motivated propaganda plan to boost public morale as was the case with Napoleonic Monuments in France'.[32] Rather, local memorial projects 'helped consolidate patriotic fervour in local areas by the discussion of the qualities of the hero'[33] and became a means of patriotism through civic endeavour. That Edinburgh took this idea of civic virtue to heart as much of the rest of the country was commented on by Cockburn in his memoirs of 1856:

> *The influence of these circumstances can only be appreciated by those who knew Edinburgh during the war . . . There were more schemes, and pamphlets, and discussions, and anxiety about the improvement of our edifices and prospects within ten years after the war ceased, than throughout the whole proceeding one hundred and fifty years . . .*[34]

The proposal for a monument to Lord Nelson was the city's first attempt at commemorating a public figure within the urban landscape in such a manner.[35] After Nelson's death at the Battle of Trafalgar in 1805 until well after the victory at Waterloo, statues, pillars and buildings were erected to commemorate the great admiral all over the country. The sentiment surrounding the proposal for the Edinburgh monument, initiated on 25 November 1805, was no different from others around the country in commemorating the great Naval and British icon and professing sadness at his sudden death.[36] The monument, which was built between 1807 and 1815, focused on a celebration of Nelson's life and his achievements, rather than any religious obligation of mourning his untimely demise.[37] This is clear from its placement in the public secular realm rather than in an ecclesiastical context,[38] and the tone of the inscription above the door of the monument is eloquent in praise of his secular virtue:

> *To the memory of Vice Admiral Horatio Lord Viscount Nelson, and of the great victory of Trafalgar, too dearly purchased with*

> *his blood, the grateful citizens of Edinburgh have erected this monument, not to express their unavailing sorrow for his death, nor yet to celebrate the matchless glories of his life, but by his noble example to teach their sons to emulate what they admire, and like him, when duty requires, to die for their country. MDCCCV.*

This celebration of Nelson's role in protecting and enhancing imperial Britain encouraged a homogeneity of sentiment to percolate throughout the country in a manner that religious memorialisation would not have achieved.[39] However, the raising of local monuments to state figures also produced variances in design that allowed regional cultural identities to be shown through symbolism, allegory and cultural association. The intertwining of state and local identity helped to maintain a sense of connection with British imperial interests at a local level, through the propagation of national sentiment by the association of national causes with civic endeavours.

This is never clearer than in the proposal for a monument to commemorate the Scottish war dead of the Napoleonic wars (1822–9). It came out of a House of Commons debate in 1815, on how to '[pay] that respect and gratitude . . . owed to the memory of those who had fallen' during the Napoleonic wars.[40] A memorial planned for this purpose in London was immediately followed with proposals for others in Dublin and in Edinburgh, so that those who could not get to the 'Metropolis of the Empire' might be able to view one of the other two memorials.[41]

> *The National Monument to be erected in London, in commemoration of the Glorious Naval and Military achievements of the late war . . . is seen and visited by a very small*

proportion only of the Scottish Nation. The ancient metropolis of Scotland ought unquestionably to be ornamented with a similar Trophy, for, as your Grace justly observed this forenoon; 'The blood and treasure of Scotland largely contributed to the purchase of the triumphs of the British arms by sea and land.' Scotsmen, therefore, as well as Englishmen, when they repair to the Capital of their Country, ought to be gratified.[42]

The institution integral to setting up the committee for the Edinburgh monument was the Highland Society of Edinburgh—now known as the Royal Highland and Agricultural Society of Edinburgh. The society's remit during the 1800s was to:

> *improve the Highlands and Islands of Scotland and the conditions of its inhabitants, an enquiry into the means of their improvement by establishing towns and villages—facilitating communications by roads and bridges—advancing agriculture—extending fisheries—introducing useful trades and manufactures, and the preservation of the language, poetry and music of the Highlands.*[43]

The institution not only intended to commemorate the war dead through a national memorial, but also considered the action as a way to fulfil its agenda of promoting Scottish interests on a British stage. This can be recognised in the agenda outlined by Mr Michael Linning of Colzium[44] to the National Monument Committee in 1816:

> *[A]s may be deemed most prudent and advisable, for the obtaining for the Metropolis of Scotland; a Pillar, Triumphal Arch, or some such Architectural Monument . . . in order that Scotchmen may be gratified with the contemplation of some striking emblem of their country's prowess and glory, and may*

read on this hallowed record, the names of those Friends, Comrades and Countrymen who, by their heroism, maintained the martial fame of their Scottish ancestors, and by their arm contributed to the overthrow of despotism, and with their blood sealed the peace of the World . . .[45]

The National Monument Committee minutes record a proposal for an arch at the west end of Princes Street by the self-proclaimed 'Architect in Scotland of the Prince Regent'[46] James Gillespie (later Gillespie Graham). A triumphal arch was originally envisioned to show 'the grand view of Princes Street through the arch',[47] which is depicted in a drawing by Gillespie.[48] However, by the time of the creation of Robert Kirkwood's 1819 map of Edinburgh New Town (Plate 4.4),[49] the arch is depicted as spanning the eastern end of Waterloo Place. The map shows a large classical structure with a central archway, flanked by double Ionic pilasters and a rectangular pediment above, no doubt for an (as yet uncomposed) inscription. To each side of the arch are smaller arches flanked by single Ionic pilasters with square tablet above. The design is not dissimilar to the arch of Constantine in Rome, but is stepped down to a lower height at the ends.

From the outset of the parliamentary debates about national monuments to the Napoleonic war dead, the view was that they should be public, and accessible to everyone.[50] Whether building or structure, there was to be a level of accessibility to a general populace that had not before been considered, as well as something of a colossal and impressive scale.[51] Designs suggested for the national monument in London, to commemorate Trafalgar in particular, encompassed both of these elements. Robert Smirke, who was involved with both the London

Plate 4.4—Robert Kirkwood, *Plan and Elevation of the New Town of Edinburgh*, 1819.
Detail showing proposed National Monument. © Courtesy of National Library of Scotland

and Dublin monuments, designed structures that had '[t]he same basic principle of a huge monolith (either an obelisk or fluted column) with the minimum of decoration, all of which is placed around the base and easily viewed by the passer-by'.[52]

However, despite London leading the way in public commemoration through national memorial, and a Parthenon on Primrose Hill at the north end of Regent's Park[53] being proposed in 1816, a monument in the guise of a 'national memorial' was never realised in the Metropolis. Instead, the money allocated was used to develop Nelson's Column and Trafalgar Square.

A report of 1838 which tried to revive the 1816 proposals for London[54] states that the reason for this was that 'the government, whilst eager to promote public enthusiasm for patriotic virtues personified by national war heroes, were also eager to avoid censure over the use of public funds for non-utilitarian projects'.[55] This was also the case in Edinburgh; the British government refused access to public money as early on in the project as 1816.[56]

After being refused funds for their cause, the National Monument Committee in Edinburgh began to debate other forms for the structure. The focus was changed from a design for 'A pillar, triumphal arch, or some such architectural monument' to a proposal for a national church, in order to attract funding through the 1818 Church Act, which included reallocated money intended for building national commemorative monuments.[57]

> The committee . . . are of the opinion that a monumental church of Ornamental Archi-tecture would be a most appropriate an[d] Hallowed place of record, for inscribing, on some durable material the names of those British Heroes, who by their signal gallantry upheld the martial fame of their ancestors.[58]

The Church Act fund was set up to address the lack of pews available to the poor in areas where industrial expansion had exponentially increased the population; and there were concerns that the lack of direct communication between the Church and the poorer classes was leading to a disaffection towards the religious teachings that played a major role in upholding the ideas of state. This was considered to have been a key factor giving rise to the godlessness that was witnessed in the revolution in France,[59] and therefore was of concern to government in maintaining the general status quo in society.

At least four proposals for a national church were submitted as the national monument in Edinburgh. These were: a design in the style of the Parthenon of Athens, supported by Lord Elgin from an earlier proposal in London by a Mr Robertson; a design in the style of the Pantheon by Archibald Elliot (Plate 4.5) which included a circular inscription hall with an extended wing leading off from the central chamber that would serve as the church; a design for a gothic church by an amateur enthusiast, Peter Spalding; and a Roman Italianate design by a Mr Thynn.[60]

However, it was the proposals for Elliot's Pantheon and Robertson's/Elgin's Parthenon that attracted most of the attention of the committee. These proposals most aptly demonstrated the sentiments of commemoration and patriotism to be achieved through the execution of this project, being 'formed on, or . . . an exact model of some of the most approved structures of antiquity'.[61]

Elliot's Pantheon-style proposal was for the national church to be placed on a gap site on the Mound, where the Royal Academy now sits.[62] He stated in an early letter to the committee that his design had given

> preference to the Pantheon at Rome or the Hall for inscriptions and sculpture . . . [as] . . . St Sophia at Constantinople . . . is a building much admired but was built in the decline of the classic age of architecture . . . [and] . . . The temple of Minerva at Athens . . . [was] . . . rejected because it is too small for a Hall and a Church and badly, if at all, lighted . . . to give it size and light . . . the character of that building would be lost.[63]

His building also fulfilled many of the symbolic criteria for commemoration, as Elliot

Plate 4.5—Archibald Elliot, *Copy of Engraving of Elliot's Unexecuted Design, for a Proposed Site on the Mound*, c. 1820.
© Courtesy of Historic Environment Scotland.

considered that '[t]he spherical form is much more indicative of the exertions and heroism performed by our countrymen in the cause of independence, liberty and religion in the various quarters of the globe than the rectangular form which has little or no meaning'.[64] This observation drew on the examples of Christopher Wren's St Paul's Cathedral in London and Jacques-Germain Soufflot's Panthéon in Paris more particularly and the Pantheon in Rome in general, as although all three buildings were used to house commemorative monuments, it was St Paul's and the Panthéon that were particularly renowned for commemorating heroes of the state.[65] Yet, though Elliot had looked to the domed magnificence of St Paul's as an example of commemorative space, its commemoration of members of state of political or military means excluded those who could be considered British heroes in the broader sense. This fact was emphasised by supporters of a structure based on the Parthenon who wished the monument to celebrate those who were considered patriots more generally.

[T]he National Monument is not intended to be confined to the celebration merely of naval and military merit, but . . . it is meant to be employed in the commemoration of public genius and virtue of every description; exactly as Westminster Abbey is in England. The precise way that this is to be done has not yet been matured, but the general idea is that besides containing a place of religious worship, it is to serve as a depository for the ashes & the busts of illustrious Scotsmen in whatever line their eminence may be displayed.[66]

As Westminster Abbey's role from the early eighteenth century was considered as 'the sole church building that could be classed as national territory',[67] this comparison further justified a monument in Edinburgh, as the Scottish equivalent.[68] By creating a building that commemorated national, rather than state (i.e. British government) triumphs, through military, political *and* cultural means,[69] a monument could be placed to inspire and perpetuate a sense of pride in citizens who might never have the opportunity to visit London, as well as cultivate friendly rivalry with other nations. This is in line with Wood's theories that citizens need to be

sublimed from the domestic apathy . . . to a state of active patriotism; and manifest their love for their country, by a gigantic effort to preserve it. They must be induced to meditate on the deeds of their predecessors, until warmed by the association; and then press forward in the same glorious path, to gain, like them, the unfading laurels of public esteem and gratitude.[70]

The idea is further emphasised in an article written by a Mr Allison for *Blackwood's Magazine*: '[W]ho has not felt the sublime impression which the interior of Westminster Abbey produces,

where the poets, philosophers, and the statesmen of England sleep with their Kings and dignify the scene.'[71]

It [The National Monument] will give stability and consistence to the national pride a feeling which when properly directed is the surest foundation of national eminence. It will perpetuate the remembrance of the brave and independent Scottish nation a feeling all others the best suited to animate the exertions of her remotest descendants. It will teach her inhabitants to look to their own country for the scene of their real glory and while Ireland laments the absence of a nobility insensible to her fame it will be the boast of this country to have erected on her own shores a monument worthy of her people's glory and to have disdained to follow merely the triumphs of that nation whose ancestors they have ere now vanquished in the field.[72]

Allison's article also discusses the choice of architectural style for a monument befitting the nation's mood. According to the author, neoclassical, rather than gothic architecture assimilates itself much more to the spirit of national pride,[73] 'recall[ing] the brilliant conceptions of national glory as they were received during the ardent and enthusiastic period of youth'.[74] In particular, the Athenian idiom's 'stern and massy form' was considered to 'befit an edifice destined to commemorate the severe virtues and manly character of war'.[75] This accords with Marc Fehlmann's extensive work on the exploitation of the Greek canon in eighteenth- and nineteenth-century Britain, where he proposes that the success of British victory was strengthened through classical justification, by associating the Napoleonic wars to the wars of Marathon, Salamis and

Plataea.[76] This is, Fehlmann argues, down to the regard that nineteenth-century Britons had for the ancient Athenian state as 'the dominant force in ancient Greece—a leading naval power that had become rich and strong through free trade and the liberty of its subjects',[77] which conveniently suited the zeitgeist that surrounded Britain's own self-perception of its naval prowess after the victories of the Napoleonic campaign. Given these associations, it is surprising that a proposal in Edinburgh to create a replica of the most famous building in Greek antiquity as a national monument was just one of two 'successful'[78] attempts to erect a Parthenon in Great Britain during the 1810s and 20s.[79] The origin of the outline plans for the Edinburgh monument was the proposal for a 'facsimile' of the Parthenon in London by a Mr Robertson, in 1816. This had been championed in Edinburgh by Lord Elgin.[80] It was stated that it had been 'universally admired' in London but deemed unsuitable for the design of a national memorial in the Metropolis due to 'the determination of Parliament to erect separate monuments for the Army and the Navy'.[81]

It is possible, therefore, that despite the general rhetoric of neoclassicism lending itself to displays of national pride, the use of the Parthenon as a monument to celebrate British victories would not be considered as an appropriate choice for a 'national monument' in a British context. As London relied on bolstering national sentiment within the masses through the erection of monuments within the public realm, the Parthenon's strong associations with places of learning and those proclaiming naval ascendancy would have excluded many who had contributed to the national campaigns. The execution of the Scottish National War Memorial

in the form of the Parthenon, therefore, must have been decided upon after consideration of other factors besides the allegorical connection with British naval success (see above).

The adoption of Hellenism as an architectural idiom in particular had been especially prevalent in Scotland during the late eighteenth and nineteenth centuries, as associations between Hellenic culture and the rational principles of the Scottish Enlightenment were supported by an antiquarian interest in the past.[82] This is considered by Naik and Stewart to have been the result of 'Scotland's lack of political autonomy . . . [which had] encouraged the assertion of its unique cultural origins'.[83] Edinburgh in particular came to be obsessed with all things Greek in the first half of the nineteenth century, being referred to as the 'Athens of the North' around the time of the development of the National Monument. Although it could be assumed that building a Parthenon on Calton Hill was meant to emphasise the similarities between the Scots and Greek capitals, it is more likely that the model of the Parthenon for the National Monument was settled upon because of the Scots interest in Hellenism. This had been fostered through cultural understanding of the Edinburgh topography, and this, coupled with connections to the sea, heavily influenced the decision over the National Monument's design.

This can be further understood when the phrase 'the Athens of the North' is more closely considered in rhetoric. One the earliest comparisons made between Edinburgh and Athens is in a comment made by the artist Allan Ramsay in 1762 to Sir William Dick of Prestonfield. He states that:

The setting up of further learned institutions such as a Riding school will render Edin-

burgh the 'Athens of Britain' where instead of the monkish pedantry of the old-fashioned Universities, young gentlemen will be initiated in the principles of useful knowledge and liberal accomplishments which qualify a man to appear in the distinguished spheres of life.[84]

Although this parallel of the advances of the intellectual community of the Scottish Enlightenment and of Ancient Athens appears from the mid eighteenth century onwards, the association between Edinburgh as a physical entity and Athens did not become common until the early nineteenth century. In fact, according to Cockburn, it was during the time of the Napoleonic wars that this idea was fully cemented:

It was about the time that the foolish phrase 'The Modern Athens', began to be applied to the capital of Scotland; a sarcasm, or a piece of affected flattery, when used in a moral sense; but just enough if it meant only a comparison of the physical features of the two places. The opportunities of observing, and the practice of talking of, foreign buildings in reference to our own, directed our attention to the works of internal taste, and roused our ambition.[85]

The likeness between the landscape of Athens and Edinburgh was paramount in cementing the comparison of the two cities. Cambridge geologist, Edward Daniel Clarke, had first pointed out similarities between the topography of the two areas in *Travels in Various Countries of Europe*.[86] He stated that 'Edinburgh exhibits a very correct model of a Grecian city and with its Acropolis, Town, and Harbour, [as] it bears some resemblance to Athens and the Piraeus.' It is this relationship between Piraeus and Athens and Clarke's comparison of these to

Leith and Edinburgh that Allison uses in support of his argument for the erection of a Parthenon on Calton Hill.

Its [Edinburgh's] position on a rock in the middle of a fertile and champagne country the vicinity of the sea and the disposition of the town at the base of the fortress resemble in the most striking manner the situation of Corinth Athens Argos and most of the Grecian capitals.[87]

The contrast of citadel and countryside, and its comparison to that of Athens can be further observed in images of Edinburgh's landscape from this period, in particular through Alexander Nasmyth's landscape watercolours of Edinburgh (see Plate 4.6). When compared with Hugh William Williams' views of Athens (Plate 4.7), the romantic interpretation of the Edinburgh topography evokes the neoclassical dreamy exoticism of Williams' Grecian countryside. However, in Nasmyth's drawings, and in Clarke's description, the comparison of the Acropolis in Athens is with Edinburgh Castle, not Calton Hill. This does not stop Allison pushing the idea of Calton Hill as a new acropolis for Edinburgh. He fits Clarke's observations to his manifesto and states the outright untruth that Clarke had considered Calton Hill's potential to become a new acropolis in his work.

To make the resemblance complete he adds it is only necessary to have a temple of great dimensions placed on the Calton Hill and such an edifice seen from all quarters and forming an object in every landscape would give a classical air to that beautiful city of which the value cannot easily be conceived.[88]

Despite Allison's stretching of the truth of Clarke's comments,[89] the homing in on the hill as a centre point during the early nineteenth

Plate 4.6—Alexander Nasmyth, *View of the City of Edinburgh*, oil on canvas, c. 1822, 141.9 x 209.9cm.
Yale Center for British Art, Paul Mellon Collection

century had slowly emerged during the development of the third New Town plan. Early versions had focused not on the development of Calton Hill, but on the road network between Leith and the city, using commemorative and triumphal architecture to emphasise this thoroughfare that included space on Leith Walk halfway between Edinburgh and Leith for the National Monument (see Part 1 and Plate 1.3a). In placing this monument instead on *top* of Calton Hill in the form of a Parthenon and adopting a Greek rhetoric, the city's connection to the Port of Leith was firmly established, as Piraeus to Edinburgh's Athens—adding further gravitas to its intellectual achievements and architectural rhetoric and emphasising Edinburgh as the 'Athens of the North'. This visually, physically and metaphorically strengthened Edinburgh's position as a naval port within the British Isles and further boosted the purpose and raison d'être of the National Monument, by celebrating the intellect and beauty of Scotland's capital, alongside the glory of the British naval fleet and, in particular, Britain's world dominance at sea.[90]

Plate 4.7—Hugh William Williams, *View of Athens*, c.1818, oil on canvas.
© Courtesy of Bridgeman Art Library

The choice of Charles Cockerell as the lead architect for the monument placed emphasis on the 'Britishness' of the project. Cockerell was a young, up-and-coming London architect, who Lord Elgin invited up to Scotland on behalf of the National Monument Committee in 1822.[91] Cockerell's appointment was somewhat pushed on the committee by Elgin who had, according to Watkin, acted prematurely in asking the Londoner to head up the scheme.[92] But as he had already made a name for himself through his 'particular knowledge in Grecian architecture & his long residence in Athens',[93] he was outright favourite to provide the accurate detail needed to replicate the Parthenon in the design of the National Monument.[94] The appointment of

Plate 4.8 (overleaf)—John Wilson Ewbank, *The Entry of George IV into Edinburgh from the Calton Hill*, oil on canvas, 1822. © www.capitalcollections.org.uk

Playfair as resident architect to produce the working drawings was therefore not only practical and cost-effective; the poetry of collaboration between an English and Scottish architect on a 'national concern of this [magnitude of] importance'[95] would not have been lost on the appointing committee.[96]

The exploitation of the classical idea, therefore, not only utilised the picturesque possibilities and views to and from the site—as Barker, Craig, Adam and Burns had done. It now also manipulated and legitimised the landscape and the monuments through collective imperial purpose, which was allied with an allegorical association with the antique—in particular, an emphasis on the cultural assimilation of Scotland to Ancient Greece.

This can be traced back to the mid eighteenth-century work of James Macpherson's 'Ossian', where he transcribed Gaelic verse as a Grecian poetic cycle.[97] At the time of publication in 1760, a comparison between Ossian and Homer's writings came to enhance the perceived connections between the classical Utopia and primitive rural Highland life, particularly with regard to poetry and folk songs. This was further emphasised by David Allan's hellenised interpretations of traditional Scottish rural pastimes.[98] The eighteenth-century literary critic, Johan Herder (1744–1803), for example, makes this comparison in musing that he 'must go to the Scottish Highlands, to see the places described by the great Ossian himself and "hear the songs of a living people". After all, "the Greeks, too . . . were savage . . . and in the best period of their flowering far more of Nature remained in them than can be described by the narrow gaze of a scholiast or a classical scholar"'.[99]

This, to many, validated Scots' own cultural roots as one of the great ancient cultures and paved the way for a romanticising of the Highlands particularly identified with Sir Walter Scott's Waverley novels. Scott's cultivating of this romantic idea during George IV's visit to Edinburgh perpetuated the assimilation of the Highlands and Greek culture; what was deemed 'the beginning of the Highland takeover of Scotland',[100] included 'Cockerell's uncompromisingly Greek temple'[101] as 'the back-cloth of the opening scene in [Scott's] romantic drama'. This is shown In John Wilson Ewbank's *The Entry of George IV into Edinburgh from the Calton Hill*, over the Bridewell and towards the Old Town and the castle (Plate 4.8). The image depicts numerous groups swathed in tartan lining Waterloo Place to welcome the king, who is sitting in an open-topped carriage to the right of the picture. Calton Hill forms the background to this mixture of Highland garb and medieval pageantry, as created by Scott.[102]

Scottish cultural identity after the Napoleonic wars therefore built on this romantic image of Scotland's fabled yesteryear and sought to dismantle the earlier eighteenth-century perception of the Highlands as a threatening savage wilderness full of Jacobean sympathisers. The rebranding of Scottish primitive life through an association with the primitive yet learned culture of Ancient Greece[103] allowed Scots to retain a Scottish identity within the union[104] that was not perceived as threatening to the political and financial integration of the 1707 Act of Union.[105] As this cultural assimilation filtered through the production of art in Scotland, the chaste style and restrained language of the architecture of the Greek Revival suited Scots' Presbyterian sensibilities. This style that established itself in the strict archaeological study of classical buildings by Stuart and Revett and Le Roy was understood alongside the emerging comparisons between the literary cultures of Scotland and Ancient Greece, and further perpetuated by the connections made between the academic advancements of the Ancient Greeks in philosophy, science and mathematics and those made during the Scottish Enlightenment. Many of the men exposed to this dialogue took on this understanding of their assimilation with the Ancient Greeks into their established careers in banking, law and positions in public office. It is therefore likely that this connection with Ancient Greece and its culture continued to encourage the Greek style for public buildings in the early nineteenth century—a genre which was the dominant source of Greek Revival buildings until Alexander 'Greek' Thomson applied his own reimagining of Grecian architecture to Glasgow in the mid to late nineteenth century.[106]

Many scholars of Scottish culture and art history who consider the emergence of the Scottish Greek Revival[107] agree that it was mutually beneficial to both Scotland and Britain to exploit this romantic, innocuous cultural identity for Scotland, as it allowed Scots to exist as a race that was removed from any commentary on Scottish political autonomy within the British state. However, John Lowrey has argued that the particular association with Athens on Calton Hill was, in fact, an attempt to demonstrate Scottish importance and prominence within the British Empire.[108] For example, in Thomas Shepherd and John Britton's *Modern Athens!* (1829),[109] the romantic era of medieval Scotland[110] is promoted alongside images of the Calton Hill and the National Monument. In the preface, it is stated that it is a 'great city of an empire' and one of our 'national capitals' and its 'history and description . . . will be important to Scotland and the whole United Kingdom.' Its text, which goes into great detail about the medieval history of Scotland and the early modern history of Edinburgh, halts at 1661, stating that 'From this time on, the only events of importance to enumerate are—the Union of the two Kingdoms in 1707, which has been attended with so many benefits to Scotland; the rebellion of 1745; and the visit of our present gracious sovereign in 1822.'

By placing not just a Greek Revival structure on Calton Hill, but a specifically Athenian structure on its summit, therefore,[111] a statement of cultural association is turned into one of political alliance that asserts Edinburgh's identity, if not superiority, within the British state. As Lowrey notes,

> [B]y assuming the identity of Athens, the implication was that Edinburgh and Scotland were superior to London and England. Scottish achievements in the Enlightenment period gave the city the right to claim that it was now the civilizing influence within Great Britain and the Empire . . . although Edinburgh was still defining itself in relation to London, it was claiming an identity that in some ways usurped the role of the capital.[112]

In creating a specific direct comparison with Athens by placing a 'Parthenon' on top of an 'Acropolis', Edinburgh became active, rather than passive, in the affairs of Empire.[113] By displaying a message of strength and fortitude in alliance with the British government, Edinburgh was asserting itself as a stronghold of Northern Britain within its own cultural terms, as well as proclaiming to be a significant city of the Empire in its own right.[114]

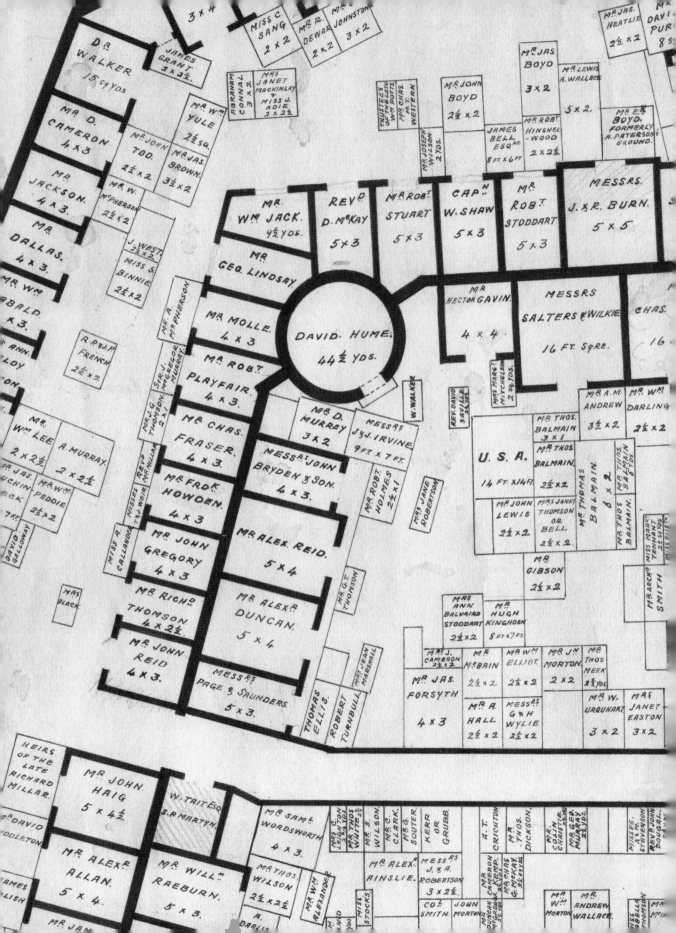

Private Burial and Public Commemoration in the Nineteenth Century

Both the Old and the New Calton burial grounds were developed during the first half of the nineteenth century, and the markers and those buried beneath them were seen as encouragements to passers-by to live good and worthy lives. The other monuments on the hill, deliberately placed outside these burial grounds, were designed to demonstrate the wider

consequences of both mourning and admiring the heroes of the day.

The Old Calton burial ground had been established in the early eighteenth century, in response to the need for new burial space for the dead of the hamlet of Calton[1] and in particular, those associated with the Incorporated Trades of Calton.[2] It was not until Robert Adam's development of David Hume's tomb (built 1777) that the burial ground became much more than simply a place of interment for local Calton tradespeople.[3] This may, in part, be a link to the area being promoted as a place of interest to visitors in the city by the 1800s, as the proximity of the Hume monument to the Nelson monument added interest to the pleasure walk around the hill.⁴ The latter's location on the summit of Calton Hill meant that it could only be reached by going past the entrance to the burial ground; an introduction to the concept of memorial and remembrance on the journey towards the monument to Nelson. This expansion of memorial space outside the confines of the burial ground was further extended with the decision to locate the National Monument on the summit of the hill in the late 1810s. These three aspects, therefore, placed the context of the broader landscape of the hill within a commemorative sphere and set the scene for the erection of further monuments there.

In the decade after the establishment of the Nelson and national monuments, three further monuments were erected, to John Playfair (1822), Dugald Stewart (1831) and Robert Burns (1831), away from their actual places of burial. In the cases of Stewart and Burns these were in addition to grand private monuments that were placed at their grave-sites. The following chapter considers these three monuments and their presence within this context, by exploring their relationship to the hill, each other and the proposed National Monument.

John Playfair and Dugald Stewart were key figures in the Scottish Enlightenment. Playfair (1748–1819), Professor of Natural Philosophy at the University of Edinburgh, was an influential member of the Edinburgh intelligentsia and president of the Astronomical Institution that had established the neoclassical observatory building on Calton Hill.⁵ Dugald Stewart (1753–1828) held the chair of Moral Philosophy at the university during the last quarter of the eighteenth century and was influential in the teaching of many prominent members of early nineteenth-century society.

Plate 5.2—William Henry Playfair,
Monument to Dugald Stewart, 1831.
© Kirsten Carter McKee

Playfair's prominence in the city was such that, on his death in 1819, a committee was set up to collect subscriptions to fund 'an architectural monument, or cenotaph, in some appropriate or conspicuous situation'⁶ in his memory. There were two options, both of which were on Calton Hill. Significantly, however, although one of the locations mooted was within the (Old) Calton burial ground (Plate 5.1), the committee did not consider the Playfair plot within the burial ground itself.⁷ Instead, the committee wanted the monument either within the enclosure of the newly established astronomical observatory on the hill's summit, or on a plot within the burial ground that belonged to an Alexander Henderson 'on the Brow of the precipitous rock to the south'.⁸

Both the committee's preferred choice of the monument's site on the summit of the hill, and the secondary proposal of erecting the memorial on another visually prominent plot within the burial ground, are telling to understanding the overall purpose of the Playfair monument in the eyes of the committee. In erecting a memorial to Professor Playfair, his admirers were not mourning Playfair's death, but rather were celebrating his achievements. That the most appropriate choice was adjacent to the site of the observatory of the Astronomical Institution— that he was instrumental in establishing— demonstrates this,[9] as does the need to erect a monument in a situation where it would have a high degree of visual impact.

This need to create visual impact through the placement of memorials can also be found in the building of a cenotaph to Dugald Stewart (Plate 5.2) some ten years later, in a position that would do 'good to Scotland'.[10] A private monument was erected at his grave in Canongate kirkyard.[11] Rather than an architectural object, the first idea was for a sculpture in a prominent internal location, such as the library of Edinburgh University. Debate ensued regarding the suitability of an external monument or an internal sculpture. Despite Stewart's wife's own preference for a statue, and her stating in a letter that Stewart himself believed that statues were more befitting of the 'merits and situation of literary men . . . than any building',[12] it was decided that a monument should be erected on Calton Hill, as it would be viewed by a larger number of people than a sculpture in the elite halls of the university.[13]

There may be another reason behind this—one influenced by the challenges faced by the committee concerning the Robert Burns

Plate 5.3—John Flaxman/Thomas Denman,
Statue of Robert Burns, 1828.
© The City of Edinburgh Council

Plate 5.4a (opposite)—
Charles Robert Cockerell (1788–1863),
Transverse Section of the National Monument, Edinburgh,
pencil, ink and wash on paper, 1822, 21.8 x 40.5cm,
1994.060. Royal Scottish Academy of Art &
Architecture collections. Image credit: Chris Park

Plate 5.4b (above)—
Charles Robert Cockerell (1788–1863),
*Transverse Section through Vestibule of the National
Monument, Edinburgh*,
pencil, ink and wash on paper, 1822, 21.7 x 40.2cm,
1994.059. Royal Scottish Academy of Art &
Architecture collections. Image credit: Chris Park

memorial. The neoclassical monument to Robert Burns situated on Calton Hill is one of three of the earliest architectural structures dedicated to the Scots poet. The others, in Dumfries and Alloway, make up a trilogy built (at earliest) twenty-five years after the poet's death, despite discussions about Burns' commemoration starting in the early 1800s.[14] From the securing of a site for the memorial on Calton Hill in 1817 by John Forbes Mitchell,[15] the form that the memorial was to take varied, back and forth, between a classical sculpture and an architectural edifice. In 1819, the monument was proposed as a classical tomb, which would hold Burnsonian relics.[16] By 1821, the design had changed from an architectural structure to a large bronze by the classical sculptor John Flaxman.[17] However, once the memorial began to be sculpted in 1824,[18] a change from bronze cast to marble statue (Plate 5.3)[19] also heralded a change in opinion as to where the memorial was to be placed. Marble was vulnerable in the damp Scottish climate, being 'a substance which fades and darkens even under the Blue of the Grecian sky',[20] and was much more vulnerable to damage, so it

Plate 5.5—William Henry Playfair, *National Monument*, 1828. © Kirsten Carter McKee

was not likely to be left outside on show.[21]

It is apparent, therefore, that the intention was to place the sculpture indoors. There were two places where it was deemed appropriate to display statues of this nature. The first was in the university library[22], but there were doubts in this case, and in fact, a number of people considered it distasteful to place him amongst people of whom he had spoken irreverently:[23]

> *Sir,*
>
> *. . . permit me to remark that I perfectly agree with you in thinking there is something extremely absurd in the idea of placing a statue of Burns anywhere in or about the college . . . Let the statue of our National Bard be placed, if not in the open air, in the National Monument. Let him stand where he will see and be seen.*[24]

The National Monument option fits with the timing of the commissioning of the statue. Cockerell had stated at the outset that he intended sculpture to be present in the building, and his drawings of the monument included these in his designs (Plate 5.4a and b).[25]

If the statue was then intended to be placed in what was to be the Scots answer to Westminster Abbey, this would also explain why there was an issue with finding somewhere for it to be placed by November 1830,[26] just two years after the statue's completion by Denman in 1828. By this point, the National Monument project had been put on hold after the building of just twelve columns of the structure (Plate 5.5), as a number of options to raise money had failed.[27] While it sat unfinished and as a grand architectural folly, its ambitions to provide an enclosed space for commemorative memorials had fallen short.[28] This left those who had commissioned marbles in the hope of theirs being one of the first on display in the National Monument at a loss for where to house them.[29]

It was around this time, when the cenotaph for Dugald Stewart was designed by William Henry Playfair, that another call for subscriptions[30] was sent out to collect further funds to erect a protective structure to house Flaxman's marble statue of Burns 'since we have as yet no Pantheon or National Edifice for the reception of Statues or Busts of Eminent Scotsmen'.[31] Flaxman's sculpture was finally placed inside the monument, designed by Thomas Hamilton, in 1833 (Plate 5.6). But even after this date, there were concerns as to whether Hamilton's Edinburgh monument was an appropriate place for a statue by such a highly respected neoclassical artist.[32] By 1846, smoke from the gasworks in the Waverley Valley below was adversely affecting the marble,[33] and so the statue was placed in the University of Edinburgh's Old College library until it was moved to the newly established Scottish National Portrait Gallery in 1882, where it has remained ever since. The empty monument that remains on Calton Hill to this day is still referred to as the Burns monument, despite being redundant as a housing for the statue. Ironically, however, after the removal of the statue, the monument was used for a number of years as a museum for Burns memorabilia, fulfilling the original vision for a classical monument that would hold relics to the bard that had been originally proposed in 1819.[34]

Comparing the design of William H. Playfair's monument to Dugald Stewart (Plate 5.2) with Thomas Hamilton's monument to Robert Burns (Plate 5.6), it is interesting to consider how both of these architects viewed the

Plate 5.6—Thomas Hamilton,
Monument to Robert Burns, 1832.
© Kirsten Carter McKee

Plate 5.7 (overleaf)—
Thomas Hamilton RSA (1784–1858),
Design for the Royal High School, Edinburgh, watercolour,
gouache and pencil on paper, 1831,
73.5 x 129.5cm, 1995.051.
Royal Scottish Academy of Art & Architecture
(Diploma Collection). Image credit: Chris Park

landscape of Calton Hill by the early 1830s. While both committees for the memorials still agreed

that Calton Hill should be the location for these structures, calling it 'a very magnificent point'[35] and stating that '[o]ur architect and artists to a man decidedly recommend that Burns' temple should be placed there',[36] the hill's status as a grand commemorative landscape appears to have shifted slightly from the previous decade, as by this point, the National Monument project was in hiatus, and the construction of Thomas Hamilton's Royal High School building (Plate 5.7),[37] halfway down the southern slope of Calton Hill, was already on its way to completion.

The location of these two monuments on the hill, therefore, were integral to their conception. Both architects looked to the Choragic monument of Lysicrates (Plate 5.8)[38] for inspiration, yet interpreted it in very different ways. Where Playfair's restrained classicism fitted in closely with his other structures on the summit of Calton Hill,[39] and with his idea of the architectural 'facsimile', most obviously the National Monument, Hamilton's monument to Burns is much more subtle and subversive,[40] and responded to the subject whom it was to commemorate, as well as to the landscape in which it was to be placed.[41]

Hamilton's request in 1831 to change the placement of the Edinburgh monument from the original plot designated by the town council to a piece of land on the hill known as Millar's Knowe[42] (Plate 5.9) may have been an attempt by the architect to repeat the spatial relationship found between the Acropolis and the Lysicrates monument (Plate 5.10) in that of the National Monument and the Edinburgh

Plate 5.8—James Stewart and Nicholas Revett, *Measured Drawing of the Choragic Monument of Lysicrates.* Taken from J. Stewart and N. Revett, *The Antiquities of Athens,* 1762.

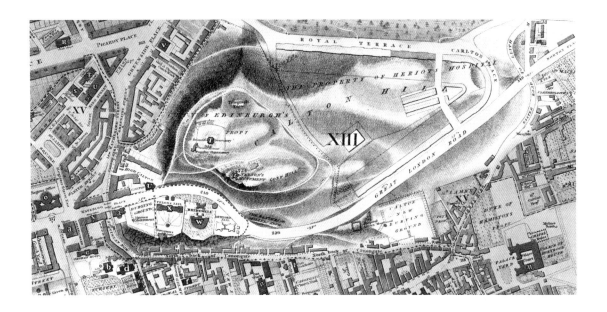

Plate 5.9—James Kirkwood, *Kirkwood's New Plan of the City of Edinburgh*, 1821. Detail showing Millars Knowe, located on the curve of Calton Hill to the east of Calton Jail. © Courtesy of National Library of Scotland

Burns monument.[43] As his request failed, and the monument was sited opposite the Royal High School on a rocky precipice, Hamilton manipulated the visual connection between the site donated by the council and the rocky precipice beneath the Temple of Vesta (or Sybill) at Tivoli in Italy.[44] By alluding to this structure in the design of his monument, Hamilton demonstrates that his structures took into consideration both the existing landscape and the placement within it, in a manner which is reminiscent of Adam's work at the end of the previous century.

While Hamilton considers how the existing romantic nature of the landscape could be enhanced through carefully chosen architectural rhetoric, Playfair, in contrast, attempts to impose a romantic landscape on the hill through the introduction of classical monuments. He believed that the presence of these classical

structures created the romantic effect on the landscape, rather than their presence merely enhancing an already romantic setting. This can be further explained through the architect's artistic representations of the site. In Thomas Allom's painting of the Burns monument and the Royal High School building (Plate 5.13), he contrasts the utopian imagery of grand classical monumental edifices, bathed in light from an unseen celestial source, with the dark shadows and ethereal mists that surround the castellated and gothic structures of the medieval old town in the distance. Classical buildings, in Allom's eyes, therefore, augment and enhance the already romantic precipitous gothic landscape of the southern side of the hill.

By contrast, Playfair's 1817 sketch of the proposed neoclassical observatory building of the Astronomical Institution (Plate 5.14)[45] depicts the structure within a fantastical exotic

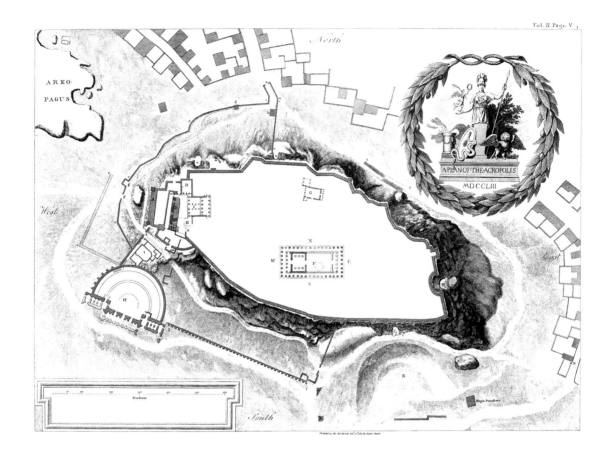

Plate 5.10 (above)—James Stewart
and Nicholas Revett,
*Plan of the Acropolis of Athens, showing Placement of the
Choragic Monument of Lysicrates.*
Taken from J. Stewart and N. Revett,
The Antiquities of Athens, 1762

Plate 5.11 (right)—Thomas Hamilton, *Framed Original
Design for the Burns Monument at Alloway*, 1818.
© Courtesy of the Trustees of Burns Monument and
Burns Cottage

Plate 5.12 (opposite)—*Design for the Burns Monument,
Calton Hill, Edinburgh*, 1832. Thomas Hamilton.
National Galleries of Scotland

Plate 5.13 (right)—Thomas Allom (1804–1872)
[supervised by Thomas Hamilton RSA (1784–1858) &
David Roberts RA HRSA (1796–1864)],
*View of the Royal High School and Burns' Monument,
Edinburgh*, watercolour and gouache on paper, c. 1830,
72.5 x 125cm, 1995.052. Royal Scottish Academy of Art
& Architecture collections. Image credit: Chris Park

landscape of Playfair's imagination, with ruinous classical structures in the background, classically swathed figures and an oriental male smoking a hookah in the near foreground. The disregard of the hill's real landscape in the drawing suggests that Playfair perceived the establishment of his classical buildings on the summit as a means to provide a romantic air to this part of the hill. His replacement of the gothic observatory with the Dugald Stewart monument in his later elevation of the Stewart monument, the astronomical observatory and John Playfair monument (Plate 5.15) further adds to the effect, as it suggests that Playfair wanted to establish a predominantly classical idiom on the summit, rather than play on the juxtaposition of the gothic and the classical as Allom does further down the south side of the hill. Although Playfair never managed to remove the Gothic observatory, it can also be no coincidence that Playfair's scale and placement of the Stuart monument on Calton Hill masks the observatory from prominent views to the hill on North Bridge (Plate 4.16). However, Playfair's focus on classical structures on the summit of Calton Hill does not by any means indicate that he was dismissive of the landscape that lay around the hill. Rather, as we have seen in the discussion of his 1819 plans in Chapter 3 (Plates 3.1a and b), he viewed the summit as separate from the contoured landscape further down the hill, which could explain why he thought it necessary to dislocate the hill's landscape in his

Plate 5.14—William Henry Playfair, *Royal Observatory, Calton Hill, Edinburgh* (watercolour on board), c.1818.
© RIAS/William Henry Playfair Collection. Courtesy of Historic Environment Scotland

pictorial representations of the observatory. By establishing a pure, utopian idea of a classical landscape towering over the city, Playfair was attempting to create a sentinel to the glory of the Enlightenment and the state, as had been envisioned by Allison, Elgin and the intelligentsia of Edinburgh,[46] which—just as the Acropolis was regarded in its closer proximity to the gods— would be loftily separate from the city and almost other-worldly in its atmosphere.[47]

The halt in the development of the National Monument in 1828 brought about a slow, but irreversible shift in the aspirations for the commemorative landscape on Calton Hill. Despite the establishment of monuments and the production of publications for the completion of the classical utopia on the hill in the five years or so after 1828,[48] interest quickly waned in the grand schemes for the hill and memorial projects were directed elsewhere in the city.

As Scottish culture in the second quarter of the nineteenth century leaned further towards the romantic idea of pre-Reformation (a culture that was, in part, perpetuated by Scott in his publications) and further away from the eighteenth-century Greek Classical, Scotland's identity was reaffirmed through appropriate imagery, in both art and architecture. According to Cookson,[49] this was responsible for the move towards a more Scottish rhetoric, such as used

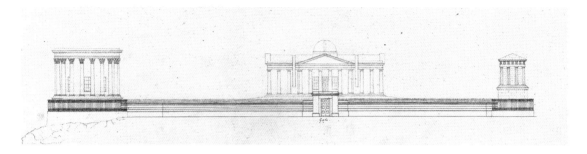

Plate 5.15 William Henry Playfair, *Elevation of the Southern Boundary Wall &c.*, 1827.
© Courtesy of Centre for Research Collections, University of Edinburgh

Plate 5.16—Monument to Dugald Stewart (located to the right of the Martyrs' Monument) from the North Bridge.
This view shows the relative scale of the monument to the Gothic Observatory behind, which it all but masks from
this viewpoint. © Kirsten Carter McKee

in the Gothic Revival design for the Scott monument in Edinburgh (1844, Plate 5.17), the monument to Bruce and Wallace in Edinburgh (1859, Plate 5.18)[50] and of the Scots Baronial in the Stirling Wallace monument (1869, Plate 5.19). With these alternative 'national monuments'[51] directing focus away from the message that Classicism in general, and the Greek Revival in particular had connected with the glorification of nation and empire in Scotland,[52] the hill had

a diminished practical and political resonance.[53]

This may also have been a consequence of the classical style falling out of fashion as a commemorative genre. From the 1830s onwards, an increase in local government powers created a culture within local councils to advance civic projects that mainly focused around persons or events with direct connections to a local area,[54] rather than the promotion of national government interests.[55] These memorialised people who

Plate 5.17—George Meikle Kemp, *Scott Monument.*
Original Design by George Kemp, c.1840
© The City of Edinburgh Council

Plate 5.18—J. Noel Paton, *National Memorial of the War
of Independence under Wallace and Bruce*, unbuilt, 1859.
© Courtesy of National Library of Scotland

Plate 5.19—John Thomas Rochead, *Monument to William Wallace erected at Stirling*, c.1861.
© Courtesy of Historic Environment Scotland

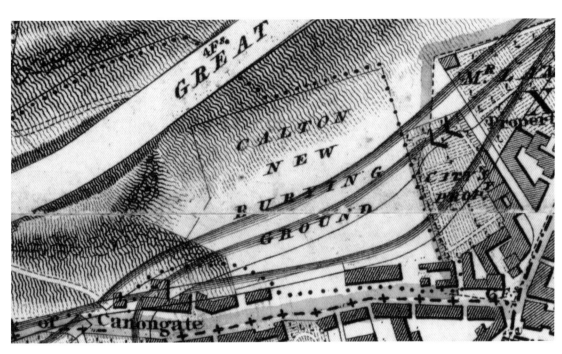

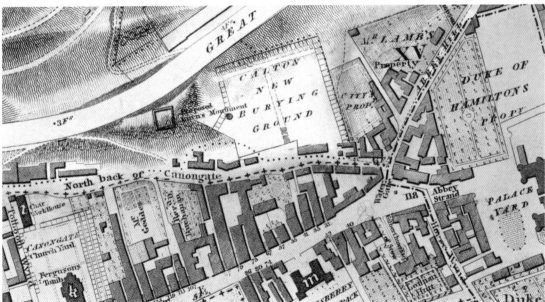

Plate 5.20 (top)—Robert Kirkwood, *This Plan of the City of Edinburgh and its Environs*, 1817. Detail delineating curtilage of New Calton Burial Ground. © Courtesy of National Library of Scotland

Plate 5.21 (foot)—James Kirkwood & Sons, *Kirkwood's New Plan of the City of Edinburgh*, 1821. Detail delineating curtilage of New Calton Burial Ground. © Courtesy of National Library of Scotland

represented specific cultural or political ideas, rather than fostering emulation and encouraging good citizenship through the abstract allegory of architectural rhetoric.[56] This is particularly emphasised in the design of the Edinburgh Scott monument (1844), which from the outset was to include a sculpture of Scott in its design, rather than using its architectural language to represent the author, suggesting that it was the author himself who was to be commemorated, rather than his position and achievements.[57] On Calton Hill, this manifested itself in the development of the New Calton burial ground. As focus shifted away from the summit of the hill, this alternative commemorative landscape was being developed on the southeastern side of the hill, where many of the burials in the first twenty years of the site are of men with a connection to the British navy.[58] This naval connection can be read as a statement of Calton Hill's links to the port of Leith, which the monument to Lord Nelson and the astronomical observatory with its associations had striven to establish.

New Calton burial ground was opened in 1817[59] by the Incorporated Trades of Calton. It was an area that was sold to the Incorporated Trades by Edinburgh town council in 1816,[60] in addition to land that had been given to them in lieu of ground lost from the (Old) Calton burial ground, during the development of Regent Road.[61] The area of New Calton is first marked out as a burial ground on the Kirkwood map of 1817, but no burial plots are identified on this map (Plate 5.20). According to Gifford et al., the burial ground was opened to visitors in 1820[62] and, by 1821, Kirkwood's map shows burial plots around the curtilage of this site (Plate 5.21). This landscape, unlike the summit, was to be 'out of view' of the new housing development higher up

the hill on Regent Terrace.[63] Its formalised layout and planting has been recognised by recent scholars of memorial landscapes as providing a different effect to other burial grounds and graveyards of a similar date,[64] which has prompted some debate over its influence in the Garden Cemetery Movement.[65] This stems from an observation about the stylistic 'House Tombs' (Plate 5.22) that are identified in New Calton, located on the burial plots laid out around the curtilage, as well as within the central area of the cemetery. In James Stevens Curl's 1983 paper, which links New Calton to the Garden Cemetery Movement, he notes the similarity of these 'House Tombs' to those found at Père Lachaise—the first real 'landscaped cemetery'.[66] However, the tombs' type in Scotland is already to be found at Greyfriars kirkyard from the sixteenth century and may be a continuation of a stylistic influence taken from European masons working on memorials in Greyfriars during this period.[67]

The thirty years after New Calton's establishment was a period of substantial development, which included the development of access routes into the site, the construction of boundary walls and the laying out of the grounds by the Superintendent of City Works, Thomas Brown.[68] Curl states that John Claudius Loudon, the founder of the Garden Cemetery Movement, 'wrote approvingly' of New Calton, which could have been influential in the development of his ideas about cemetery reform in the 1840s. The publication of Curl's article has since resulted in New Calton being considered as a possible precursor to his influential theories on cemetery design, but this has never been wholly substantiated. The quotes in Curl's article are not, in fact, from Loudon, but from a 'Mr. Brown, Esq.' in an article published in *Gardeners Magazine* on

Plate 5.22—House tombs at New Calton Burial Ground. © Kirsten Carter McKee

the cemeteries of Edinburgh and Leith, dated to 1842.[69] It is therefore likely that Thomas Brown, the Superintendent of City Works and the person associated with the laying out of New Calton was the author of the text. As Loudon was editor of the journal in which the article was published, he would no doubt have been aware of Brown's article, but there is no mention of either New Calton or Thomas Brown's article in Loudon's seminal work on the Garden Cemetery Movement to suggest that the layout of New Calton burial ground was influential to his theories. It is more likely that Brown's work on the cemetery was a continuation of his methods in his landscaping of Princes Street Gardens, which he carried out with Playfair, Hamilton and William Gilpin, the English artist and landscape designer.[70] In this way, therefore, he was contemporaneous to Loudon in his application of landscape theory to memorial landscapes, although his output was nowhere near as influential in the later development of this field.

CONCLUSION

The transposition of the memorial from grave-yards and churches into the urban setting came about contemporaneously with the fervour surrounding the late eighteenth-century cam-paigns against the French, and in particular the Napoleonic wars. Memorial structures were displayed to celebrate the success of British gov-ernment policies in the Napoleonic campaigns, in order to instil confidence in the state and mon-archy, and to evade the threat of civil unrest.

Within this context, the monuments of Calton Hill followed the practice of placing structures within an urban setting, in an area designed to better establish Edinburgh's role within Britain, and promote its importance within the Empire (as we have seen in Part 1). However, with the exception of the monument to Lord Nelson, those who were to be commem-orated here were not representative of the British state, but rather marked the significance of the Scottish contribution to the 'British Idea'. In this manner, the allegorical nature of the classical ar-chitecture used on this site conducted a dialogue which was not only to glorify the successes of the British state, but also to claim Scotland's role within that success.

This striving to define Scotland's identity within Britain began to evolve through its cultural outputs in more definitive ways, as the nineteenth century continued. Through the influence of the literature of Sir Walter Scott, and the increasing industrialisation of the city with the establishment of the railways in the 1850s,[1] Scots moved away from the use of classical allegory towards the gothic romanticism associated with pre-Reformation Scotland for characterising its identity. This looked to specific characters and used cultural heroes to make outward displays of nationhood, rather than the abstract architectural rhetoric of Greek Revival Classicism used by those involved in the development of the site. The result of this was that within a decade of being conceived, and before it was even finished, the classical landscape of Calton Hill was out of touch with Scottish notions of what represented Scottish identity. As a result, the hill never achieved the ambitions of the Scottish elite to become an urban Arcadia—instead, project proposals halted and interest in the completion of the National Monument waned, as its classical architecture came to be seen as a representation of the British elite, and those who supported and ran it, rather than the Scots nation as a whole. This became ever more defined as the nineteenth century continued and the gothic Baronial came to represent a Scottish identity that tapped into a culture of romanticising a golden era of Scotland in a pre-Reformation pre-union age. This reinvented medieval visual culture and looked to influences from former allies on the European mainland, further substantiating Scotland as a separate cultural entity from the established British identity, which for the main, tended to be reflective of English culture. By the early twentieth century, therefore, Scotland had developed an identity which sat more comfortably within the cultural melting pot of British imperial society, rather than as an intrinsic part of the British state. ⁓

PART 3

Unionism to Nationalism

Around the early 1830s, Scottish society began to define Scottish nationhood through different cultural markers from those used in the immediate post-Napoleonic period. As the nineteenth century ended and the twentieth century progressed, a shift away from Classicism as the default style of Scottish identity, sprung from collective unionist-nationalist pride in the early nineteenth century, became ever more prominent. While Scottish culture further separated itself from the collective culture of a unified British state that was displayed through neoclassical architecture, it instead looked to revivalist aesthetic styles that were more closely associated with a Scottish medieval 'golden age' as a better representation of Scottish culture and Scotland as a nation.[1] As a result of this, the classical structures on Calton Hill were no longer being viewed as part of Scotland's role in the British state, but instead were believed to represent elite governance and control over Scottish affairs.

Despite Calton Hill being viewed largely as a pleasure ground throughout the nineteenth century. This aesthetic had been created by a laissez-faire governance system of local organisations that managed Scottish society, in the absence of a focus on specifically Scottish affairs at Westminster during the nineteenth century. The grandiose vision of Calton Hill as an exclusive space, by those in positions of influence, was thwarted, however, by the site continuing to be used and populated by the lower tiers of Edinburgh society.[2] The conscious class divide between those with the decision-making powers and those who used Calton Hill on a daily basis exacerbated the sense of disjunction on the hill, as the existence of these lower-class pursuits alongside the classical architecture only served to highlight the extreme poverty and wretchedness of the poorer classes in nineteenth-century society. Rather than an area dedicated to the glorification of the British state, it instead highlighted the flaws in the governance of the Scottish populace at both a state and municipal level.

Plate 6.1—Robert Forrest, *Robert the Bruce and the Monk of Baston*, c.1832. © Joe Rock

Calton Hill as Utopia?
The Urban Reality

In 1831, the monumental sculptor, Robert Forrest, was invited by Michael Linning as head of the National Monument Committee to open a 'public exhibition of statuary' at the site of the National Monument.[1] Forrest had gained recognition in Edinburgh in the late 1820s for his sculpture of Lord Melville (Henry Dundas) for William Burn's 1822 Melville monument in St Andrew Square,[2] and it was hoped that his exhibition would encourage interest and public support of the site's development as a national pantheon to house 'monumental busts and statues'.

Forrest's exhibition, which was mounted in 1832, consisted of four equestrian statues in grayish Lesmahagow sandstone, known as liver rock, placed in the area behind the completed columns.[3] The statues were a blend of Scottish cultural folklore and British political triumph,[4] fused together with classical references in the costume and composition of the subjects (see Plates 6.1 and 6.2).[5] The idea to place the statues at the site of the National Monument was at the outset considered to be a mutually beneficial one, as focus on the summit of Calton Hill and the monument would be sustained through continued public interest, by a thematically relevant exhibition, while Forrest would have somewhere to display his work and boost his reputation as a sculptor. However, as the construction of the National Monument

Plate 6.2—Robert Forrest, *Duke of Wellington*, c.1832. © Joe Rock

continued to be on hold throughout the 1830s, Forrest further added to his collection on the hill[6] to the point where his occupation was considered a blight on the landscape—particularly in the case of the large wooden hut that had been erected in front of the National Monument to house his sculptures (Plate 6.3).

By the time proposals for the completion of the National Monument were mooted in the 1840s, Forrest's (now large) collection of statues from history and fiction—initially received positively by the public[7]—was considered to bring down the 'tone' of the hill[8] and to put the completion of the monument in jeopardy.[9] Though heavily condemned, first by art critics,[10] then by the National Monument Committee, Forrest's exhibition was not the reason the monument project failed, or why focus on the development of Calton Hill as a national landscape fell out of favour so soon after 1828. It was not a straightforward

Plate 6.3—T. Picken after J. Harding, *The National Monument on Calton Hill*,
showing the rear of the wooden hut erected in front of the National Monument.
Taken from J. P. Lawson, *Scotland Delineated in a Series of Views*, 1847

matter of cause and effect. Instead, it brings focus to a continuing problem on the hill during its development in the late eighteenth and early nineteenth century—that of perceived 'ownership' by Edinburgh's inhabitants.

The ownership of Calton Hill and the land to its north has been defined, in legal geographical terms in Part 1, showing that most of the site by the late eighteenth century was owned and managed by the city as public ground, or by influential charitable institutions within Edinburgh. This meant many of the decisions about the initial development of its landscape were made by those who sat on the boards of these trusts, or on Edinburgh town council committees tasked with overseeing what happened with the site. However, decisions about the placing of structures on

the hill during the late eighteenth and early nineteenth centuries were not only made by those who owned the land. In fact a complicated matrix of municipal, civil and quasi-'national' organisations facilitated the establishment, funding and design of the structures, which came to embody the political perspectives and aspirations of those within these bodies.

Graeme Morton's book on the governance and management of urban Scotland during the nineteenth century looks at the roles of these groups, which filtered into every aspect of society from the late eighteenth century on.[11] Termed as Scotland's 'civil society', they ranged from council committees, set up to oversee the management of municipal projects, to scientific and literary institutions run by academics and

Plate 6.4—Henry Raeburn,
Portrait of Sir James Stirling of Larbert,
oil on canvas, c. 1800.
© Courtesy of www.phillipmould.com

learned gentlemen, to institutions established by the kirk focusing on benevolent and charitable causes.[12] In common with most contemporaneous Scotland-wide bodies, those operating in Edinburgh were made up of 'an active elite', who formed a mode of self-governance at a local level that was outside of central state control.[13] It seems likely, therefore, that decisions surrounding the development of the city, and in particular Calton Hill, tended to be made to benefit this elite group, rather than the city and its people as a whole.[14] In the case of the hill, this is particularly obvious looking at those involved in the National Monument scheme, since despite its name, the National Monument was never, in fact, a national project. Rather, it was a project

run and supported by organisations fronted and steered by those within the top layers of society.[15]

The process of decision-making on urban development projects on Calton Hill in the late eighteenth century brought prestige to those involved on the town council, as well as the council itself. Henry Raeburn's portrait of Sir James Stirling of Larbert (Plate 6.4),[16] is a good example of this. It shows Stirling sitting in a room with a window that frames a view of Robert Adam's Bridewell outside—a project that was commenced and built while he was Lord Provost of Edinburgh. It is also evident in the city's sanctioning of an observatory on Calton Hill in the 1770s as a public work and the subsequent rapid disengagement with it when the project failed in later in the decade.[17] In the early nineteenth century, and particularly after the triumphs of the Napoleonic wars, prestige deriving from the large urban development projects within the third New Town was claimed by those involved in the broader 'administrative management' of Scottish society—Graeme Morton's 'civil society'. In the early years of the site's development therefore, decisions were made that suited elite political agendas as well as the economy of the city and major landowners. Where previously the council could hand-pick projects that were of interest and benefit to them and their time in office, those who would directly prosper from the stronger connections to Empire, through economics and political power, pushed focus on the collective national consciousness of Empire-building as the cause for city development.[18]

The debate about the relocation of the Royal High School building to Calton Hill in the early 1820s emphasises the role that the local elite played in the promotion of personal

Plate 6.5—*Royal High School, Infirmary Street*.
Taken from W. Steven, *The History of the High School of Edinburgh*, 1849

agendas through urban expansion. Prior to its placement on Calton Hill, the Royal High School maintained close physical and academic links with Edinburgh University—the two institutions were established in Kirk O'Fields within five years of each other, in the sixteenth century.[19] When Robert Adam's new university premises were built on the southern side of the Old Town in the late eighteenth century, the High School was also rehoused in a building that sat roughly across from the entrance (Plate 6.5).[20]

By the early 1820s, however, discussions were under way to relocate the High School. A demand for a larger premises to accommodate the growing numbers of pupils[21] was cited, along with the need for a more 'centrally' located

building that could be accessed easily from all corners of the expanding city.[22] In particular, it was thought unacceptable that the school was in what was considered an increasingly insalubrious part of the city, exposing students to the repugnance of Old Town life on a daily basis.[23] However, looking at Edinburgh Town Council minutes,[24] it is apparent that the real push came from proposals to erect a new academy at the north end of the New Town.[25] This was the project of Lord Henry Cockburn and Leonard Horner,[26] who proposed that the site for the Edinburgh Academy would be at the farthest point from the Old Town. Location, along with its high fees, would exclude people living in the Old Town.[27] As the majority of High School

Plate 6.6—Thomas Hamilton, *Proposal for a Royal High School in St James Square*, c.1825.
© Edinburgh Royal High School

pupils in the early nineteenth century lived in the New Town,[28] it was considered that this exclusivity would appeal to those in the higher class of society, and therefore be of detriment to the High School.[29]

The council's attempt to retain control over the city's educational establishments brought forth a proposal in 1822 that the new academy be under the aegis of the High School and two separate schools would be created—the original Old Town premises, and a newly built establishment in the New Town.[30] Thomas Hamilton was commissioned to prepare designs for the new High School, which was proposed on the site of St James Square, adjacent to Robert Adam's Register House (Plate 6.6),[31] but this was rejected due to concerns over the class segregation that would result from having two separate schools within different areas of the city.[32]

In addition to an exclusive location for the new academy, proposers also intended to provide an exclusive style of education. For a number of years, there had been concerns about the Latin bias at the High School—in particular, the 'Scots' pronunciation of Latin, and a preference for Latin over Greek in its classical curriculum. The academy would provide a more Etonian, anglicised style of education so that pupils from elite Edinburgh families would be able to 'challenge the stranglehold' of English public schools on Oxbridge, and access the influence and power that an Oxbridge education fostered. It was therefore this challenge to an English stronghold on establishment power in Great Britain and the British Empire that those who were behind the development of the academy really looked to achieve in the building of a new school for the city.[33]

Plate 6.7—Archibald Elliot, Regent Bridge/Road, c.1817.
Detail showing niches in retaining walls, © Kirsten Carter McKee

The suggestion of 'convert[ing] the Parthenon of Athens into the great hall of our National Academy' on the Mound into the new Royal High School,[34] which would 'combine the splendour of classic, with the glories of our own times, in the young and ardent associations of our sons' therefore further fostered the idea that a new establishment would be built to educate Scots to become the British leaders of tomorrow,[35] rather than provide a feeder school for Edinburgh University. Subscribers to the National Monument were appealed to, to help to support and raise funds for the new High School to be established as part of the National Monument, as 'there is no

purpose to which it can be supplied so appropriate as the erection of a great national school, in which the youth, not of Edinburgh, but from every quarter in Scotland, are to be trained to serve their country in all departments of public life . . . let the fabric be connected with the youth of the country'.[36]

As the town council did not build the proposed new structure in time to satisfy the subscribers to the new academy building, Cockburn and Horner commissioned William Burn to design and build it on their original plot at the north end of the New Town. This, in essence, freed up the council to develop a new

Plate 6.8—Julien-David Le Roy, *Sketch of the Propylaea, Athens*.
Taken from J.-D. Le Roy, *Les Ruines des Plus Beaux Monuments de la Grèce*, 1758

High School building on their own terms on Calton Hill. Yet, the design also incorporated aspects that it believed would satisfy the aspirations of its elite students. The hill's proximity to the National Monument and its location in an imperial landscape were no doubt part of that message the Council wished to convey to the students of the Royal High School. In addition, as the only educational establishment on the hill up to this point had been Joseph Lancaster's school for educating the poor, it provided further opportunity to establish elite control over the educational presence on the hill.[37] Rather than the route to the city school passing through the seedy area on the North Bridge, pupils would walk along Waterloo Place, past Archibald

Elliot's retaining walls for the Old Calton burial ground (Plate 6.7), in which would be placed memorial busts and statues of characters of great inspiration, piety and patriotic valour.[38] On reaching the school, they would be confronted by a building 'of ornamental character . . . [which would] be a conspicuous object from many points, and particularly prominent on entering the town by the splendid approach of the Regent's Road . . . [which] harmonize[s] . . . with the magnificence of the surrounding scenery'.[39]

The site that was decided upon for the new High School at Calton Hill therefore elevated local concern regarding a local institution to a national level, and also attempted to incorporate the old establishment order. The space afforded by siting it here meant that only one building would be required and there would be no need to split the school between two sites in the Old and New Town,[40] while its placement on the hill allowed the architect, Thomas Hamilton, to create both visual and geographical links with the National Monument on the summit. Hamilton's insightful proposal placed the school on a curve in Regent Road,[41] halfway up the hill (Plate 5.7). His interpretation of Le Roy's Propylaea (Plate 6.8), the gateway to the Athenian Acropolis provided opportunity to contribute to Calton Hill's Ancient Greek eminence, while its horizontal dominance satisfied William Stark's contention that structures are 'finer when seen from a moderate elevation . . . skirting the brow of the hill'.[42] In addition, the Propylaea's purpose as a gateway building to the Acropolis no doubt provided appropriate references to the school's purpose of education as a gateway to imperial opportunities, whilst also displaying a renewed emphasis on Grecian Classicism within the curriculum. By fully removing its geographical association with the university and placing the structure on Calton Hill, the school no longer sat in the shadow of academia, but instead basked in the celestial light of imperial grandeur.

Further examples of elite autonomy guiding the development of the hill can be identified in the proposed resiting of the gothic fifteenth-century Trinity College church on Calton Hill during the early 1850s. Following the driving of the railway through the church's original site within the Waverley Valley in 1848 (Plate 6.9), and an outcry at its planned demolition, an alternative location for this pre-Reformation structure was needed.[43] A number of places were considered.[44] They included two sites on the south side of Calton Hill—the first, near the foot

of the access steps to the top of the hill, and the second on the site of the Burns monument.[45]

A watercolour showing a proposed site for Trinity College was prepared by David Bryce (Plate 6.10).[46] This shows the church at the entrance to the steps leading up to the Arcadian classical summit,[47] a 'commanding position . . . [it would] be seen, not only along Waterloo Place, but from several quarters of the city'.[48] The second site on Calton Hill was where the already built Burns monument sat, which was to be removed and placed elsewhere.[49] Of the two, the latter would have made more sense overall, as a plan of the area (Plate 6.11) demonstrates that this would have resulted in the church being adjacent to the New Calton burial ground, providing a small parish church and a burial site for the residents of Greenside. The proposals for placing Trinity in such prominent positions on Calton Hill show that the gothic structure was considered of architectural or historical merit. This is supported by Robert William Billings in his publication *The Baronial and Ecclesiastical Antiquities of Scotland*, where he states that 'with the exception of Holyrood Chapel, Trinity College Church was the finest example of Gothic architecture in Edinburgh',[50] since, with detailing similar to that of Rosslyn chapel, but on a larger scale, its ornamentation was considered worthy of minute examination and study.

Despite the opinion of Billings, and the town council's appreciation of Trinity's grandeur, the resiting was challenged when it was apparent that in removing the kirk from the Canongate, it would provide a place of religious worship for the inhabitants of Calton Hill to the detriment of those who lived in some of the poorest conditions in the city. The church, which had been founded in 1462 by Mary of Guelders, consort of James

Plate 6.9—Robert William Billings, *Trinity College Church, Edinburgh, South West View*, 1847.
© Courtesy of Historic Environment Scotland

II, was closely associated with the charitable trust of Trinity Hospital, set up to give alms to the poor.[51] The church and the trust continued their work here until the church and hospital's removal in 1845.[52] Removing the church from near the Canongate, and placing it on the hill for the benefit of those residing in the exclusive properties at Playfair's Royal, Regent and Carlton Terraces would make it inaccessible to those who needed the most help, both financially and spiritually.

> [T]he parish [currently] attached to the Trinity church is one of the most destitute in Edinburgh, and one the most devoid of religious ordinances. In passing through the Canongate, countrywards on a Sabbath afternoon, we have seen more of the people who never attend any church lounging at the close-heads than would have filled the church of the Holy Trinity thrice over. But not such the character of the locality in which it is proposed to re-erect it. The inhabitants of Regent and Carlton Terrace belong mainly to the upper ranks,—the people of Norton Place and comely green to the Middle classes; they are church goers already; and a new church in the district would be of no use to them, and would bear no moral effect on the community at large . . .[53]

Hugh Miller's[54] comments in his 1856 article opposing the resiting of Trinity chapel[55] further highlights the social discrepancies between those

Plate 6.10—David Bryce and Louis Joseph Ghémar, *Proposal for Trinity Church at the Foot of Calton Hill*, 1852
© www.capitalcollections.org.uk

who were to benefit from urban redevelopment in the city, and those who actually needed it. By placing the chapel in a prominent position on the south side of the hill, the town council showed that their priorities lay with enhancing the urban landscape, rather than providing poor relief and investment where it was sorely needed.[56] In fact, despite the council's efforts to resurrect the complete structure on Calton Hill—which included the careful recording, photographing[57] and numbering of the stones

during its demolition for the railway[58]—when Robert Billings was finally commissioned to rebuild the chapel in the Old Town in 1872, only the original apse of Trinity was used. It is possible that a reduced version was built since it was not considered right to place what was considered an impressive and grandiose building in such a poor area.[59]

With the establishment of the Royal High School and Playfair's observatory on Calton Hill, it had been believed that such an elite

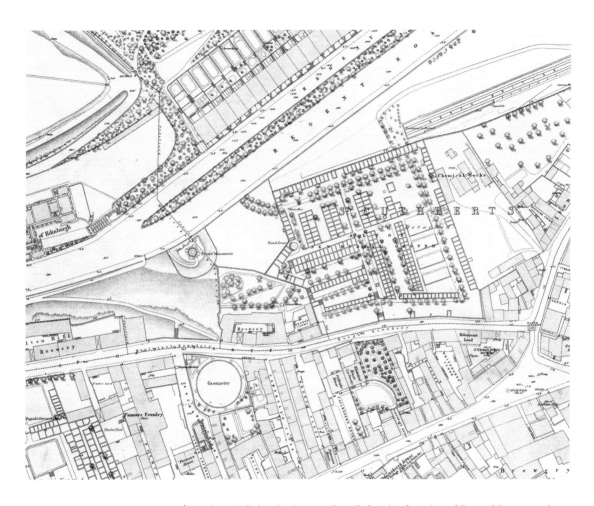

Plate 6.11—Ordnance Survey, *Town Plan of Edinburgh*, 1849–53. Detail showing location of Burns Monument in relation to New Calton Burial Ground. © Courtesy of National Library of Scotland

presence would discourage the seedier elements of the community, who had easy access from the Old Town at Jacob's Ladder, from using the area. The image of the Royal High School in *Modern Athens!*[60] (Plate 6.12), for example, illustrates this attempt to disengage the hill from the Old Town, by distancing the emblem of Enlightenment knowledge[61] from the grim reality in the Canongate below.[62] G. M. Kemp's image of Calton Hill from Salisbury Crags (Plate 6.13) around 1830 betrays a consciousness of this

opposition by setting the Arcadian aspirations of the National Monument Committee in a distant celestial light but removing the Old Town completely by cleverly obstructing all but the castle from view. Yet despite best efforts to create an ornamental landscape on Calton Hill by the New Town intelligentsia, the poor had been a constant presence throughout the process.[63] Images of the hill from a closer viewpoint provide an alternative perspective of those who frequented and used Calton Hill in their day-

Plate 6.12—W. Tombleton after Thomas Shepherd, *Royal High School, Calton Hill, Edinburgh*.
Taken from Thomas Shepherd and John Britton, *Modern Athens! Displayed in a Series of Views*, 1829

to-day lives. J. M. W. Turner's 1819 sketch of *Edinburgh from Calton Hill & Heriot's Hospital* (Plate 6.14) and Francois A. Pernot's sketch entitled *Edimbourg. Vu du Calton Hill* from 1827[64] (Plate 6.15), for example, capture the presence of washerwomen—as commented on by Robert Mudie—alongside other characters who, by their dress, are evidently from the lower classes, and would have lived in the Old Town. These must surely be more realistic portrayals of the hill.

By 1847, around the time of the proposals for Trinity, a second panorama from Calton Hill was published. It showed that despite best efforts to endow the hill with an elevated character through its architectural enhancement, in reality nothing had changed (Plate 6.16). Respectable couples still promenaded a hill frequented by washerwomen and barefooted children, and the hill's architecture became a picturesque backdrop to a touristic pleasure walk, used by the broad spectrum of the populace for a variety of activities.

Its draw as a tourist site by the mid 1830s resulted in the building of Maria Short's camera obscura[65] beside the rapidly expanding exhibition of Forrest's statuary,[66] and the

Plate 6.13 (overleaf)—George Meikle Kemp, *Calton Hill, Edinburgh, with the Proposed National Monument*, c.1830.
© Courtesy of Historic Environment Scotland

Plate 6.15—Francois A. Pernot,
Edimbourg: Vu du Calton Hill, 1826.
© Courtesy of National Library of Scotland

presence of these attractions, alongside the Nelson monument, further removed any serious opportunity for the development of national discourse. [67] Nevertheless, these two structures, demonstrate that even before the arrival of Maria Short's 'wooden showbox'[68]—as Lord Cockburn disparagingly called it[69]—there were two tiers operating on the site; one for the elite gentleman scholar, and one for the common populace.

This division of gentlemanly and populist pursuits was particularly represented in the establishment and use of the astronomical observatories on Calton Hill in the last quarter of the eighteenth century. Despite the failure of Thomas Short's proposals to construct an observatory that would house his optical lens, subsequent remedial work by Short's son James Douglas Short, in 1792, completed both Craig's octagonal structure, and the gothic tower, housing the optical lens within the tower and advertising it as a popular observatory, or 'camera obscura' for public viewings, to pay for the upkeep of the structures.[70] When the area was handed over to the Astronomical Institution in 1812,[71] James Craig's octagon was demolished to make way for the Royal Observatory[72] by William H. Playfair (Plate 5.14), and the tower was retained as a popular observatory for the masses. However, the serious financial situation of the Astronomical Institution by the mid nineteenth century resulted in the camera obscura being

Plate 6.14 (overleaf)—Joseph Mallord William Turner,
Edinburgh from Calton Hill & Heriot's Hospital, 1819.
© National Galleries of Scotland

Plate 6.16 (above)—Anon, *Edinburgh: A Complete View of the City and Environs as seen in a Walk Round the Calton Hill*, 1847. © Lammerburn Collection, Edinburgh

Plate 6.17 (below)—Thomas Begbie, *Washerwomen on the Calton Hill*, 1887 © www.capitalcollections.org.uk.

sold, dismantled and removed.[73] The Royal Observatory never really reaching its full potential to contribute to astronomical science. Once the new Royal Observatory was completed on Blackford Hill to the south of the city in 1895, the Playfair building and the ancillary domes were no longer used at all for academic study, and all of the working machinery in the Calton Hill observatories was instead used by members of

Plate 6.18—David Octavius Hill and Robert Adamson, *Calotype of Monument to Dugald Stewart and Gothic Observatory*, c.1840s. By permission of University of Glasgow Library, Special Collections

Plate 6.19—David Octavius Hill and Robert Adamson, *Calotype of Nelson Monument*, c.1840s. By permission of University of Glasgow Library, Special Collections

washerwomen bleaching sheets on Calton Hill (Plate 6.17)[77] show that the practices of the lower classes living nearby continued uninterrupted, well up to the end of the nineteenth century.

Begbie's evocative images were not the only instance of photographic legacy. During the 1840s, a photographic studio was established on Calton Hill in Rock House, by David Octavius Hill and Robert Adamson. Much of their work focused on experimenting with the calotype technique and processes through a series of photographs of external structures that included images of the Dugald Stewart monument and the observatory (Plate 6.18), the Nelson Monument (Plate 6.19) and the political Martyrs' Monument (Plate 6.20) on the hill, as well as a number of panoramas and views to and from the site. But it was their capturing of human character through photography work, spurred by the photographic portraits for David Octavius Hill's painting of the Disruption of the Kirk,[78] which have since been acknowledged as insightful and evocative pieces of artwork. In particular, Hill and Adamson's studies of working men and women at Newhaven Harbour are often referenced as particularly significant in early photographic portraiture. These beautifully raw images of the 'fisherfolk' of Newhaven included portraits of many of the local fishwives, which captured the rugged characters and fragile wretchedness of women who were considered not much better than prostitutes and on the lowest rung of society.[79]

Inspiration for these calotypes could have come about from Hill and Adamson's exposure to the ravages of hard work and poverty that were so apparent against the classical back-drop on the summit of Calton Hill. No images of the hill washerwomen are known to exist in Hill and Adamson's collection of negatives, but,

the public who practised astronomy as a hobby.

Overshadowing the significance of the hill's monuments, and those that they commemorated, [74] was what was classed in disparaging terms by local councillors as the 'peep show' of Short's camera obscura, [75] which was considered no more than an attraction for persons of ill repute. Some attempt was made to 'clean up the hill' with the presence of a constable, and a 'suitably attired' guide to point out monuments and places of interest to visitors.[76] But, despite these measures, Thomas Begbie's 1887 photographs of

considering the location of the photographic studio at Rock House, and that Hill and Adamson
prepared a number of images of Calton Hill's
landscape and architecture,[80] they must have
frequently tramped around the area. As in the
successful development of calotype photographs, the bleaching of linen also requires good
light and so it is not a big leap that the constant
presence of these working women on Calton Hill
were the inspiration for their later studies down
at Newhaven.[81] The grand architecture on the hill
would have highlighted the plight of the lower
classes, now preserved for posterity.

The influence of both those who developed
the Calton landscape, and those who experi-
enced the hill on a daily basis shaped the
perception of the hill, culturally and socially
throughout the remainder of the nineteenth
century. The unionist/nationalist aspirations
reflected in the classical structures became
further obscured by a growing cultural affiliation
with pre-Reformation Scotland that many felt
was best represented in art and architecture by
the medieval gothic and romantic figures of
that time. With this loss of clarity in the elite
aspirations for the hill's development, and the
growing presence of populist activities, its status
as an Arcadian landscape of imperial aspiration

Plate 6.20—David Octavius Hill and Robert Adamson,
Calotype of Martyrs Monument, c.1844. By permission of
University of Glasgow Library, Special Collections

lost out to the city's tourist trade, for which
many of the structures supplied little more than
a picturesque backdrop.

Cultural Nationalism and the 'Municipal State'

Scots' sense of identity was further focused in the latter part of the nineteenth century after 1840s legislation establishing boards to monitor local services of poor relief, public health and mental welfare. Concern for the wretchedness and poverty of the lower classes[1] began to raise questions about the management and control of internal social problems within Scotland. Where previously national ambition had turned to Scotland's external reputation within the British Isles and its role in imperial expansion, the lack of autonomy and power that the Scots had over national affairs brought focus to the problems of legislation through government based outside of Scotland.

Scottish National Identity of the late nineteenth century was largely founded on a vision of the Scots as an 'imperial race'. Scottish achievements in the Empire formed a focus of national pride; it was claimed that the Scottish militia played a prominent role in its conquest and defence, the workshop of the Empire furnished it with manufactured goods, Scottish governor generals administered vast territories, Scottish colonists formed significant parts of the new dominion nations and Scottish missionaries spread Presbyterianism to all quarters of the globe. Such a self-congratulary [sic] view of the nation, however, was becoming increasingly difficult to sustain as the gradual emergence of mass democracy forced contemporaries to look at the reality of life in Scotland. Slum housing, poverty and disease painted a very different picture which was becoming hard to ignore.[2]

By the 1830s, proposals and discussions for the completion of the National Monument no longer attempted to portray the structure as a representation of Scottish autonomy within the British state. Some looked to it as a symbol of British sovereignty, for example Michael Linning, secretary to the National Monument Committee, in his published memoirs of 1834, states that its role in the building of the structure was much more politically focused in 'promot[ing] the cause of domestic colonisation', than in perpetuating cultural affiliations. Mr Fairholm in 1837 (Plate 7.1)[3] proposed a statue of Britannia astride the finished monument—a figure that he believed was 'suited to the national object to which this structure was intended'. This unsuccessful design was followed in 1840 by another of with a similar fate by James Raeburn, a scheme which proposed to turn the National Monument into a memorial to the Duke of Wellington. This would have added 'six columns to the twelve already executed, dividing the interior by a central wall into two porticoes . . . to give the whole the appearance of a triumphal porch—on the centre of the pediment the equestrian statue of the duke would be placed'.[4] In some respects, this could be viewed as fulfilling the intention of the monument to commemorate the Napoleonic wars, and in particular the battle of Waterloo. Scottish contribution to this battle would have been acknowledged in the 'decisive charge of the Scots Greys at Waterloo' depicted on the western tympanum, balanced by another group of soldiers associated with a Scottish regiment on the eastern side. However, in making the man

who was previously described by Robert Forrest as representing 'the ancient honour and glory of the English nation'[5] the focal point of the structure, rather than the Scots who fought for the British state, it completely contrasted with the 1820s intention for the monument. By making the Scots regiments of secondary importance to Wellington and establishing a Roman triumphal porch rather than an Athenian temple,[6] prominence was placed on a hero who represented the British state, and Britain as a colonial power, rather than the contribution of the Scots nation to the success of British campaigns.

With this gesture the monument would demonstrate, through its architecture, the British state's claim to authority over Scottish affairs. Scots tended to look more to the past to define their culture, rather than to their present political construct—which resulted in a further distancing of the idea of 'Scottishness' from that of 'Britishness' within the union. As political reforms looked to internal, rather than national affairs, by the mid nineteenth century, Scottish national identity within the British state had further evolved to become a predominantly cultural concept. An understanding of Scottishness as it had been set out by Sir Walter Scott in the early nineteenth century[7] perpetuated this notion, largely removing Scottish national identity from the politics of the relationship between nation and state, and instead focusing on historical references. This emerging form of national identity is recognised in architectural terms through the growing prominence of the gothic architectural style[8] alongside monuments to commemorate specifically Scottish heroes during the latter part of the nineteenth century.[9] On Calton Hill, this strengthening of cultural nationalism, already identified in Forrest's exhibition during the 1830s, and in the proposals in the early 1850s to place Trinity Kirk on the hill, was substantiated in the 1846 proposal for the completion of the National Monument as a gallery of monumental busts and statues.[10] As the structure was a classical one, emphasis was placed on the concept of nationhood, commemorating distinguished people of all nations and periods through sculptural art, rather than representing this through its architectural style. By amending the original Act of Parliament of the 1820s,[11] this subtle shift allowed a rebranding of the structure to sit within a historical cultural context, rather than the political one that had been pushed by those involved with the original design. For example, it is stated in George Cleghorn's[12] 1852 publication on the National Monument that the aims of the resurrected project were no longer to promote Scotland and Edinburgh as 'North British', such as was the original proposal for an Athenian building, but instead to emphasise Scots' independent culture in its own right.[13]

This distancing of Classicism from Scottish cultural identity resulted in the stylistic classical outputs of the late eighteenth and early nineteenth centuries being thought of in Scotland as representing unionist aims. In particular, the displaying of a number of statues to Tory heroes who represented and perpetuated policies that benefited and strengthened the union, such as Lord Melville (Henry Dundas), William Pitt and George IV in the first New Town[14] emphasised the British state as the prime political entity.[15] John Dick Peddie's painting *Improvements to the City* (c.1870, Plate 7.2) focuses on the 'Classical' and 'British' landscape in Edinburgh, by including a proposal for a hotel that would sit at the terminus to the North British Railway line between Edinburgh and Berwick—the northernmost part of the main line between London and Edinburgh.[16] By aligning the picture to cut out the Nelson monument, and removing the non-classical elements of the gothic observatory and the curtilage walls (replacing these with regulated classicised walls of smooth ashlar) Peddie depicted a suitably British backdrop to his proposal for a hotel catering for those travelling between England and Scotland.[17] Proposals for the National Monument since, and including the 1846 proposal, no longer contained the allegorical representation of Greek Classicism as defining Scotland within the nation-state. Instead, the question of whether and how Calton Hill and its structures related to Scottish national identity and the British state was reflected in the wide ranging proposals for this site from the late nineteenth century on.

After those of 1846, the next substantive proposals for the development of the National Monument did not appear until the beginning of the twentieth century, when William Mitchell—Edinburgh lawyer and secretary to the Cockburn Association[18]—proposed that the monument be completed to house a new national gallery building. This was made into a pamphlet in 1906,[19] and suggested how the work might be funded. Mitchell argued that any notion of the structure as a national monument should be rejected on the grounds that it represented the successes of the British military against 'Scotland's auld friends', the French. He proposed that it should

Plate 7.2 (overleaf)—John Dick Peddie RSA (1824–1891), *Suggestions for the Improvement of Edinburgh* (design for the Waverley Market, Edinburgh), pencil, ink and watercolour on paper, c.1870, 52.2 x 76.7cm, 1994.032. Royal Scottish Academy of Art & Architecture (Diploma Collection).
Image credit: Chris Park

Plate 7.3a—William Mitchell and Henry F. Kerr, *Proposal for the Completion of the National Monument*, 1906

be redefined as a Scottish national gallery that would celebrate Scottish achievements. It would house the national collection, busts of the great and good of Scotland, the National School of Art and the collection of casts of the Scottish Antiquarian Society.[20] Mitchell's financial calculations sat alongside designs by Henry F. Kerr for development of the gallery on Calton Hill, which suggested completing the rectilinear structure with a Grecian frieze and pediment, topped with *acroteria angularia* (Plate 7.3a). A smaller entrance hall with a Doric portico would have sat to the south, and a funicular railway would have served as access for the gallery and to the hill (Plate 7.3b).

However, the 1906 National Gallery of Scotland Act[21] specified a change of use to the Royal Institution building in front of the National Gallery on the Mound as the preferred option for the Royal Academy building, which essentially put to rest any plans for the National Monument as a gallery. This did not deter Mitchell from his mission to develop Calton Hill, as a second scheme was produced in a 'deluxe edition',[22] which included a proposal to use half of the £100,000 Usher bequest to develop a national gallery on Calton Hill alongside a concert hall, creating a cultural 'hub' on the top of the hill. Kerr's 1907 amendments (Plate 7.4) therefore include access from the east, a semi-circular bay to the north of the main building of the National Monument,[23] and a domed hall to the

DRAWING No. I.

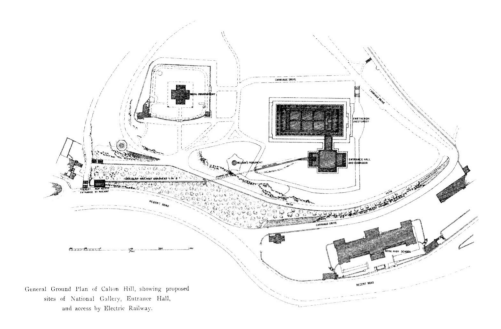

General Ground Plan of Calton Hill, showing proposed
sites of National Gallery, Entrance Hall,
and access by Electric Railway.

Plate 7.3b—William Mitchell and Henry F. Kerr, *General Ground Plan of Calton Hill, Showing Proposed Sites of National Gallery, Entrance Hall and Access by Electric Railway*, 1906

south, close to the entrance hall in the 1906 plan.

By 1909, Kerr had given up on the development of the monument, instead focusing his vision for the whole hill as a 'cultural Valhalla', including delineation of the footprint of the Parthenon by tree planting (Plate 7.5). However, the ever-determined Mitchell continued with his vision for the monument's completion. In 1911, he again proposed that it be built, but this time as a memorial to Queen Victoria—something he had previously suggested, in 1900.[24] This was to include ample inside room to pay tribute to the country's 'gallant and illustrious sons as a memorial of the past and incentive of the future heroism of the men of Scotland'.

When taken in context with the other designs for the National Monument over the previous century, Mitchell's proposals further demonstrate Graeme Morton's argument that since its establishment within the British state, 'Scotland [has been] forced to re-invent its national identity again and again.'[25] In particular, Mitchell attempted to place Scottish identity within a nationalist ideology that defined a separate relationship between Scotland and Europe from that found between Britain and Europe. This suggests that by the early twentieth century, Scottish identity was not only considered to co-exist with other national identities of the British state but was also seen (in the eyes of the Scots at least) as belonging to a separate functioning nation within a European context.[26]

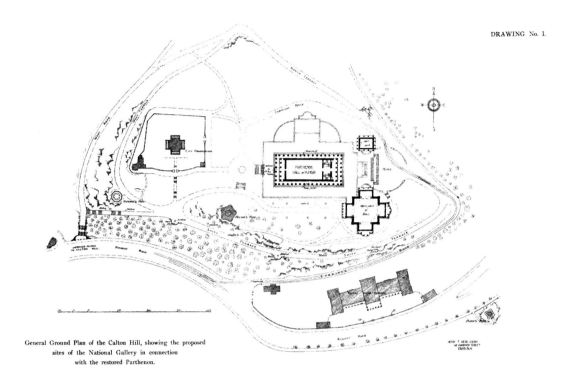

DRAWING No. I.

General Ground Plan of the Calton Hill, showing the proposed
sites of the National Gallery in connection
with the restored Parthenon.

Plate 7.4—William Mitchell and Henry F. Kerr, *General Ground Plan of the Calton Hill, showing the proposed sites of the National Gallery in Connection with the Restored Parthenon*, 1907

Mitchell's proposals for the site to become, if not a Scottish national gallery, then a memorial to Queen Victoria, also placed Scottish identity at the core of the monument's development. In celebrating the imperial monarch, rather than the achievements of the governing state, Scottish identity would be celebrated in a similar vein to that of a colonial nation of the Commonwealth and would reassert itself as a separate entity from England.[27]

Yet, where Mitchell sought to reassert Scottish identity and significance within early twentieth-century polities, Frank Mears and Ramsay Traquair's proposals considered Scottish identity to be linked to its geographical and social context. Their 1912 article for Patrick

Geddes' magazine, *The Blue Blanket* provided a critique of Mitchell's interpretation and use of the National Monument.[28] They state that great men should be commemorated in or near the places that they are most closely associated with. Mears and Traquair believed that the development of the 1820s classical suburb of the New Town and particularly Calton Hill had resulted in an abandonment of Edinburgh's true history, it had no connection with the Old Town people or events it sought to commemorate there. For instance, memorials to lawyers should be situated near the law courts, memorials to professors near the university, and memorials to military men near the castle. Yet they also believed that monuments to great men had a purpose in the urban scene, providing commentary to those in positions of governance.

> *The commemoration of famous men by stat-
> ues or buildings is a proper part of civic life.
> In such activities, a higher ideal of corporate
> unity is reached than in the routine of admin-
> istration, or even schemes of philanthropy.
> Here some degree of beauty and of idealism
> can still penetrate the practical armour of a
> municipal government, and the community
> would be dead which had so lost the spirit of
> reverence that it could no longer rise to en-
> shrine the memory of its great men.* [29]

Mears and Traquair's own proposals for the National Monument (Plate 7.6), which were displayed in the Royal Scottish Academy annual show of 1912, therefore continued the dialogue started by Mitchell on the relationship between the monument and the question of Scottish national identity. Mears and Traquair had considered that 'The Calton Hill, in time, will become historical, and we may make it truly so by raising there monuments to modern men, and by using it for modern functions.'[30] Their fantastical design of an open courtyard, with small niches for medieval and romantic sculpture surrounding a rectilinear water feature, gave the effect of a takeover of Celtic art nouveau on the site, further emphasising Scottish identity within a European cultural context. A bronze statue of seated Caledonia, defiantly facing westwards towards the Doric columns of the 1820 classical development, appears to show the spirit of the Scots nation challenging the previous dominance of the British unionist state on the site. Yet the columns' incorporation in the design, rather than their disregard, also serves a purpose in acknowledging this part of history. Mears and Traquair's comments on the suitability of Calton

Hill as a place for memorial had expanded not only to include the tangible connections with Scotland's past, but also connections with Scotland as a nation in its present. The part-completed nineteenth-century structure within the overall effect of the site left Mears and Traquair's interpretation of Scottish identity as a dominant feature, with the unionist facet a small part of the whole. This representation of state as peripheral served as a reminder to those in the governing elite that it should place its people or nation above the state.

It is in this context that the criticism of George Washington Browne's proposals for the Scottish National War Memorial (SNWM, built at Edinburgh Castle) can be better understood. The architects invited to submit proposals for the SNWM[31] had all favoured interpretations of historic Scottish styles in their earlier work—with the forerunner in the competition, Sir Robert Lorimer, having already been knighted for his Thistle Chapel (executed in the Scottish Gothic) at the High Kirk of St Giles in Edinburgh.[32] When Browne revealed his idea for the SNWM as a classical adaptation of Playfair's National Monument on Calton Hill (Plate 7.7),[33] it appears anachronistic—particularly as a proposal for this specific national war memorial.[34] Browne's frieze and level cornice, which were to be added to the completed columns of the existing classical structure, along with a great quadriga (classical sculpture of a chariot drawn by four horses) in the centre of the open screen (partition which separates the structure into sections)[35] was a far cry from the interpretation of Scottish identity within the union, which those erecting a specifically Scottish war memorial tried to show.[36]

This new understanding and interpretation

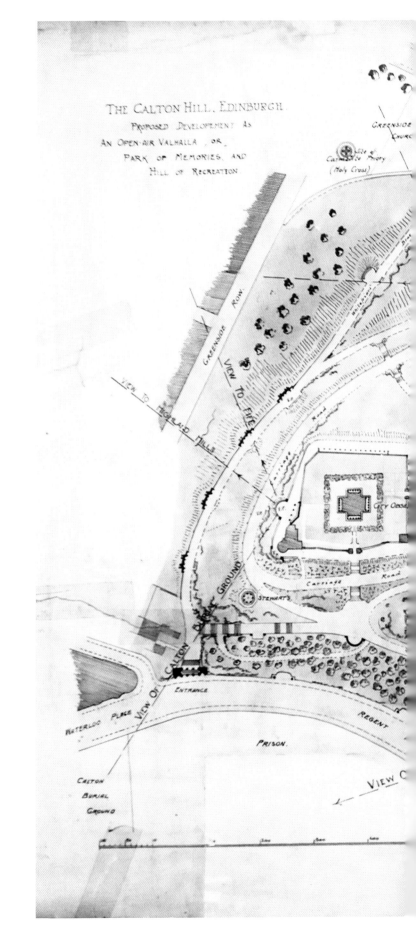

Plate 7.5—William Mitchell
and Henry F. Kerr,
*Proposed Development of
Calton Hill as
an Open Air Valhalla or
Park of Memories
and Hall of Recreation*,
1909

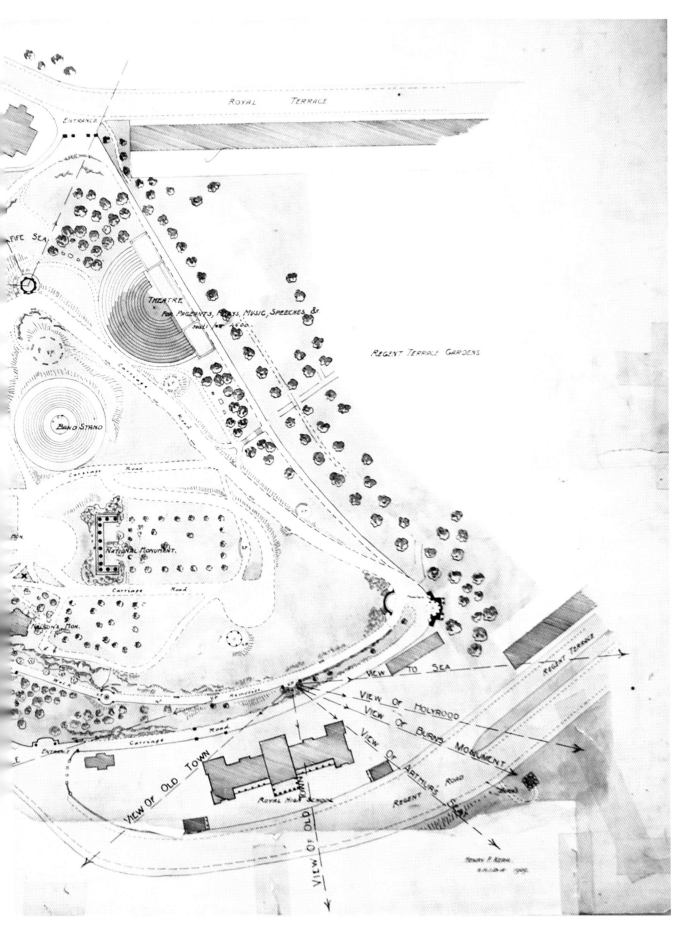

ROYAL TERRACE

ENTRANCE

FIFE SEA

REGENT TERRACE GARDENS

THEATRE
FOR PAGEANTS, PLAYS, MUSIC, SPEECHES &c.
seats for 1600.

BAND STAND

Carriage Road

Carriage Road

NATIONAL MONUMENT.

Carriage Road

NELSON'S MON.

VIEW TO SEA

VIEW OF HOLYROOD

VIEW OF BURNS MONUMENT

REGENT TERRACE

VIEW OF OLD TOWN

VIEW OF ARTHUR'S SEAT

ROYAL HIGH SCHOOL

REGENT ROAD

VIEW OF OLD TOWN

ENTRANCE

Carriage Road

HENRY F. KERR.
1907.

Plate 7.6—Ramsay Traquair and Frank Mears, *A Scheme to Complete the National Monument on the Calton Hill*, pen and watercolour, 1912

of nationalism in the early twentieth century continued to be a very strong theme in the erection of the SNWM—designed by Sir Robert Lorimer and completed in 1927.[37] Lorimer's redesign of the Billings building as a 'hall of honour' retained the original footprint of the surviving barracks, and added a seven-bay apse to the north elevation as a shrine (Plate 7.8.)[38] It was executed by skilled Scottish craftsmen and artists, personally picked by Lorimer, many of whom he had met as students or tutors at Edinburgh College of Art.[39] The decoration of the building took pains to separate Scots identity within the union by expressing its role as a separate contributor to imperial expansion, in order to demonstrate that Scotland, had 'willingly answered the call to arms and proudly played her part in the war'.[40] This idea is demonstrated in the entranceway of the SNWM, which depicts Scotland on equal terms within

the union, by placing a unicorn holding a shield engraved with the St Andrew's cross on the left of the front steps, and a lion brandishing a Union Jack on the right. Every image placed within the memorial had direct connection with Scotland's military history; from William Wallace to those who had served in Scottish regiments during the First World War. These sat alongside a 'Tree of Empire',[41] which dominated the back wall of the shrine entrance.[42]

The location of the monument at Edinburgh Castle as 'the very focus of Scottish Traditions and Memories'[43] was also thought particularly important in maintaining a Scottish identity for the memorial. The Earl of Rosebery's commentary on Browne's proposal not only rejected the stylistic choice of the design, but also the choice of site, stating that: 'Edinburgh Castle is National property, and not Edinburgh property. Glasgow will never give a penny to help on a thing like the Calton Hill.'[44]

This opinion is particularly significant for understanding the perspective that some had on the role Calton Hill played by this time. Specified as Edinburgh property, the hill and its monuments were not considered as being representative of nation or state per se. Rather, the hill represented the municipality of Edinburgh and an achievement of its bureaucratic elite—particularly one involved with state governance. This became a prominent factor in the fate of the site's development during subsequent decades.

There had been little interest in the idea of home rule in Scotland during the nineteenth century.[45] Municipal affairs regarding the management of the urban environment, policing, education and health continued to be administered through the numerous organisations sustained within Scottish civil society, bolstered by town councils, the kirk and the Scottish legal system, as well as (after the Poor Law of 1845) the parochial boards.[46] However, the lack of political control over these boards—and the management of Scottish concerns in general—led to a feeling that ministerial powers were needed within Westminster to represent and promote specifically Scottish affairs.[47] This resulted in the re-establishment of a Secretary for Scotland in 1885,[48] to support the boards by providing more access to parliamentary time in order to ensure that Scottish affairs were appropriately considered in draft legislation. However, the post was a largely symbolic one that still left the management of many affairs to the parochial boards. As a form of Scottish administrative devolution it barely succeeded, while the grisly realities of first the Boer War and then the First World War further 'undermined the ideological foundations of laissez-faire in social policy' that

had kept Scotland running up to this point.[49] The malnourished, poorly educated majority of local recruits to imperial wars, and the manner in which whole communities were recruited throughout Britain left many questioning the priorities of government and the nature of state management in Scotland.[50]

As in the surge of local monuments to national heroes in the early nineteenth century (see Part 2), the role that local pride played in fuelling national identity grew after the First World War. This duality of local allegiance perpetuating interest in national issues became prominent in the nationalist dialogue after 1918 throughout Britain,[51] which in Scotland manifested itself in the fixing upon a need for a separate Scottish National War Memorial.

The Englishman does not concern himself with the affairs of his neighbours. He is proud of his native county; he holds in affectionate remembrance the village or street where he was born, and the garden or green where he played as a child. But, if he was born in Lancashire, he is not particularly interested say, in Middlesex, or for that matter, in London itself, and vice versa . . . The County is the unit, not the country . . . But Scotland has a different way of ordering these matters, for she is . . . small enough to be acutely conscious of herself as a whole . . . never a Scottish regiment comes under fire but the whole of Scotland feels it. Scotland is small enough to know all her sons by heart. You may live in Berwickshire, and the man who died may have come from Skye; but his name is quite familiar to you. Big England's mourning is local; little Scotland's is national.[52]

Nationalist feeling was invigorated by

Plate 7.7—
George Washington Browne,
*Proposal for the Scottish National
War Memorial*, 1918
From *The Builder* 26 July 1918

Plate 7.8 (overleaf)—
Robert Lorimer, *Edinburgh
Castle Reconstruction of
Disused Barracks as Scottish
National War Memorial*, n.d.
© Courtesy of Historic
Environment Scotland

OLD NORTH ELEVATION

NORTH

WEST ELEVATION

SOUTH

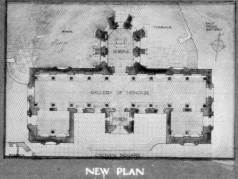

NEW PLAN

EDINBURG
RECONSTRUCTION C
SCOTTISH NATIO

ATION

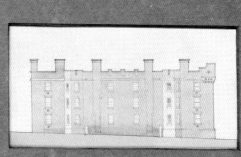

OLD SOUTH ELEVATION

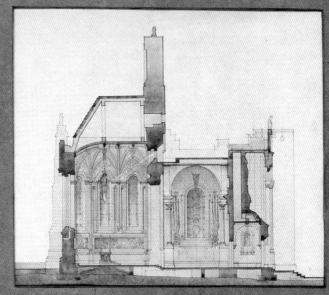

SECTION

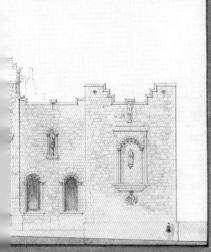

TION

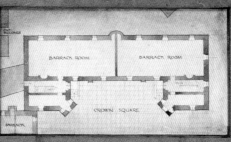

OLD PLAN

CASTLE
USED BARRACK AS
WAR MEMORIAL

SIR ROBERT LORIMER ARA
ARCHITECT

parliamentary discussion about the establishment of separate nations under the imperial umbrella, such as had been proposed for Ireland and India.[53] As Finlay has stated, 'Scottish national identity of the late nineteenth century was largely founded on a vision of the Scots as an "Imperial race".' The acknowledged importance of Scots in imperial campaigns sat alongside a discontent about the mismanagement, or ignoring of, Scottish concerns that had resulted from the misery of the Great Depression in the 1920s.[54] Home rule, as it was being debated for other countries of the Empire, was an option that would enable an active government to look after Scottish concerns and to promote and improve social policies in areas such as health, education and housing. Between 1892 and 1928, a 'Government for Scotland' Bill was discussed in Parliament on nearly thirty separate occasions.[55] It was argued that self-governing rights that were being given to Ireland should also be given to Scotland and was also made clear that, since the 1890s, it had been 'desirable, while retaining intact the power and supremacy of the Imperial Parliament, to establish a Legislature in Scotland for dealing with purely Scottish affairs'.[56] By 1927, a Bill granting home ruling powers was no longer on the cards, and instead, in 1928, on the advice of John Buchan[57] Westminster decided to convert proposals for the centralisation of department offices, mainly made up of the now subsumed Edinburgh boards,[58] into one administrative building, to appease nationalist sentiment by providing an 'outward and visible sign of Scottish nationhood'.[59] The Scottish Office would be built on Calton Hill in Edinburgh. In what has been described as a 'sop' to national identity, this structure would bring government closer to people, without compromising the existing constitutional setup, by providing a symbol of the Scottish nation under state control.

The story of the development of the Scottish Office building, known as St Andrew's House, is discussed in detail in David Walker's comprehensive study of the structure.[60] Walker details the struggle between the London government, and the Scottish populace—led by a number of Scottish peers—for control over the design of a structure to house administrative government offices alongside the Sheriff Court and the National Library of Scotland. The first proposal was drawn up by an in-house architect within the London administration, and was put on exhibition in model form, but did not include any contextual illustrations as to how its perspective related to the landscape of Calton Hill. Pat Ronaldson, then a student at Edinburgh College of Art, produced the missing perspective designs on the instruction of his lecturer, John Summerson. These were subsequently published in the *Scotsman* in 1930 (Plate 7.9).[61] The sheer scale and mass of these proposals, placed on such a prominent site, caused public furore. In good Scottish tradition, a civil committee of the great and the good of the country, including the kirk, nobility and influential members and organisations in Scottish society banded together to form a Scottish national committee to voice their strong objection to the proposals.[62] After attempts to reduce the size of the monolithic structure by finding alternative sites for the Sheriff Court and the National Library, the proposals were finally withdrawn by the end of 1930, and in 1933, a competition for a new design for a department for the Scottish Secretary of State was held. The resulting complex (Plate 7.10), designed by the Scottish architect, Thomas S.

Plate 7.9—Pat Ronaldson, *Perspective Drawing of the Proposed Government Offices on Calton Hill*, 1930.
Taken from C. McKean, *The Scottish Thirties*, 1987

Tait, is described by McKean as one of the 'finest Thirties buildings in Scotland'.[63] Facing onto Regent Road, it consists of a large hollow square of building, with two long wings extending east and west, terminated by flat-topped stair towers. Walker identifies the style as 'American Beaux Arts Modern',[64] which may be partially down to the flat overhanging roofs, thought to have been influenced by Tait's acquaintance with Frank-Lloyd Wright.[65] However, its style also recalls Henri Paul Nénot's 1927 design for the League of Nations building, and in particular, Tait's own competition designs for Norwich municipal buildings and for a block of flats on the Brook House site of London's Park Lane.[66]

Its resonance with these buildings and the materials and design in its construction created a dialogue that linked the structure both to the roots of its history and to the aspirations for its future use. Tait's modernised Classicism made a distant connection with the classical structures already found in the New Town. The Darney Stone used was a close and sympathetic match to Craigleith sandstone,[67] while also giving the building a distinctively separate air to others found in the city. In addition, elements of international modernism also ensured that St Andrew's House did not wholly appear as a representation of Westminster governance. Rather, it provided a new chapter in Scottish government administration, bridging Scottish governance under the unionist flag within the wider world.

Its decoration follows the example of the SNWM in its use of Scottish sculptors and heraldic artists, albeit to a much more restrained extent than in Lorimer's structure.[68] On the northern, Regent Road side, the building's relationship with government administration is acknowledged through the half-length figures by W. Reid Dick that are placed on top of mullions that rise from the first floor representing Architecture, Statecraft, Health, Agriculture, Fisheries and Education.[69] However, it is the south side of the building that has received greatest praise by architectural critics. No doubt

NEW GOVERNMENT OFFICES ON CALTON HILL, EDINBURGH.
NOW IN COURSE OF ERECTION FOR HIS MAJESTY'S OFFICE OF WORKS, ETC.
VIEW FROM SOUTH.
REPRODUCED BY PERMISSION OF THE COMPTROLLER H.M. STATIONERY OFFICE.
A.3736.

Plate 7.10—Anon, *New Government Offices on Calton Hill, Edinburgh . . . View from South*.
Image of Thomas S. Tait's St Andrew's House, 1933. © St Andrews University Library

keeping in mind the comments of Queen Mary, who in 1930 had helped the campaign against the earlier proposals by stating that she 'hope[d] that nothing unsightly would be built on the flank of Calton Hill that might spoil the outlook from her palace at Holyrood',[70] Tait's design is commended as having 'real imagination and grandeur' which merits 'comparison with [Hamilton's] Royal High School'.[71]

As McKean remarked, Tait had developed 'the seat of the secretary of State for Scotland and his administration, with a dignity and quality never originally envisaged'.[72] Both the manner in which this building was constructed, and the structure itself reflected the mood of the Scottish nation in gaining recognition and governance over Scottish affairs within the unionist state. Its placement on the demolished site of the Calton jail,[73] halfway up the southern side of the hill was fortuitous, in that it was already the proposed location for a new administrative hub of government offices. Although chosen for its central location and generous space, a site that was already seen as an area controlled by municipal government for the purpose of the state would also have provided a somewhat muted commentary on the role of the building, and the significance of its work within a wider government construct. A proposal for plain administrative state offices had therefore developed into a building with a substantial expression of the importance to Scots of national identity over state control, in cultural terms at least. Where Scotland lacked control over its political autonomy, its civil society had ensured control over its cultural environment.

CONCLUSION

The role of the Scottish elite in the urban development of Calton Hill, and the manner in which the site and its structures were used, provide examples of how civic and municipal affairs were managed by Scottish civil society in the nineteenth century. Through the examples discussed in Part 3, it is possible to understand how decisions were made based on the perceived benefit to the upper classes, which at times was to the detriment of those in the lower classes. Both the proposed and the executed structures on the hill reflected the interests of those higher up the social ladder in boosting Scottish interests on an imperial stage for both economic and political gain, which resulted in a heightened national consciousness and a call for greater Scottish autonomy over its national affairs by the end of the long nineteenth century.

Despite the efforts of the elite to take control of the hill, people from the many different tiers of society continued to use the hill throughout and after its development. There was an obvious dissonance between the classical architecture on the hill and the dreadful Old Town slums, which merely drew attention to the enormous differences in people's lives. This dialogue was captured in both painted and photographic mediums, which show that the grandiose ambitions of the Scottish elite were never fully realised here.

However, the architecture of Calton Hill did retain its association with those who fronted Scottish civil society. They were involved in the governance and management of local municipal affairs on behalf of the state; the hill and its structures, therefore, represented the British state. This was further supported by the classical style of architecture favoured, which appeared to symbolise a British identity, rather than a Scottish one.

Reaction to the site in the twentieth century, therefore, either built on the idea of Calton Hill as being representative of the state, or sought to dismiss it outright. This can be seen in proposals for the National Monument before the First World War, and during discussions for the Scottish National War Memorial, as well as during the establishment of the Scottish Office in the 1930s. Tait's St Andrew's House, although considered an architectural triumph for the architect, and for those who had objected to earlier government designs for the structure, was viewed as a political failure by supporters of the idea of Scottish home rule. Considered a building housing the old managerial order under the administrative umbrella of state, St Andrew's House was a focal point for state government, participating in Calton Hill's reputation as a representation of state control over Scottish affairs. It was therefore only a matter of time before those who objected to British state autonomy restored a sense of Scottish national identity to Calton Hill, as an act of defiance against Westminster control.

Plate 8.2—Stan Warburton (Photographer), *Slogan Painted on the National Monument on Calton Hill in Edinburgh*, 1968.
© The Scotsman Publications Ltd

Defining Calton Hill

In his 1989 publication on the Greek Revival in America, Roger Kennedy states that:

Though Edinburgh delighted in calling itself 'The Athens of the North' throughout the revolutionary age, Scotsmen, including scholars, are apt to look baffled or even annoyed when asked about the political implications of Greek forms . . . The filaments of ideas tying the American Greek Revival to that of Scotland—the only nation in which it was as empathetic, conspicuous and long lasting in the United States—were not political.[1]

Through a better understanding of the role that the Greek Revival played in Calton Hill's development, it is possible to refute Kennedy's view that there was no political resonance in early nineteenth-century Scottish Greek Revival architecture. It has become apparent that the political commentary found in the development of Calton Hill was more nuanced and indirect than that in structures in Washington or Virginia, since Scottish national identity of the nineteenth century was much more acquiescent in the governing set-up of the British state.

The architectural output of Calton Hill therefore represented Scotland's identity within that state and the imperial idea of the British governing system. As the nineteenth century progressed, this rhetoric evolved, and as a result of this, its resonance within the cultural and

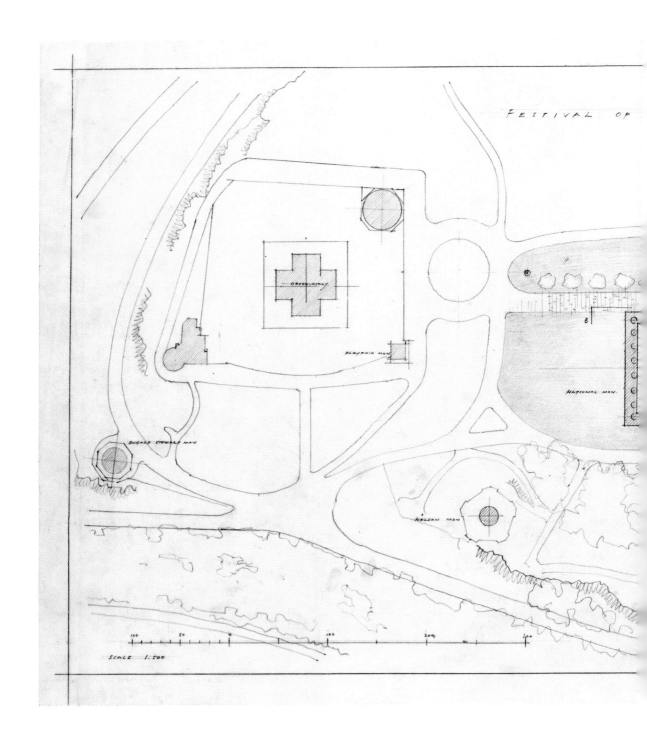

Plate 8.1—Alan Reiach, *Festival of Britain: Proposed Development on Calton Hill, Edinburgh.* 1949
© Courtesy of Historic Environment Scotland (Alan Reiach Collection)

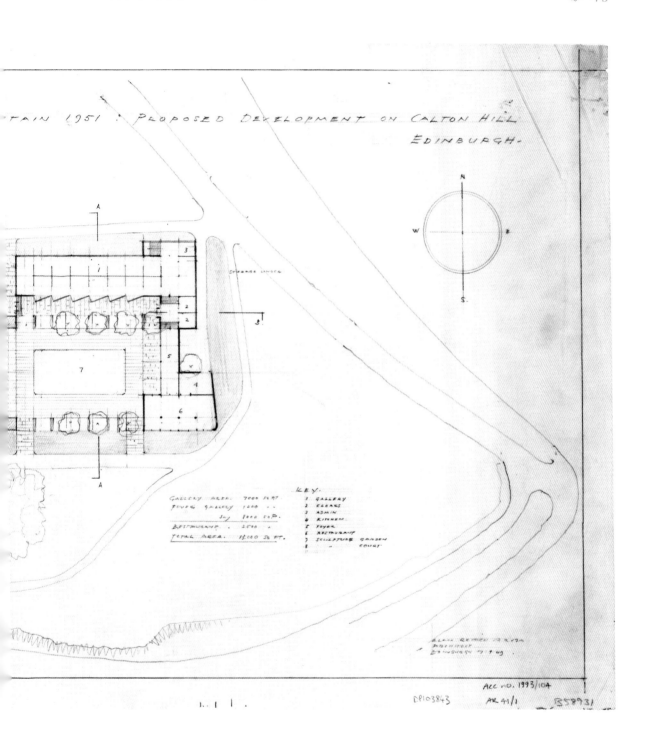

...TAIN 1951 : PROPOSED DEVELOPMENT ON CALTON HILL

EDINBURGH.

GALLERY AREA.   7000 SQ FT
FOYER GALLERY   1000 ..
                Say 1000 SQ FT.
RESTAURANT .   2500 .
TOTAL AREA .   18,000 SQ FT.

KEY.
1 GALLERY
2 CLOAKS
3 ADMIN
4 KITCHEN
5 FOYER
6 RESTAURANT
7 SCULPTURE GARDEN
8   COURT.

political elements of Scottish society shifted in its interpretation. In the mid nineteenth century, national identity was reflected in the strong sense of cultural representation that manifested itself through proposals for sculptural art galleries and the resiting of pre-Reformation structures. By the early twentieth century, this site had again become political, through the hill's role in the debate about Scottish political autonomy within state and empire, and the need to better address societal issues within Scotland through the establishment of its own government departments.

Throughout the rest of the twentieth century, there are numerous further examples of the hill reflecting contemporaneous notions of Scottish identity, which become more acutely focused as this achieves greater synonymity with Scottish nationalism. The proposed redevelopment of the site as a war memorial after the Second World War[2] and Alan Reiach Architects' 1949 plans for developing the National Monument during the 1951 Festival of Britain[3] (Plate 8.1) are the last known schemes that are synonymous with the British state as a whole. After the Second World War, as support for the Scottish National Party (SNP) grew (Plate 8.2),[4] there was a resurgence in overtly Scottish cultural output, which is reflected in art works, music and literature, as well as political discourse. For example, cultural associations as statement of national identity are found in Kate Whiteford's installation on Calton Hill in 1987 (Plates 8.3a, b), which used the ground space in front of the National

Monument to create works associated with 'Scottishness' through Scotland's Celtic past. Jane Brettle's installation *Allegorical Blueprint*, for the 1995 Fotofeis exhibition (Plate 8.4),[5] on the other hand, overtly separated cultural from state imagery, to demonstrate that schism in reality during the mid 1990s.[6]

Calton Hill's largest contribution to Scottish national identity during the twentieth century was to have been in 1979, by the establishment of a debating chamber in the Royal High School for the proposed Scottish Assembly. As the school had outgrown Hamilton's structure by the 1950s and moved to a new site at Barnton at the end of the 1960s, the building's vacant status and proximity to St Andrew's House highlighted it as a logical and sensible option for the proposed devolved parliament.[7] However, in the end, it was the failure of the 1979 referendum—that would have established the Scottish Assembly on the site—that attracted further attention to the hill as a symbol of nationalist politics. After the fourth Conservative victory at Westminster in 1992, a vigil by members of the Democracy for Scotland campaign group (Plate 8.5)[8] was held adjacent to the vacant 'home' of the non-existent Scottish Assembly at the Royal High School (Plate 8.6), which continued until the devolution referendum of 1997 then achieved Scottish parliamentary home rule. The vigil was commemorated in 1998 by the erection of a democracy cairn on Calton Hill (Plate 8.7). It was the use of the hill as a place of protest against Westminster government that

Plate 8.3a (opposite top)—Kate Whiteford creating installation on Calton Hill, 1987. Alan Macdonald.
© The Scotsman Publications Ltd

Plate 8.3b (opposite foot)—Aerial view of Kate Whiteford's installation on Calton Hill, 1987. Alan Macdonald
© The Scotsman Publications Ltd.

Plate 8.4—Jane Brettle, *Allegorical Blueprint*, Fotofeis Exhibition, 1995.
© Jane Brettle

resulted its being allegedly seen as a 'Nationalist Shibboleth' by 1997,[9] and its rejection as the site for the new Scottish parliament in favour of the development at Holyrood, at the foot of the hill (Plate 8.8).[10]

The architecture and landscape on this hill therefore represents—and holds a dialogue with—the definition and perception of Scottish national identity throughout the last 250 years. Whether creating interpretations of Scottish romanticism, defining the Scottish nation within the British state, or exploring Scottish cultural identity as an output for Scottish civic nationalism, this site has been integral in reflecting the overall consciousness of Scottish identity throughout its architectural and urban evolution.

Plate 8.5—Anon, *The Vigil for Scottish Parliament on Calton Hill, Edinburgh*, 1997.
© National Museums Scotland

Plate 8.8—Scottish Parliament showing location with reference to Calton Hill, 2018.
© Kirsten Carter McKee

Plate 8.6—Debating chamber in ground floor of former Assembly Hall, Royal High School, Regent Road, c. 1979. View from north. © Crown Copyright: Historic Environment Scotland.

Plate 8.7—Democracy Cairn, Calton Hill, 1998.
© Kirsten Carter McKee

Notes

Introduction

1   Approximate height above sea level provided by https://www.freemaptools.com/elevation-finder.htm

2   Malcolm Sinclair Irvine, *The Calton of Caldtoun of Edinburgh 1631–1887* ([Edinburgh: s.n.], 1887).

3   Henry M. Paton, 'The Barony of Calton, Part I', *Book of the Old Edinburgh Club* XVIII (1932): 33–78; Henry M. Paton, 'The Barony of Calton, Part II', *Book of the Old Edinburgh Club* XIX (1933): 92–141.

4   B. McQueen, 'Appendix 1—Archival and Documentary Research', in *Calton Hill Conservation Plan*, ed. LDN Architects for City of Edinburgh Council (1998). This mainly outlines the information held within the archives of Edinburgh City Council.

5   AOC Archaeology Group, 'Appendix 5—Archaeological Analysis', in *Calton Hill Conservation Plan* (1998).

6   Ibid. 25.

7   Between the 'common-way and passage on the west' (Greenside) and 'the low ground betwixt the rock of Craigengalt' a flat piece of ground was given to the city as a jousting ground by James II on 13 August 1456 for performing 'tournaments, sports and other warlike deeds'. Grant, *Cassell's Old and New Edinburgh*: 102.

8   John Slezer: Edinburgh—*The North Prospect of the City of Edenburgh* (National Library of Scotland, 1693) depicts sheep and shepherds on the summit of Calton Hill. See Plate 1.5.

9   See such examples as 'Articles and Conditions of Roup [Auction/Sale] for a Tack [Lease] of the Lands of Calton Hill and of Green Gate Site, Belonging to the Town, 29th October 1756, Moses', Edinburgh City Archives.

10 John Slezer, *The North Prospect of the City of Edenburgh*.

11 James Gordon, 'Edinodunensis Tabulam', Amsterdam? (National Library of Scotland, 1647).

12 Leith Walk Research Group, *Leith Walk and Greenside: A Social History* ([Edinburgh]: [The Group], 1979): 1. 'Mud Island' is denoted and depicted as a cluster of buildings in Alexander Kincaid, *A Plan of the City and Suburbs of Edinburgh*, 1819 [Plate 3].

13 (d. 1649). One of a number of peers of the realm behind the instigation of the Scottish National Covenant of 1638.

14 This was later to be entitled the 'Incorporated Trades of Calton'. See Note 19. See Paton, 'The Barony of Calton, Part I.' and Irvine, *The Calton of Caldtoun of Edinburgh*: 9.

15 Grant, *Cassell's Old and New Edinburgh*, vol. 5: 131.

16 Royal Commission on the Ancient and Historical Monuments and Constructions of Scotland, *An Inventory of the Ancient and Historical Monuments of the City of Edinburgh, with the Thirteenth Report of the Commission* (Edinburgh: HMSO,1951): lx–lxi. This kirk was a similar distance from the church at Restalrig.

17 Paton, 'The Barony of Calton, Part II'.

18 As religion played a large part in the daily running and recording of Scottish society up until the mid nineteenth century, this burial ground and the hamlet of Calton still had to be associated with a parish to record births, deaths and marriages. This, along with the lands of Restalrig to the east of Calton were part of the parish of South Leith, hence bodies interred in Calton burial ground are recorded as 'Leith'.

19 A society that worked in the interests of the tradesmen, or freemen of the hamlet of Calton.

20 See Paton, 'The Barony of Calton, Part I' and Paton, 'The Barony of Calton, Part II'.

21 Irvine, *The Calton of Caldtoun of Edinburgh*.

22 It should be noted that you did not have to be a freeman of Calton to be interred in the burial ground.

23 William Edgar, *City and Castle of Edinburgh*, 1765 (http://maps.nls.uk/towns/detail.cfm?id=312).

24 Edinburgh Town Council Minutes, 17 August 1722, 7 September 1722, 6 January 1725 and 3 February 1725, SL1, Edinburgh City Archives. Balmerino was a staunch Jacobite, who was beheaded in 1746 at the Tower of London for his support of Charles Stuart. It is possible that he had sold this land off to raise money for the Jacobite cause.

25 Provost James, Earl of Arran and the bailies of the city conveyed both the lands and the chapel at Greenside to John Malcolme, Provincial of the Carmelites and his successors by charter. Grant, *Cassell's Old and New Edinburgh*, vol. 3: 102.

26 Hugo Arnot, *The History of Edinburgh, by Hugo Arnot, Esq; Advocate* (Edinburgh: 1779): 197. No trace of either the monastery or the hospital remains, although the sites of both are still noted on 1:500 Ordnance Survey maps and archaeological excavations in 2009 located a number of graves thought to hold the remains of the hospital's inhabitants. See Leith Walk Research Group, *Leith Walk and Greensid*; and Sorina Spanou, 'Edinburgh Trams Project: South Leith Parish Church Graveyard, Constitution Street', in *Discovery and Excavation in Scotland*, Volume 11 (2010): 69.

27 Irvine, *The Calton of Caldtoun of Edinburgh*.

28 Paton, 'The Barony of Calton, Part I' and Paton, 'The Barony of Calton, Part II'.

29 Ann K. Mitchell, *The People of Calton Hill* (Edinburgh: Mercat Press, 1993).

30 A. J. Youngson, *The Making of Classical Edinburgh, 1750–1840* (Edinburgh: Edinburgh University Press, 1988).

31 Connie Byrom, *The Edinburgh New Town Gardens: 'Blessings as Well as Beauties'* (Edinburgh: Birlinn, 2005).

32 Peter Reed, 'Form and Context: A Study of Georgian Edinburgh', in *Order in Space and Society*, ed. Thomas A. Markus (Edinburgh: Mainstream, 1982): 115-53.

33 Marc Fehlmann, 'A Building from which Derived "All that is Good": Observations on the Intended Reconstruction of the Parthenon on Calton Hill', *Nineteenth Century Art Worldwide* 4, no. 3 (Autumn, 2005): http://www.19thc-artworldwide.org/ autumn05/207-a-building-from-which-derived-qall-that-is-goodq-observations-on-the-intended- reconstruction-of-the-parthenon-on-calton-hill and John Gifford, 'The National Monument of Scotland',

Architectural Heritage 25 (2014): 43–83.

34 David Myles Gavine, 'Astronomy in Scotland 1745–1900' (PhD thesis, Open University, 1982); D. J. Bryden, 'The Edinburgh Observatory 1736–1811: A Story of Failure', *Annals of Science* 47 (1990): 445–74.

35 Joe Rock, *Thomas Hamilton Architect 1784–1858* ([Edinburgh?]: J. Rock, 1984); Ian Fisher, 'Thomas Hamilton', in *Scottish Pioneers of the Greek Revival*, ed. David Walker and Scottish Georgian Society ([Edinburgh]: Scottish Georgian Society, 1984): 37-42.

36 Alison Yarrington, 'The Commemoration of the Hero 1800–1864: Monuments to the British Victors of the Napoleonic Wars' (Oxford: Garland, 1988). PhD thesis.

37 Thomas A. Markus, 'Buildings for the Sad, the Bad and the Mad in Urban Scotland 1780–1830', in *Order in Space and Society*, ed. Thomas A. Markus (Mainstream, 1982): 25–114; Alex Tyrrell and Michael T. Davis, 'Bearding the Tories: The Commemoration of the Scottish Political Martyrs of 1793–94', in *Contested Sites: Commemoration, Memorial and Popular Politics in Nineteenth Century Britain*, ed. Paul A. Pickering and Alex Tyrrell (Aldershot: Ashgate, 2004; 25-56; David Walker, *St Andrew's House: An Edinburgh Controversy, 1912–1939* (Edinburgh: Historic Buildings and Monuments, Development Department for the Secretary of State for Scotland, 1989); and Charles McKean, *The Scottish Thirties: An Architectural Introduction* (Edinburgh: Scottish Academic Press, 1987).

38 Iain Gordon Brown, 'David Hume's Tomb: A Roman Mausoleum by Robert Adam', *Proceedings of the Society of Antiquaries of Scotland* 121 (1991): 321–422; Betty Willsher, 'Midlothian and Edinburgh', in *Survey of Scottish Gravestones* (National Monuments Record for Scotland, c. 1985).

39 Michael T. R. B. Turnbull, *The Edinburgh Graveyard Guide* (Edinburgh: Scottish Cultural Press, 2006); John Smith, *Epitaphs and Monumental Inscriptions in Old Calton Burying Ground, Edinburgh* (handwritten and self-published, 1907); J. F. Mitchell, *Some Edinburgh Monumental Inscriptions* ([Edinburgh]: self-published,1961); John F. Mitchell, *Edinburgh Monumental Inscriptions (pre-1855). Vol. 1, Old Calton Burial Ground, New Calton Burial Ground*, ed. Stuart E. Fleming (Edinburgh: Scottish Genealogy Society, 2003).

40 Susan Buckham (ed.), *The Edinburgh Graveyards Project, 2013* (Edinburgh: World Monuments Fund, Edinburgh World Heritage, 2011).

41 John Smith, *The Calton Hill, Edinburgh and Its Monuments* (Edinburgh: n.d.); David Gavine and Laurence Hunter, *A Caledonian Acropolis: The Story of Calton Hill* (Edinburgh: Scotland's Cultural Heritage, 1982).

42 University of Edinburgh, Department of Extra-Mural Studies; Edinburgh New Town Conservation Committee, 'The Calton Conference: National Shrine, City Park and Outstanding Vantage Point: Does Edinburgh Make the Most of This National Asset?' (Edinburgh: Edinburgh New Town Conservation Committee, 1983).

43 Law-Dunbar and Naismith (LDN) Architects, 'Calton Hill Conservation Plan' (Edinburgh, 1999).

44 John Lowrey's analysis of the urban design of Calton Hill is one of the few published sources to discuss Nash's contemporaneous development of Regent's Park and its similarities to the development at Calton Hill. However, the length and scope of the article did not afford opportunity to explore this topic in detail, or to discuss the broader resonance of these outside factors in the development of this site. John Lowrey, 'The Urban Design of Edinburgh's Calton Hill'. Paper presented at the St Andrews 'Studies in the History of Scottish Architecture and Design. The New Town Phenomenon: The Second Generation'. [St Andrews], 2000; Richard J. Morris and Graeme Morton, 'The Re-Making of Scotland: A Nation within a Nation, 1850–1920', in *Scotland, 1850–1979: Society, Politics and the Union*, ed. Michael Lynch (London: The Historical Association, 1993): 13-18.

45 'Three key events shaped eighteenth century Scottish politics: the union of 1707, the defeat of the Jacobite rising of 1745 and the British wars against France': Alice Brown, David McCrone and Lindsay Paterson, *Politics and Society in Scotland*, 2nd edn (Basingstoke: Macmillan, 1998): 3.

46 This is further considered in numerous discussions about Edinburgh's New Town development, such as Charles McKean's suggestion that James Craig's original Union Jack plan was to appeal to the unionist sympathies of the judging panel. See Charles McKean, 'The Incivility of Edinburgh's New Town', in *The Neo-Classical Town: Scottish Contributions to Urban Design since 1750*, ed. W. A. Brogden (Edinburgh: Rutland, 1996): 41. Peter Reed also suggested that the plan was intended to be purely classical in form, in its hierarchical layout. Reed, 'Form and Context'.

47 Holger Hoock, 'The British Military Pantheon in St Paul's Cathedral: The State, Cultural Patriotism, and the Politics of National Monuments, c.1790–1820', in *Pantheons: Transformations of a Monumental Idea.*, ed. Richard Wrigley and Matthew Craske (Aldershot: Ashgate, 2004): 81–105; Linda Colley, *Britons: Forging the Nation, 1707–1837*, 2nd edn (New Haven, CT and London: Yale University Press, 2005); Yarrington, 'The Commemoration of the Hero 1800–1864; John M. MacKenzie, 'Empire and National Identities: The Case of Scotland', *Transactions of the Royal Historical Society* 8 (1998): 215–31; Michael Fry, *The Scottish Empire* (East Linton: Tuckwell Press, 2001); Martha McLaren, *British India & British Scotland, 1780–1830: Career Building, Empire Building, and a Scottish School of Thought on Indian Governance*. Series on International, Political, and Economic History (Akron, OH: University of Akron Press, 2001).

48 James Buchan, *Capital of the Mind: How Edinburgh Changed the World* (London: John Murray, 2003): Ch. 1.

49 Stewart Lamont, *When Scotland Ruled the World: The Story of the Golden Age of Genius, Creativity and Exploration* (London: HarperCollins, 2001); Buchan, *Capital of the Mind*; Mary Cosh, *Edinburgh: The Golden Age* (Edinburgh: John Donald, 2003); E. Patricia Dennison, *Holyrood and Canongate: A Thousand Years of History* (Edinburgh: Birlinn, 2005).

50 For example, see McKean, 'The Incivility of Edinburgh's New Town'.

51 Such as Youngson, *The Making of Classical Edinburgh*. Patrick Geddes' work on the re-introduction of university residences into the heart of the Old Town is one of the few urban redevelopments which tried to replicate this Enlightenment community. See Jim Johnson and Louis Stanley Rosenburg, *Renewing Old Edinburgh: The Enduring Legacy of Patrick Geddes* (Glendaruel [Edinburgh]: Argyll

Publishing; Scottish Centre for Conservation Studies, 2011).

52 Cosh, *Edinburgh: The Golden Age*; Buchan, *Capital of the Mind*; Morris and Morton, 'The Re-Making of Scotland'; Fry, *The Scottish Empire*; Lamont, *When Scotland Ruled the World*.

PART 1
Introduction

1 With the exception of a short article comparing Calton Hill's development to that of John Nash and Decimus Burton's Regent's Park design. See Lowrey, 'The Urban Design of Edinburgh's Calton Hill'.

2 Arnold, *Rural Urbanism*; Yarrington, 'The Commemoration of the Hero'.

3 Ibid.

Chapter 1

1 It is possible that older structures may have been placed on this site but these are not fully verifiable and are only identified through aerial photography.

2 This is often referred to as 'Old Observatory House' or 'James Craig House', but both of these names are not fully correct and can be considered misleading. This building is therefore referred to as 'the gothic tower' throughout this book.

3 A popular observatory was an observatory that would be used as a tourist attraction. This is in contrast to an astronomical observatory, which would be closed to the public and was for scientific calculation only.

4 See 'Petition of Thomas Short, Optician of Edinburgh for a Feu of Half an Acre of Ground on Top of Calton Hill to Build an Observatory. With Plan of the Ground Etc', 1 January 1776, D015R, *Macleod Bundles,* Edinburgh City Archives. Also, Anon., 'Edinburgh Observatory', *Caledonian Mercury*, 8517, 3 June 1776: 4. James Short was a renowned instrument maker, based in London. His death in the late 1760s had resulted in his brother, Thomas Short, inheriting the London business along with the task of completing a lens intended for Christian VII, King of Denmark. By the time the lens was finally completed, Christian had been removed from his throne and the commission was no longer required. This left Thomas Short with the 'twelve-foot focus reflector' reputedly worth 12,000 guineas. On the advice of friends, Short applied to set up the telescope on Calton Hill for the general public to view at a small sum, which would glean some profit from the bequest given to him by his brother, in addition to recouping some of the expense of completing this instrument after his brother's death. O.D.E. & P.A.R. 'Account of the Observatory on Calton Hill', *Scots Magazine*, 50, December 1788: 606.

5 Bryden, 'The Edinburgh Observatory 1736–1811; D. J. Bryden, 'James Craig's Original Design for the Observatory on Calton Hill, May 1776', *Book of the Old Edinburgh Club* 7 (new edn) (Edinburgh: self-published, 2008): 161-6.

6 Gavine, 'Astronomy in Scotland 1745–1900'.

7 Both trace the history of the development of an observatory in Edinburgh back to the seventeenth century and describe in detail the efforts of Colin MacLaurin (Professor of Mathematics at the University of Edinburgh) to raise funds to erect one at the University between 1734 and 1744.

Gavine's article also provides detailed financial accounts for the costings in erecting the structures that were eventually to be placed on the hill.

8 'Act in Favour of Thomas Short for a Tack of Half an Acre of the Calton Hill', Edinburgh Town Council Minutes, 29 May 1776, SL1/1/93.

9 Arnot, *The History of Edinburgh, by Hugo Arnot*: 310. Gavine reports the funds standing at approximately £700 after interest. See Gavine, 'Astronomy in Scotland 1745–1900': 220.

10 O.D.E. & P.A.R. 'Account of the Observatory on Calton Hill': 606. This was to be built at a cost of £110. For a reference to this initial design and costs for masonry and timber work.

11 O.D.E. & P.A.R., 'Account of the Observatory on Calton Hill', *Scots Magazine*: 606.

12 Anon., *Caledonian Gazetteer* 1 (31 May 1776); Anon., *Edinburgh Evening Courant* (1 June 1776); and Anon., *Caledonian Mercury* 8517 (3 June 1776).

13 For a list of these, see Kitty Cruft and Andrew G. Fraser, 'The Ingenious Architect of the New Town of Edinburgh': *James Craig 1744–1795* (Edinburgh: Mercat Press, 1995).

14 O.D.E & P.A.R., 'Account of the Observatory on Calton Hill': 633. Technical specifications for the building were by John Robinson, the Professor of Natural Philosophy at Edinburgh. See Bryden, 'The Edinburgh Observatory 1736–1811: 462.

15 Only three sides can be identified in the image, but the other sides are assumed from Laurie's plans of the site (see Plates 1.3a and b) and contemporary descriptions of the building.

16 Untitled pamphlet, n.d: 23, 263, Gough Scotland Bodleian Library archives, University of Oxford. There is no date for this sketch, but it is known that the foundation stone for this building was placed on 25 July 1776. See *Scots Magazine* 38, July 1776: 393-4.

17 James Stuart and Nicholas Revett, *The Antiquities of Athens Measured and Delineated by James Stuart F.R.S. and F.S.A. and Nicholas Revett Painters and Architects*, 4 vols (London: John Haberkorn, 1762), vol. 1: Ch. 3. This building is described as possibly originally being a Clepsydra, described in Vitruvius as 'an astronomical instrument, by which hours are measured' (15).

18 Sometimes spelled 'Lawrie'.

19 'Plan of Half the Acre of Ground at the Top of Calton Hill—Site of the Observatory—John Laurie, 20 April 1776, D0105R, Macleod Bundles, Edinburgh City Archives. NB Accounts for James Craig's designs for the observatory mention that the design for an observatory was carried out by Craig in 1775—a year earlier than Short's arrival or application to the town for a feu of ground on Calton Hill.

20 'The interests of the university in having an observatory that would be used for teaching and astronomical research were represented in an expansion to Craig's initial design, with pavilions added to east and west of the dome for the apparatus required for regular scientific observation' (Bryden, 'James Craig's Original Design for the Observatory on Calton Hill, May 1776': 162).

21 This plan is also held in a different location. 'Plan of Half the Acre of Ground at the Top of Calton Hill—Site of the Observatory—John Laurie, 20 April 1776, SL12/211,

Edinburgh City Archives.

22 Arnot, *The History of Edinburgh, by Hugo Arnot*.

23 The octagonal observatory designed by Craig was abandoned halfway through its construction in order to commence building on the fortified curtilage. The building can be identified in Robert Barker's panorama of the late 1780s. See Bryden, 'James Craig's Original Design for the Observatory'. Barker's panorama is also discussed in further detail below.

24 No elevations remain of this original design, but the southwest tower survives as a house in (mostly) its original external form, with some later extensions added in the nineteenth century. In addition, there are a number of early drawings of the structure prior to the later nineteenth-century extensions that provide information on the building's original form.

25 There is currently debate amongst experts in the field as to whether this would have been completely lime washed, or whether some protrusion of stone would have been visible. Personal communications: James Simpson, Simpson and Brown Architects, and Dorothy Marsh, former Senior Curator, City of Edinburgh Council Museums and Galleries Division.

26 See Ian Campbell and Margaret Stewart, 'The Evolution of the Medieval and Renaissance City', in *Edinburgh: The Making of a Capital City*, ed. Brian Edwards and Paul Jenkins (Edinburgh: Edinburgh University Press, 2005). In particular, see the central colour inset which is a mock-up of Mar's written proposals for the site.

27 Edmund Burke, 'A Philosophical Enquiry into the Origin of Our Ideas of the Sublime and Beautiful' (London: printed for R. and J. Dodsley, 1757). http://ezproxy.lib.ed.ac.uk/login?url=http://galenet. galegroup.com/servlet/ ECCO?c=1&stp=Author&ste=11&af=BN&ae= T042248&tiPG=1&dd=0&dc=flc&docNum= CW109732666&vrsn=1.0&srchtp=a&d4=0.33&n= 10&SU=0LRK&locID=ed_itw.

28 William Kay, 'Robert Adam: Some Responses to a Scottish Background', *Architectural Heritage: The Journal of the Architectural Heritage Society of Scotland* 4 (1993): 23-38.

29 John Summerson, *Architecture in Britain, 1530 to 1830*, 9th edn (New Haven, CT and London: Yale University Press, 1993): 407.

30 Adam's watercolour collections of picturesque landscapes, now held in collection at the National Gallery of Scotland, depict a number of views that can be considered strongly reminiscent of Calton Hill and the surrounding Edinburgh landscape. In *Landscape with a River and Castle and Sailing Boat in the Foreground*, the hill in the distance to the left hand side of the picture could be interpreted as similar to the silhouette of the Salisbury Crags. *A Lake with a Castle, Bridge and Sailing Boats* is a similar view found when looking below the ridge of Edinburgh Castle along the Old Town from west to east, including Mylne's North Bridge of the early 1770s and Calton Hill on the left hand side. As for Calton Hill in particular, *Landscape with a Castle, Lake and Farm Animals* does resemble the hill in both its layout and its use at the time of Adam's work, and *Landscape with a Castle on a Cliff on the Right and Another Castle on the Opposite side of the River* also could be considered an exaggerated

version of rolling hills coming to an abrupt climax at a summit, on top of which sits a castellated building with a circular turret and enclaves.

31 Accounts for the construction of both of these buildings are held in the Edinburgh City Archives. See letter and account from James Craig for making designs for two observatories built on Calton Hill. With letter from James Douglas, 1 January 1792, 186/D015R, Macleod Bundles, Edinburgh City Archives.

32 See Bryden, 'The Edinburgh Observatory 1736–1811'.

33 Letter and account from James Craig for making designs of two observatories built on Calton Hill. With letter from James Douglas, 1 January 1792, Macleod Bundles.

34 Craig's design for the octagonal observatory was described as a tower with wings in O.D.E. & P.A.R. 'Account of the Observatory on Calton Hill': 606.

35 Cruft and Fraser, 'The Ingenious Architect of the New Town of Edinburgh'.

36 Arnot, *The History of Edinburgh, by Hugo Arnot*: 320.

37 Ibid.: 320.

38 A. R. Lewis, 'The Builders of Edinburgh's New Town 1767–1795', PhD thesis (University of Edinburgh, 2006): 188.

39 See Dr Joe Rock's research pages for further information on this: https://sites.google.com/site/historicaltimelines/home/ botanical-cottage-leith-walk/botanic-cottage-analysis-of- the-evidence

40 Cruft and Fraser, 'The Ingenious Architect of the New Town of Edinburgh': 114.

41 The Adams' working with other architects and builders in the city in this way appears to have been a common occurrence within Edinburgh building circles during this period: 'There can be little doubt of the power and influence of the Adam family's buildings and patronage of tradesmen in Edinburgh. John, Robert and James Adam were able to influence tradesmen who aspired to be builders, and architects themselves'. Lewis, 'The Builders of Edinburgh's New Town 1767–1795': 255.

42 Brown, 'David Hume's Tomb'.

43 See Alistair Rowan and Soane Gallery, 'Bob the Roman': *Heroic Antiquity & the Architecture of Robert Adam* (London: The Soane Gallery, 2003); Alistair John Rowan, *Vaulting Ambition. The Adam Brothers: Contractors to the Metropolis in the Reign of George III* (London: Sir John Soane's Museum, 2007) for further information on this.

44 Brown, 'David Hume's Tomb': 409.

45 'When the eye is to be confined within the frame of a picture . . . we want a castle, or an abbey, to give consequence to this scene'. William Gilpin, Prebendary of Salisbury Gilpin, *Observations on the River Wye, and Several Parts of South Wales . . . Relative Chiefly to Picturesque Beauty; Made in the Summer of . . . 1770* (London, 1782): 14.

46 Although the language of landscape evolved within aesthetic theories throughout the second half of the eighteenth century, the notion of the picturesque discussed by Gilpin in his 1782 publication was not formalised in urban landscape terms until at least the 1790s. Calling Adam's approach as 'romantic' therefore defines his understanding of the site as a rural backdrop to the city, rather than the 'rus in urbe' it became in the nineteenth century under William Henry Playfair (see Chapter 3).

47 Brown, 'David Hume's Tomb': 410.

48 John Lowrey, 'Robert Adam and Edinburgh', *Rassegna* 64 (1995): 26–33.

49 Gilpin, *Observations on the River Wye.*

50 See the discussion below regarding Adam's proposals for a connecting bridge to Calton Hill from the New Town.

51 This semi-rural state of picturesque landscape is discussed in papers published in the eighteenth century as theories of the Picturesque evolved. For example, Sir Uvedale Price, *An Essay on the Picturesque as Compared with the Sublime and the Beautiful: And on the Use of Studying Pictures for the Purpose of Improving Real Landscape,* 2 vols (London: Hereford, 1794); Richard Payne Knight, *The Landscape: A Didactic Poem, Addressed to Uvedale Price* (London, 1794); Humphry Repton, *A Letter to Uvedale Price, Esq. [Commenting on his 'Essay on the Picturesque', Etc.]* (London, 1794).

52 Markus, 'Buildings for the Sad, the Bad and the Mad': 65–88.

53 James Craig, 'Plan for a General Bridewell' ([Edinburgh?], 1780). According to the town council minutes in the Edinburgh City Archives, James Craig was paid 'to [make] a design of a Bridewell for the City of Edinburgh 2 stories high, plans of different floors, Elevations & sections & to survey . . . the area contiguous to the present correction house where it is intended to be built': see Edinburgh Town Council Minutes, 28 January 1780, SL1/1/98. However, the reference to Craig as the author of the published pamphlet is possibly wrong—there is a handwritten acknowledgement that this would have been done by David Steuart, Lord Provost of Edinburgh, between 1780 and 1782. As we know that Steuart was definitely responsible for the second pamphlet, published in 1782 (see D. Steuart and A. Cockburn, 'General Heads of a Plan for Erecting a New Prison and Bridewell in the City of Edinburgh') it is also likely that he was the author of this earlier pamphlet.

54 Markus discusses six styles, but a later study by Sandy Kinghorn published online has argued that there could have been up to eight different proposals for this site. See https://sites.scran.ac.uk/ada/documents/castle_style/bridewell/bridewell_designs.htm.

55 See Plate 1.19 for final constructed version of Bridewell.

56 Steuart and Cockburn, 'General Heads of a Plan for Erecting a New Prison'. This consisted of a radial layout of cells, which were centred on a 'keeper's house', the courtyard for which was entered from the south, through a gatehouse in the old city wall.

57 His suggested designs within the 1777 report included cells with vaulted arcades on the ground floor that would allow exercise in wet weather and improve the circulation of air. See John Howard, the Philanthropist, *The State of the Prisons in England and Wales, with Preliminary Observations, and an Account of Some Foreign Prisons* (Appendix) (Warrington, 1777): 42.

58 Allan Brodie et al., *English Prisons: An Architectural History* (Swindon: English Heritage, 2002): 37.

59 An overall study of Scottish prison designs is yet to be carried out to evaluate fully the influences of the designs proposed for these penitentiaries. However, an excellent survey of the architectural history of English prisons has been researched and published by English Heritage, which provides useful information on the contemporaneous social considerations and philosophies of late eighteenth century prison reform, which is useful in contextualising these early designs, and the 1790s proposals for the Bridewell (ibid.).

60 This had been taken from traditional monastic plans and had become standard for a number of institutional buildings during this period. Harriet Richardson and Ian H. Goodall, *English Hospitals 1660–1948: A Survey of their Architecture and Design* (Swindon: Royal Commission on the Historical Monuments of England, 1998): 16–20

61 Adam had visited this building en route to Edinburgh in 1791. Ranald MacInnes, 'Robert Adam's Public Buildings', *Architectural Heritage: The Journal of the Architectural Heritage Society of Scotland* 4 (1994); 13–14.

62 In particular Adam's designs for Barnbougle. Although generally considered to be Barnbougle Castle, *'Fortified Castle or Palace, Surrounded by a High Wall, Corner Towers and a Central Gateway'* retains elements of the completed Bridewell, such as the turreted circular towers and the arched detailing for the fenestration and the recesses including twin towers with pitched roofs, recessed arched fenestration decoration, a single storey entranceway and castellated towers at the corner points of the outer walls.

63 Jeremy Bentham, *Panopticon: Or, the Inspection-House. Containing the Idea of a New Principle of Construction Applicable to Any Sort of Establishment, in which Persons . . . Are to Be Kept . . . and in Particular to Penitentiary-Houses, Prisons . . . in a Series of Letters, Written in . . . 1787 . . . by Jeremy Bentham* (Dublin: Thomas Byrne, 1791).

64 Ibid., 73–84.

65 'A fortress thus secured would have collateral use. In times of riot, it would afford an asylum, where obnoxious persons or valuable effects might be lodged in perfect safety against everything but cannon' Ibid., 525 fn.

66 Ibid., 520–5.

67 Correspondence of John Paterson to Robert Adam, dated 26 Feb. 1790. Paterson Papers, private collection. I am indebted to Dr Allen Simpson for access to these papers.

68 This could be Paterson confirming that the unfinished gothic tower on the summit of Calton Hill was 'partly designed' by Adam, as has been considered above.

69 Correspondence of John Paterson to Robert Adam, dated 26 Feb. 1790. Paterson Papers, private collection.

70 This has been described as the 'Court Revival style', and linked to his studies of such buildings as Holyrood Palace. See MacInnes, 'Robert Adam's Public Buildings': 15.

71 'An Act for Building and Maintaining a Bridewell and Correction-House, in and for the City and County of Edinburgh' (Edinburgh, 1791). Item 16 D0021 Macleod Bundles, Edinburgh City Archives.

72 'The choice of the Calton Hill site was preceded by public debate and contention, mainly couched in practical and sanitary terms. But it is clear that the issue really was whether a jail could and should occupy a visible, central city site, or be peripheral—in the tradition of earlier institutions . . . Calton was a compromise and can be seen as the acceptance of social surveillance of the prison by the gaoler of the inmates. Its presence would be both a reminder of the order being achieved and a deterrent. Of course, this gave the architect the problem of finding a suitable formal expression for such a central, civic site'

(Markus, 'Buildings for the Sad, the Bad and the Mad': 66).

73 For example, Jacques François Blondel, *Cours d'architecture; Ou, traité de la décoration, distribution & construction des bâtiments*, 2 vols (Paris, 1771). This was particularly common for many prisons built after John Howard's publication on the state of prisons. John Howard, *The State of the Prisons in England and Wales, with Preliminary Observations, and on Account of Some Foreign Prisons* (Warrington, 1777). See Brodie et al., *English Prisons*; Markus, 'Buildings for the Sad, the Bad and the Mad' for further discussion on this.

74 Despite a suggestion by John Paterson to add a clause into the 1791 Edinburgh Bridewell Act which would include the construction of an access route, this bridge was not realised for a further twenty-five years until the development of a second prison on the Calton Hill.

75 For further discussion of this, see John Lowrey, 'Robert Adam and Edinburgh'.

76 Correspondence of John Paterson to Robert Adam, dated 26 Feb. 1790, Paterson Papers, private collection.

77 This is extremely faint and provides no stylistic detail; it only considers where the bridge may be placed over Low Calton.

78 These are held in the Soane Museum Archives in London.

79 *Bridge over (?) from Princes Street at (?) Calton Hill Edinburgh*, vol. 2, no. 50, Soane Museum Archives, Sir John Soane's Museum, London.

80 This is similar to Adam's plan for the South Bridge, where its scale and detail dominate the landscape, and its classical facade creates a monumental *via triumphalis* into the New Town.

81 The dome was never constructed by Adam and instead was eventually built by Robert Rowand Anderson in the late nineteenth century. See Andrew G. Fraser, *The Building of Old College: Adam, Playfair & the University of Edinburgh* (Edinburgh: Edinburgh University Press, 1989). The David Hume Monument is represented as a classical temple with a domed roof, rather than the open-roofed structure that it is now. Arnot notes in *The History of Edinburgh*, 'the height of the walls conceal[ing] the roof' of the David Hume Monument, but no evidence of a roof being fitted on the structure has previously been found in Adam's designs for the monument. See Brown, 'David Hume's Tomb'.

82 This has also been commented on by Stephen Astley, in the published catalogue of Robert Adam's castle styles from the Sir John Soane Museum. See Stephen Astley, *Robert Adam's Castles* ([London]: Soane Gallery, 2000): 34.

83 The magistrates were not so convinced by the grand ideas that were put forward by Adam as they did not think that the value of the land could be redeemed. They believed that the design issues surrounding the Bridewell had also not been taken into consideration within these proposals. See Correspondence of John Paterson to Robert Adam, 6 Nov.1790, Paterson Papers, private collection. It may be unsurprising that they were so cautious of Adam's grand schemes, considering this grand idea of speculative building was in a similar vein to Adam's London Adelphi development, which ended in the bankruptcy of the Adam business in the 1770s. See Rowan, *Vaulting Ambition*.

84 www.objectlessons.lib.ed.ac.uk/barker.htm. In fact, you can see Craig's unfinished octagonal observatory in the 1787 panorama.

85 Thomas A. Markus, *Buildings & Power: Freedom and Control in the Origin of Modern Building Types* (London: Routledge, 1993): 214.
http://www.oxforddnb.com.ezproxy.webfeat.lib.ed.ac.uk/view/article/1411?docPos=4

86 As the word is considered in the present day. According to Wolfgang Stechow, in Wolfgang Stechow, *Dutch Landscape Painting of the Seventeenth Century* ([London]: Phaidon, 1966): 33–49, the term 'panorama' originally referred to seventeenth-century Dutch landscape paintings that show a distant scene with an extended view along the horizon. See Scott Barnes Wilcox, 'The Panorama and Related Exhibitions in London', MLitt thesis (Edinburgh: University of Edinburgh, 1976): 2. This can also be identified in Scottish art. See James Holloway, Lindsay Errington and National Gallery of Scotland, *The Discovery of Scotland: The Appreciation of Scottish Scenery through Two Centuries of Painting* (Edinburgh: National Gallery of Scotland, 1978): 14. However, Wilcox notes that the Dutch scenes were intended to be more expressive, as opposed to the later panoramas on cityscapes, which were intended to be informative.

87 Sir Joshua Reynolds, quoted in 'The Panorama, with Memoirs of its Inventor, Robert Barker, and his Late Son, Henry Aston Barker', *The Art-Journal 3* (1857): 46. For further information on the development of the panorama and its success in the nineteenth century, see Wilcox, 'The Panorama'. This provides a satisfactory analysis of the panorama's place in the history of art, but does not consider any further analysis on its impact within the wider cityscape.

88 Fintain Cullen, 'Union and Display in Nineteenth Century Ireland', in Dana Arnold (ed.), *Cultural Identities and the Aesthetics of Britishness* (Manchester: Manchester University Press, 2004): 115.

89 Barker had realised that controlling the manner in which the painting could be observed provided a much more satisfactory manner in which to display and view landscape painting. His first purpose-built structure, the Rotunda, was designed by Robert Mitchell and opened in Leicester Square in 1793. An inverted cone skylight lit the top panorama and a glazed annular ring the lower one. See Wilcox, 'The Panorama' for further information and plans of this.

90 See Wilcox, 'The Panorama'. This includes views of British and foreign cities and scenic views, such as Bath (1794), Paris (1803), Mexico (1825) and Niagara Falls (1833), and scenes such as *Lord Nelson's Attack of Copenhagen* (1802), *Battle of Paris* (1815), *Lord Exmouth's Attack upon Algiers* (1818) and *Procession of the Coronation of His Majesty George the Fourth* (1822).

91 Ibid., 174–6.

92 Ibid., 178.

93 See John Ainslie, *City of Edinburgh,* 1780 and Alexander Kincaid, *A Plan of the City and Suburbs of Edinburgh,* 1784: http://maps.nls.uk/towns/#edinburgh-city s.

94 Nelson Pillar Minute Committee Book, 3 March 1806. Edinburgh City Archives.

95 The site of the structure was on the site of a former telegraph pole, which was a visual form of telegraph using flags and semaphore. Electrical telegraph was not invented until

later on in the nineteenth century. This can be seen in John Ainslie, *Old and New Town of Edinburgh and Leith with the Proposed Docks* (1804) [Plate 4 here].

96 In January 1839, Sir David Milne recommended that a time ball on a mast could replace the long uphill trek from Leith by mariners to check their chronometers against the clock in the transit house window, but there were no funds to build this until the middle of the nineteenth century. Gavine, 'Astronomy in Scotland 1745–1900': 344. This was to provide the ships docked at Leith with accurate timekeeping. The ball would drop at exactly 1pm, allowing ships to set their clocks, facilitating accurate navigation. This was accompanied shortly after by a single cannon shot from Edinburgh Castle, which still fires at 1pm every day. See www.oneoclockgun.com.

97 Building work commenced in 1807, but was halted through lack of funds. It was eventually completed by Thomas Bonnar in 1814–16.

98 John Gifford et al., *Edinburgh*. The Buildings of Scotland: Pevsner Architectural Guides (London: Penguin, 1991): 437–8.

99 Ibid.

100 James Nasmyth and Samuel Smiles, *James Nasmyth, Engineer. An Autobiography*, popular edn (London: John Murray, 1897).

101 Ibid.: 44–5.

102 'The Sub committee having considered the two plans of Mr Naysmith and Mr Burn, with the specifications of the work and estimates given in, of the expence [sic] of executing the same . . . While they highly approve of the plan given in by Mr Naysmith, regret that the narrowness of the subscription prevents them from carrying it into execution and therefore to accept the plan by Mr Burns (Nelson Pillar Minute Book, 30 July 1807, 9.41 62u, Handlist of Historical Records, Edinburgh City Archives).

103 Yarrington, 'The Commemoration of the Hero 1800–1864'.

104 Ibid.: 101.

105 See, for example, the Black's guide to Scotland in the mid nineteenth century, Charles Black, *Black's Picturesque Tourist Guide of Scotland. With . . . Map; Engraved Charts and Views . . . Plans of Edinburgh and Glasgow and a Copious Intinerary* (Edinburgh: A. & C. Black, 1840). This idea for the monument as a tourist draw has also been commented on by John Gifford (personal communication), and it is evident from Barker's panorama that the area was already being used as a pleasure walk and tourist attraction, where it had been used to educate on the planets of the solar system (Plate 1.20).

Chapter 2

1 Henry Cockburn, *Memorials of His Time* (Edinburgh: Adam and Charles Black, 1856): 241. Lord Henry Cockburn was an influential peer in the city.

2 Anno 53 George III c.77, 'An Act for Erecting and Maintaining a New Gaol and Other Buildings for the County and City of Edinburgh' (21 May 1813).

3 At a site to the east of Libberton's Wynd to the rear of the Justiciary Court.

4 It appears that to help his petition to Parliament for the new jail, the Sheriff had undertaken a study tour of a number of jails in England. See Anon., 'New Jail', *Scots Magazine and Edinburgh Literary Miscellany* 76 (May 1814): 393–4.

5 As opposed to Calton Hill, which was already owned by the city. In particular, it is likely that a 'New Town' venue would be thought unsuitable for what would be considered an 'Old Town' institution—both in its original placement, as well as its purpose.

6 Timon, 'View of Different Proposals for the Situation of the New Jail, with the Plan of a Bridge and Road across the Calton Hill', *Scots Magazine and Edinburgh Literary Miscellany* 76 (January 1814): 4–5.

7 Government of Great Britain, *Journal of the House of Commons*, 'An Act for Erecting and Maintaining a New Gaol and Other Buildings for the County and City of Edinburgh' (4 November 1813–1 November 1814) Anno 54 George III c.53: 151. See also Anon., 'New Jail', *Scots Magazine and Edinburgh Literary Miscellany* 76 (May 1814): 393 4. http://gateway.proquest.com/openurl?url_ver=Z39.88– 2004&res_dat=xri:hcpp&rft_ dat=xri:hcpp:fulltext:journals_hol_index-000008:233

8 Byrom, *The Edinburgh New Town Gardens*.

9 'Access to the extensive lands connected with the Calton Hill, valuable both as building grounds and as a delightful city walk, has long been a desideratum': taken from Robert Stevenson's report to Heriot's Hospital, noted in David Stevenson, *Life of Robert Stevenson, Civil Engineer.* (Edinburgh, 1878): 77.

10 This was most likely influenced by the posthumously published report by William Stark on the hill, dating to 1814. This is further discussed in detail below.

11 Stevenson, *Life of Robert Stevenson*: 82.

12 Roland Paxton, J. Shipway and Royal Commission on the Ancient and Historical Monuments and Constructions of Scotland, *Scotland—Lowlands and Borders*, Civil Engineering Heritage (London: Thomas Telford, 2007): 151. See also Stevenson, *Life of Robert Stevenson*: 74–91.

13 More on this topic is discussed below.

14 '[T]his road should not be less than seventy-five feet in breadth, or similar to Princes Street . . . Princes Street, including sunken areas, measures ninety-five feet in breadth . . . but the narrowing of the street even to sixty feet in width . . .'. Taken from Robert Stevenson's report to Heriot's Hospital, noted in Stevenson, *Stevenson, Life of Robert Stevenson*: 82–3.

15 Ibid.

16 1761–1823. According to Colvin, Elliot was 'one of the leading Edinburgh architects during the first quarter of the nineteenth century' Howard Colvin, *A Biographical Dictionary of British Architects 1600–1840* (New Haven, CT: Yale University Press, 1995): 350.

17 Completed in 1817. This followed much of the rhetoric of the adjacent Bridewell, but with a less rusticated approach to the exterior stonework. In Elliot's design, the 'Court Revival' style defined by MacInnes in Adam's Bridewell made way for a more restrained castellation that seemed to incorporate Burn's interpretation of Adam's style through his Nelson Monument. MacInnes, 'Robert Adam's Public Buildings'.

18 These consist of central semicircular arches, flanked by Corinthian columns and framed either side by Ionic colonnades.

19 Nash had first implemented the ideas of picturesque in urban design during the development of Blaise Hamlet near Bristol, along with Humphrey Repton, in the 1790s. John Nash has been mainly attributed the development of Marylebone Farm, but recent work by Dana Arnold has highlighted the importance of the team effort of the group of architects, builders and surveyors, led by Nash, Decimus Burton and S. P. Cockerell, that went into this project, and its significance to the urban planning of London as a whole. See Arnold, *Rural Urbanism: London Landscapes in the Early Nineteenth Century*.

20 As Nash is the sole author of the proposals of 1809, then this discussion will refer to him only. Where the need arises to discuss the actual development, the group will be referred to as Nash et al.

21 The similarities between these two views have previously been highlighted in John Lowrey's paper on the urban design of Calton Hill, where he discusses the significance of these developments in the implementation of the 'picturesque' in urban design during the early nineteenth century. Lowrey, 'The Urban Design of Edinburgh's Calton Hill': 6.

22 Nash's plan was thought to demonstrate how urban design could be implemented as a 'national object'. See Terence Davis, *John Nash. The Prince Regent's Architect*. (London: Country Life, 1966). See below for further discussion on this.

23 Arnold, *Rural Urbanism*: 77.

24 'Compared to mainstream contemporary Scottish urbanism, Edinburgh's plan was distinctly English'. Charles McKean, 'Twinning Cities: Modernisation Versus Improvement', in Brian Edwards and Paul Jenkins (eds), *Edinburgh: The Making of a Capital City* (Edinburgh: Edinburgh University Press, 2005): 47 See also Charles McKean, 'Improvement and Modernisation in Everyday Enlightenment Scotland', in Elizabeth A. Foyster and Christopher A. Whatley (eds), *A History of Everyday Life in Scotland, 1600 to 1800* (Edinburgh: Edinburgh University Press, 2010).

25 Sir Gilbert Elliot Minto, 'Proposals for Carrying on Certain Public Works in the City of Edinburgh' (Edinburgh, 1752).

26 Ibid.: 36.

27 John Lowrey and Anthony Lewis, 'James Craig: Architect of the First New Town of Edinburgh', *Architectural Heritage: The Journal of the Architectural Heritage Society of Scotland* 5 (1994): 39–50; Cruft and Fraser, 'The Ingenious Architect'.

28 This bridge was designed by William Mylne, but it partially collapsed soon after opening and had to be rebuilt by John Smeaton (1724–1792), eventually re-opening in 1772. In 1894–7, this bridge was again rebuilt by Cunningham, Blyth and Westland to its current state. Paxton et al., *Scotland—Lowlands and Borders*: 144–5.

29 Quote from a letter written by Thomas Gray, c. 30 September 1765. Footnoted in Malcolm Andrews, *The Search for the Picturesque: Landscape Aesthetics and Tourism in Britain 1760–1800* (Stanford, CA: Stanford University Press, 1989): 207.

30 Lowrey has previously commented that Samuel Johnson's scathing remarks on the thoroughfares in Edinburgh provide a direct and precise counter to the development of the North and South Bridges of the city: '[Johnson's]

observation [in his 1775 publication, *A Journey to the Western Isles of Scotland*] that the highway to London was the most welcome sight a Scotsman ever saw, is not only a criticism of what he considered the backwardness of Scotland, but a reference to the way London was seen by many Scotsmen, namely, as a place of opportunity and a standard against which developments in Scotland were measured.' John Lowrey, 'From Caesarea to Athens: Greek Revival Edinburgh and the Question of Scottish Identity within the Unionist State', *Journal of the Society of Architectural Historians* 60, no. 2 (2001): 147.

31 This arch was later incorporated into the entrance of the university building.

32 It has been noted that the southernmost wall of Adam's (Old) College building for the University of Edinburgh would have been viewed as part of the city wall on entering the city from the south. This wall is much more ornate than the northernmost wall, which would not have been seen on entering the city.

33 Designed by Adam c. 1785 and built by Alexander Laing, architect, between 1786 and 1788. Paxton et al., *Scotland—Lowlands and Borders*: 143.

34 Robert Mein, *The City Cleaned, and Country Improven. By Following out this Proposed Method, for Paying only One Penny per Week, for an 8l. Rent, and so Proportionally by the Possessors of each Bounds, Consisting of 800l. Of Yearly Rent, which is 50 Houses, at 16l. Rent* (Edinburgh, 1760).

35 See inset on Mostyn John Armstrong, Andrew Armstrong and Thomas Kitchin, *To the Nobility, Gentry & Clergy of the Counties of Haddington, Edinburgh and Linlithgow This Map of the Three Lothians Is* ([Edinburgh], 1773).

36 'The society of Edinburgh has never been better, or indeed so good . . . the exclusion of the British continent which made this place the favourite resort of strangers'. In Cockburn, *Memorials of His Time*: 212.

37 'The wars against France were a catalyst for British nation-building. Scotland had participated actively in that process . . .'. Richard Rodger, *The Transformation of Edinburgh: Land, Property and Trust in the Nineteenth Century* (Cambridge: Cambridge University Press, 2001): 471–2.

38 Minto, 'Proposals for Carrying on Certain Public Works in the City of Edinburgh'. Specific works to improve Leith docks can be found in 'An Act for Enlarging and Improving the Harbour at Leith; for Making a New Bason, Quays, Wharfs or Docks; for Building Warehouses; for Making New Roads and Widening Others; Leading to and from the Said Harbour; and for Empowering the Lord Provost, Magistrates and Council of the City of Edinburgh to Purchase Lands, Houses and Areas; and to Borrow Money for these Purposes' (Edinburgh, 1788).

39 See Gordon Jackson, *The History and Archaeology of Ports* (Tadworth: World's Work, 1983): Ch. 3.

40 '[B]etween 1750 and 1800, [Scotland's] overseas commerce expanded by 300 per cent, England's by 200 per cent.' Colley, *Britons: Forging the Nation*: 123.

41 Its increase in shipping trade is remarked on in *Plan and Estimate for Enlarging and improving the Town and Harbour of Leith By Charles Henry Kerr*, [Edinburgh], 1787.

42 John Rennie was engaged to do this. See Paxton et al., *Scotland—Lowlands and Borders*: 156. The decision was to sell it or turn it into a trust. By 1826, the Leith Dock Commission

had been created and in another twelve years it was financially independent of the city.

43 The line of the road was created during the threat of invasion from Oliver Cromwell in July 1650, when General David Leslie had ordered two deep defensive trenches be dug from Calton Hill to Leith Walk. There are claims that the walk was built on top of the trenches, but evidence has been found that the level of the walk was much lower than that of the present one. Leith Walk Research Group, *Leith Walk and Greenside: A Social History*, [Edinburgh]: [The Group], 1979.

44 The earliest known use of Leith Walk as a street dates to 1695, when the town council ordered payment of £60 Scots yearly to James Lauder 'to be the keeper and overseer of the walk betwixt Edinburgh and Leith, for laying chanell (gravell) thereon'. Quoted in *Leith Walk and Greenside*: 3.

45 The route is still identified as a gravel walk as late as 1760, in Robert Mein's pamphlet on improving trade and commerce in the city (Plate 2.6). Robert Mein, *The Edinburgh Paradise Regain'd, on the City Set at Liberty, to Propagate and Improve her Trade and Commerce . . . By a Merchant-Citizen . . .* (Edinburgh, 1764).

46 As the infrastructure projects within Edinburgh were prioritised over the dock redevelopment, this resulted in the mismanagement of funds and only two out of three docks were ever completed (Jackson, *The History and Archaeology of Ports*: 54). This may be mainly due to the cost of the bridge linking Calton Hill and Princes Street, which had been financially draining on other commitments. See Reed, 'Form and Context'; and Byrom, *The Edinburgh New Town Gardens*: 315.

47 See J. Ainslie, *Old and New Town of Edinburgh and Leith with the Proposed Docks*, Edinburgh, 1804, Plate 1.26 for detail on specific boundaries and extents of the landowners.

48 See Reed, 'Form and Context': 135.

49 Minutes of Committee for feuing Calton Hill Grounds & Co., 15 January 1811, Shelf 32 9/41, 'Fishsupper', Edinburgh City Archives. Also taken from Peter Reed, 'Georgian Edinburgh', in Thomas A. Markus (ed.), *Order in Space and Society*: 135.

50 According to Reed, a similar scheme had been carried out for the second New Town. Ibid: 152.

51 The full list notes local papers as *The Edinburgh Courant, Mercury, Advertiser* and *Correspondent* and the London papers as *The Courier, St James' Chronicle, London Chronicle* and *The Times*. Minutes of Committee for feuing Calton Hill Grounds & Co., 15 January 1811, Shelf 32 9/41, 'Fishsupper', Edinburgh City Archives. 22–3

52 It is not possible to give an exact number of proposals as not all are mentioned in the record book, but it appears that around half a dozen hopefuls submitted more than one and that submissions six and seven were counted as one submission, placing the number around forty-one or forty-two designs.

53 The four joint competition winners were: William Reid (Plate 2.7), Richard Crichton (Plate 2.8), Alexander Nasmyth (Plate 2.9) and James Milne and Benjamin Bell (Plate 2.10).

54 These were: Robert Reid, John Baxter, William Burn, James Gillespie, John Paterson and William Stark, although Stark's report was not included in the comments at the back

of this book. See 'Entry of the Plans for the New Buildings in the Order in which they were Received by Macritchie & Little, 1813, GD113/1/325, National Archives of Scotland, Edinburgh.

55 Timon, 'View of Different Proposals': 4–5.

56 Minutes of Committee for Feuing Calton Hill Grounds & Co., Shelf 32 9/41, 23. A flagstaff was located on the summit of Calton Hill until the 1820s.

57 This resulted in the committee deciding that the prize money should be shared out between the four proposals that were considered to have interesting and preferential parts to their designs, but which were not wholly acceptable as a plan for the area. It was therefore suggested that the first prize of £300 should be shared by William Reid (Plate 2.77), Alexander Nasmyth (Plate 2.8) and Richard Crichton (Plate 2.9) and the £100 second prize should go to a jointly submitted plan by James Milne and Benjamin Bell (Plate 2.10). This would mean that all 'winners' received £100 apiece. These designs are discussed in detail in Reed, 'Form and Context' and Byrom, *The Edinburgh New Town Gardens*.

58 Stark (1770–1813) was a Fife-born architect whose father was a merchant and mill owner in Glasgow but who had family connections in the Midlothian area. His architectural portfolio was in the main Glasgow structures, such as the Glasgow court house, the Hunterian Museum at Glasgow University and St Georges Tron Church in Buchanan Street. His work in Edinburgh consisted of the interiors of the Signet Library and the Advocates Library (now the upper Signet Library), and his role on the committee for the development of the lands of Calton Hill. Colvin, *A Biographical Dictionary of British Architects 1600–1840*: 977.

59 William Stark, *Report to the Right Honourable the Lord Provost, Magistrates, and Council of the City of Edinburgh, and the Governors of George Heriot's Hospital . . . On the Plans for Laying out the Grounds for Buildings between Edinburgh and Leith* (Edinburgh: Printed by A. Smellie, 1814): 16.

60 'To the stranger occupied in the examination of the present New Town, it would import little to be informed when looking along George Street, that it is precisely parallel to Prince's Street and Queen's Street; or, if admiring Charlotte Square to be told that it forms exact counterpart upon the ground plan to St Andrew's Square.' Stark, *Report . . . On the Plans for . . . Edinburgh and Leith*: 8.

61 Ibid.: 16.

62 Ibid.: 6.

63 Ibid. It is thought that William Playfair may have been the 'friend' who had added the post script, as he was apprenticed to Stark at the time.

64 Colvin, *A Biographical Dictionary of British Architects 1600–1840*: 977. Quote cited but not referenced.

65 Ibid.

66 McKean, 'Twinning Cities': 55.

67 See Byrom, *The Edinburgh New Town Gardens*: 315 for further discussion on this.

Chapter 3

1 Further discussion on this in Part 2. According to Byrom, this 'received unanimous approval', as reported in the *Edinburgh Evening Courant* dated 12 Feb 1818. See Byrom, *The Edinburgh New Town Gardens*: 316.

2 Minutes of Committee for Feuing Calton Hill Grounds &

Co., 8 May 1818, Shelf 32 9/41, 'Fishsupper'.

3　William Playfair, *Report to the Right Honourable the Lord Provost, Magistrates, and Council of the City of Edinburgh . . . On a Plan for Laying out the New Town between Edinburgh and Leith, Etc.* (Edinburgh, 1819). NB Playfair produced two reports, a rough draft in April 1819 (Plate 3.1a) and this one, in December 1819 (Plate 3.1b).

4　Ibid.: 5.

5　Ibid.: 3.

6　Ibid.: 7.

7　'Above these public buildings, and rising from the trees, is a handsome row or terrace, sufficiently elevated to give a prospect over the tops of the houses immediately below, and enjoying an extensive view of the more distant country.' Ibid.: 2.

8　John Nash, '1st Report to H.M. Commissioners of Woods, Forests and Land Revenues' (1809). Taken from John Summerson and John Nash, *John Nash: Architect to King George IV,* 2nd edn, p. 299, pl. XVI (London: George Allen & Unwin, 1949).

9　The development of the land had already been determined by the project Trustees early on in the venture (hence why the site is a strange zig-zag shape on the eastern side, where landowners had agreed, or not to be part of the development).

10　Summerson and Nash, *John Nash*: 126.

11　The name 'Carlton' has caused numerous issues in the referencing and understanding of the hill, as it has often been confused with the namesake of Calton and its origins. A simple Google search demonstrates how commonly this mix-up occurs.

12　Playfair, *Report . . . on a Plan for Laying out the New Town*: 2.

13　It appears that a wall was built to separate the private from the public land, but this was shielded on the private gardens side by the Ha Ha. It is possible that these were built at the same time, as the wall is noted in place from as early as 1840. See http://www.scran.ac.uk/database/record.php?usi=000–000–0126–115-C.

14　'I have also . . . introduced large public gardens, trusting that by judicious and careful planting, an assemblage of trees and buildings may be obtained, without which architecture is deprived of half its beauty'. Playfair, *Report . . . on a Plan for Laying out the New Town*: 5.

15　Playfair further associates his plan for the Hillside Terrace gardens with Stark's proposals, by including the same group of elm trees that Stark mentions in his 1814 report: 'Going down the walk, we first come to that part of Mr Allan's property, which is so much adorned by a double row of elms. These I would most carefully preserve'. Ibid.: 3. It is possible that these are preserved to this day, in what is now known as London Road Gardens.

16　Ibid.: 6.

17　See Cockburn, *Memorials of His Time*: 185.

18　See discussion on the panorama, above.

19　Davis, *John Nash: The Prince Regent's Architect*: 64.

20　Arnold, *Re-Presenting the Metropolis*: 47.

21　This incorporation of commemorative architecture was to become a real focus for the development of the city in the late 1810s and early 1820s and is central to the discussion in the next section.

22　Playfair, *Report . . . on a Plan for Laying out the New Town*: 3.

23　Ibid.: 4.

24　It should be noted that Hillside Road was later renamed London Road. Playfair provides separate, more detailed drawings on this area and its public buildings. See Playfair Drawings Collection, Centre for Special Collections, Univer

PART 2
Introduction

1　Lord Henry Cockburn (1779–1854), Scottish lawyer, judge and literary figure. Highly influential figure in nineteenth-century Edinburgh.

2　Henry Cockburn, *A Letter to the Lord Provost on the Best Ways of Spoiling the Beauty of Edinburgh* (Edinburgh: Adam & Charles Black, 1849).

3　Ibid.: 7.

Chapter 4

1　This often occurred when the city was overcrowded and the threat of plagues made it a necessity to separate the infectious dead from the living.

2　A kirkyard situated to the south of the city and consecrated in 1562, which served the population of the burgh up to the nineteenth century.

3　From as early as the 1616, the Dean of Guild in Edinburgh had assumed control over the style and form of the monuments erected in Greyfriars kirkyard and only monuments erected to a particularly high standard and by the wealthiest of families would be permitted within the site. Anne Boyle et al., *Ruins and Remains: Edinburgh's Neglected Heritage* (Edinburgh: Scotland's Cultural Heritage, 1985): 17.

4　This was erected in Greyfriars by his nephew, Robert Milne (also a royal master mason) in 1667.

5　John Lowrey, 'Architect's Monuments at Greyfriars', paper presented at Death, Commemoration and Memory Conference (University of Edinburgh, 2010).

6　James Brown, *The Epitaphs and Monumental Inscriptions in Greyfriars Churchyard, Edinburgh.* (Edinburgh: J. Moodie Miller, 1867): 249.

7　Nigel Llewellyn and Victoria and Albert Museum, *The Art of Death: Visual Culture in the English Death Ritual c.1500-c.1800* (London: Reaktion, 1991): 48, 54.

8　Matthew Craske also explores this idea from an English context, where he argues that the use of funereal effigies and memorials within English churches also served as a public and official proclamation of lineage and inheritance. Matthew Craske, *The Silent Rhetoric of the Body: A History of Monumental Sculpture and Contemporary Art in England, 1720–1770* (New Haven, CT and London: published for the Paul Mellon Centre for Studies in British Art by Yale University Press, 2007).

9　'Old' is there to distinguish this burial ground from the 'New' Calton burial ground that was established in the early nineteenth century (see below).

10　This is substantiated by the names and occupations found on grave markers in Old Calton from this period, as well as from records of interments through the Incorporated Trades Minute Books. See Smith, *Epitaphs and Monumental Inscriptions*; Mitchell, *Edinburgh Monumental Inscriptions*.

Edinburgh City Archives, SL110.

11 The Incorporated Trades of Calton used the money collected from trade dues (the annual payment for the privilege of being freemen of Calton), the renting of burial plots, the provision of mortcloths for the dead and the interment of the recently departed within the (Old) Calton burial ground to help the freemen of Calton and their families who were poor, infirm or widowed. Further information on this group and how they functioned can be found in two volumes of the *Book of the Old Edinburgh Club* from the 1930s, in M. S. Irvine's the *Caldtoun or Calton of Edinburgh* and many of the meeting minutes and account transactions of the Incorporated Trades that still survive in the Edinburgh City Archives. This latter resource includes records of those buried within the (Old) Calton burial ground, and of those who paid for burial plots. It should be noted that you did not have to be a freeman of Calton to be interred in the burial ground.

12 Robert Monteith, *An Theatre of Mortality: Or, the Illustrious Inscriptions Extant upon the Several Monuments Erected over Dead Bodies (of the Sometime Honourable Persons) Buried within the Greyfriars Church-Yard; and Other Churches within the City of Edinburgh and Suburbs* (1704).

13 Barbara S. Groseclose, *British Sculpture and the Company Raj: Church Monuments and Public Statuary in Madras, Calcutta, and Bombay to 1858* (Newark and London: University of Delaware Press; Associated University Presses, 1995): 25.

14 These were being erected from as early as 1737. The monuments to William Shakespeare and John Milton, for example, were built without any notion of the body being interred alongside (John Milton is buried in the Church of St Giles' Cripplegate in London and William Shakespeare is buried in the Church of the Holy Trinity in Stratford-upon-Avon).

15 This reputation is considered to have inspired the development of later galleries of national 'celebrities' throughout Europe (such as the Panthéon in Paris and Walhalla in Regensberg) and in America (United States Capitol in Washington DC), and has even been taken into today's popular culture from this period. See Uta Kornmeier, 'Madame Tussaud's as a Popular Pantheon', in Richard Wrigley and Matthew Craske (eds), *Pantheons: Transformations of a Monumental Idea* (Aldershot: Routledge, 2004): 81–105.

16 '[T]he Abbey's function [was] not only honorific, but integrative: [uniting] individual achievement to the life of society as a whole'. Richard Jenkyns, *Westminster Abbey*, Wonders of the World (London: Profile Books, 2004): 85.

17 Matthew Craske, 'Westminster Abbey 1720–1770: A Public Pantheon Built upon Private Interest', in Richard Wrigley and Matthew Craske (eds), *Pantheons: Transformations of a Monumental Idea* (Aldershot: Routledge, 2004): 57.

18 'Go into Westminster Abbey, and you will find that what raises the admiration of the spectator is not the mausoleums of the English kings, but the monuments which the gratitude of the nation has erected to perpetuate the memory of those illustrious men who contributed to its glory.' François Marie Arouet de Voltaire (1694–1778) (1909–14), 'Letter XXIII—On the Regard that Ought to be Shown to Men of Letters', in *Letters on the English*. The

Harvard Classics: http://www.bartleby.com/34/2/23.html.

19 Hoock, 'The British Military Pantheon in St Paul's Cathedral': 81–106.

20 In Treasury letter book T.27/53.400 reports from the committee can be found in Treasury minutes, e.g. T.29/505.527, and its activities easily followed in the index to Treasury letters for each year. Margaret Dickens Whinney, *Sculpture in Britain, 1530–1830* (Harmondsworth: Penguin, 1964): 199.

21 Hoock, 'The British Military Pantheon in St Paul's Cathedral': 82.

22 This is referred to as 'The Cult of the Hero' (ibid.). It has not only been identified in commemorative monuments, but also in other forms of material culture of the period, such as paintings, texts and panoramas. These matters were addressed in a conference held in 2012 at the Tate Britain: 'Contested Views: Visual Culture and the Napoleonic Wars'. See http://www.tate.org.uk/whats-on/tate-britain/conference/contested-views.

23 Dana Arnold, *The Metropolis and its Image: Constructing Identities for London, c. 1750–1950* (Oxford: Blackwell, 1999); Dana Arnold, *Re-Presenting the Metropolis;* Dana Arnold (ed.), *Cultural Identities and the Aesthetics of Britishness.* Studies in Imperialism (Manchester and New York: Manchester University Press, 2004).

24 In particular those that had strong connections with the British navy. See Yarrington, 'The Commemoration of the Hero 1800–1864'; Colley, *Britons: Forging the Nation, 1707–1837.*

25 Hoock, 'The British Military Pantheon in St Paul's Cathedral'.

26 Such as the naming of streets after key successes in battle (Waterloo Place, Trafalgar Square etc.).

27 Yarrington, 'The Commemoration of the Hero 1800–1864': 326.

28 Arnold, *The Metropolis and its Image.*

29 William Godwin, *Essay on Sepulchres: Or, a Proposal for Erecting some Memorial of the Illustrious Dead in All Ages on the Spot where their Remains have been Interred* (London, 1809).

30 William Wood, *An Essay on National and Sepulchral Monuments* (London: William Miller, 1808).

31 'It is not only by the sword that a country be defended: when true patriotism is properly excited, the most obscure and feeble individuals will devise their own means of assisting the public cause.' Ibid.: 6.

32 Yarrington, 'The Commemoration of the Hero 1800–1864': 103. Yarrington's PhD thesis concentrates on case studies of monuments to Lord Nelson in London and Bristol, but also briefly considers the Edinburgh monument within the wider context of the phenomenon of the commemoration of Nelson at that time.

33 Ibid.: 103.

34 Cockburn, *Memorials of His Time*: 288–92.

35 As discussed above and in Part 1, the establishment of the David Hume monument on Calton Hill was the first instance on the hill and in the burgh environs where memorial became a public display of veneration as well as a symbol of commemoration. However, it is not thought that Adam's intention was to create an emotive visual trigger through the remembrance of Hume in the construction of

this monument, in as much as his design was to add to a broader landscape that would provide emotive stimulus in picturesque terms.

36 'We . . . regret the loss of that highly illustrious hero, Lord Viscount Nelson . . . [whose] . . . superior skill and intrepidity led our fleets to victory . . . it was inter alia resolved that a subscription shall be opened for the erection of a statue, Naval Pillar, or other monument to the memory of Lord Nelson as a lasting mark of the affection of this metropolis.' Minutes of the Nelson Pillar committee, 25 November 1805, 9.41 62u, Handlist of Historical Records, Edinburgh City Archives.

37 This may explain why, by the early nineteenth century, the Hume monument in (Old) Calton burial ground was noted in numerous travel guides as a monument to visit to commemorate the 'celebrity' of Hume as a hero, rather than appreciate the broader drama of the landscape to which it contributed, as Adam had intended.

38 Two sites had been suggested, one at the west end of Princes Street, the other on Calton Hill. Personal communication, Prof. Charles McKean.

39 Due to the number of denominations of the Christian church found in Britain, as well as other religions with varying views on idolatry.

40 T. C. Hansard, 'Parliamentary Debates'. 29 June 1815, vol. 31, cc 1048. 'Address for a National Monument, and Monuments to Officers who Fell in the Battle of Waterloo: http://hansard.millbanksystems.com/commons/1815/jun/29/address-for-a-national-monument-and#S1V0031P0_18150629_HOC_30.

41 Ibid. 29 June 1815, vol. 31, cc 1055.

42 Minutes of the National Monument Committee, 24 February 1819, SL103/1/1, Edinburgh City Archives: 18.

43 See http://www.rhass.org.uk/information/thesocietysfoundation.

44 An estate near Kilsyth, in North Lanarkshire.

45 'Proceedings of the Highland Society of Scotland Regarding the Application for a Monument to be Erected in Honour of the Victory of Waterloo. Chaired by Earl of Wemyss, attended by 120 noblemen & gentlemen, members of the society'. Minutes of the National Monument Committee, 9 January 1816, SL103, Edinburgh City Archives.

46 Colvin, *A Biographical Dictionary of British Architects 1600–1840*: 440.

47 Letter from James Gillespie to Michael Linning. Minutes of the National Monument Committee, 4 March 1816, SL103/4/10, Edinburgh City Archives. The cost for this was estimated at £10,000.

48 A copy of this drawing was held by Prof. Charles McKean, who obtained it from a collection at the offices of Frank Mears/Naismith. These images are now held in the National Library of Scotland but, despite numerous attempts to locate this drawing, it appears to have vanished.

49 The archway drawn on this map was a proposed design that was never executed.

50 'The interior . . . would be admirably calculated to contain any monuments hereafter to be erected by the Nation to departed heroes, as well as those by which St Paul's and Westminster Abbey are now encumbered, if they could with propriety be removed; and from which the Public are

virtually excluded, except during the hours of divine service.' Andrew Robertson, *The Parthenon Adapted to the Purpose of a National Monument to Commemorate the Victories of the Late War; Proposed to be Erected in Trafalgar Square or Hyde Park [with Plans]* (London, 1838): 25.

51 'the intention was to erect a pillar, or triumphal arch, some architectural monument, in fact, suitable to the magnificence of the nation, and which, of course, would not be confined within the walls of a church'. Minutes of the National Monument committee 9.1.1816 SL103/1/1: 1.

52 Yarrington, 'The Commemoration of the Hero 1800–1864': 200.

53 The building would have served as a monument to the victory over Bonaparte and was to be placed on a platform to the north end of London's Regent's Park on Primrose Hill. The author praised the Parthenon as 'the taste of the purest age of Athens; the production of the very ablest artists the world ever saw, acting under the guidance of the most accomplished patrons. It is admitted, beyond all dispute, to be the perfection of Greek architecture: and now that a large proportion of the original sculpture belonging to it is deposited in the British Museum, it is equally beyond all cavil, that these ornaments of the temple are of the highest scale of excellence' (Anon., signed 'B.', *The Times*, 8 April 1817).

54 Robertson, *The Parthenon Adapted to the Purpose of a National Monument*.

55 Yarrington, 'The Commemoration of the Hero 1800–1864': 327–8.

56 Correspondence between the British government and the monument committee in Edinburgh shows that the 'application for public aid was unsuccessful and [they] resolve to continue efforts to accomplish their objective by means of subscription or in such other way as may be deemed most advisable'. See Minutes of the National Monument Committee, June 1816, SL103/1/1, Edinburgh City Archives: 6.

57 'Mr Tierney gave notice, that soon after the holydays he intended to move, that the sum granted by parliament for the erection of a monument to commemorate our victories by sea and land, be laid out in the erection of a parish church or churches . . . The Chancellor of the Exchequer[s] . . . own opinion was that nothing could be more fit than that national monuments should be rendered applicable to purposes of general utility . . . The right hon. gentleman then moved, 'That his Majesty be enabled to direct exchequer bills, to an amount not exceeding one million, to be issued to commissioners, to be by them advanced, under certain regulations and restrictions, towards Building, and promoting the Building, of additional Churches and Chapels in England.' (http://hansard.millbanksystems.com/commons/1818/mar/16/building-of-new-churches).

58 'Proposals for Building in Scotland a Monumental Church of Ornamental Architecture in Commemoration of the Naval and Military Victories of the Late War', Minutes of the National Monument Committee, 20 April 1818, SL103/1/1, Edinburgh City Archives: 8.

59 M. H. Port, *600 New Churches: The Church Building Commission, 1818–1856*, new edn (Reading: Spire Books, 2006): Ch. 1. Churches in Scotland were not explicitly

included in the specifics of this Act, which stated that it was to fund churches in England. It appears that those involved in the National Monument just presumed the monies would be available to all who required it. This is supported by an application in Edinburgh in 1824 to build St Mary's Church in Bellevue Crescent. This resulted in a query about whether the Act did actually included Scottish churches—the Treasury confirmed that it did (215).

60 Spalding's designs are mentioned in the footnotes and 'Mr Thynn proposed a Roman Italianate style'. M. Linning, *Memoranda Publica* ([Edinburgh: s.n.], 1834). No trace can be found of either of these designs, but the models for Mr Spalding's gothic church were included in the inventory for his house at 1 Heriot Row. It has since been discovered that Mr Thynn worked as William H. Playfair's draughtsman and was busy designing churches in Leith at the same time as his proposal for the national monument. Personal communication, Joe Rock, 18 10 Oct. 2012.

61 Letter from Mr Elliot to National Monument Committee. Minutes of the National Monument Committee, 22 July 1819, SL103/4/78, Edinburgh City Archives: 39.

62 In fact, this site was also mooted for the national monument as Parthenon, alongside the discussions for the new Royal High School. 'It is disposed therefore, not as an indispensable part of any plan for removing the High School to the only open space in the midst of the city, but as a subject for consideration that the great hall or national monument be placed near the north end of the Earthen Mound, opposite to the opening of Hanover Street. In that situation it would be visible from a great many parts, and over a considerable extent of the Old and New Town: it would add another to the very few public buildings which it contains, while it would not interfere with any other view or object, but would give, in the very bosom of the city, a character more truly attic to our metropolis than any other edifice which it contains. Above all it would unite utility with ornament . . . (A Letter to the Lord Provost on the Mischievous Tendency of a Scheme for Abolishing the High School of Edinburgh', Edinburgh, 1822: 25).

63 Letter from Mr Elliot to National Monument Committee. Minutes of the National Monument Committee, 10 February 1819, SL103/1/1, Edinburgh City Archives.

64 Ibid., 15 June 1821, SL103/4/115, Edinburgh City Archives.

65 St Paul's replacing Westminster Abbey as the public pantheon for the commemoration of the stately war dead in Britain from 1795 onwards: see Holger Hoock, 'The British Military Pantheon in St Paul's Cathedral: The State, Cultural Patriotism, and the Politics of National Monuments, c.1790–1820, in Richard Wrigley and Matthew Craske (eds), *Pantheons: Transformations of a Monumental Idea* (Abingdon: Routledge, 2004): 81–105 ; and Dominique Poulot, 'Pantheons in Eighteenth-Century France: Temple, Museum, Pyramid', in Wrigley and Craske, *Pantheons*: 143–6. The Panthéon was originally designed to replace the Abbey of St Geneviève as a votive church for Louis XV and was only 'secularised' after the Revolution by Quatremere de Quincy.

66 Lord Henry Cockburn to Mr Niven. Lord Henry Cockburn, Bonaly-by-Callington, 2 May 1822, SL103/4/200, Edinburgh City Archives.

67 Craske, 'Westminster Abbey 1720–1770': 57.

68 '[T]his edifice . . . which as it commemorated the victories of Marathon and Salamis in ancient, so will its representative, commemorate as it is destined to do, those of Trafalgar and Waterloo in modern Athens, while it will, as to monumental purposes serve as "the Westminster abbey of the north" and like it, will have its "poet's corner".' Linning, *Memoranda Publica*: 57–8.

69 Ibid.

70 Wood, *An Essay on National and Sepulchral Monuments*: 5.

71 Sir Archibald Allison, 'On the Proposed National Monument at Edinburgh', *Blackwood's Edinburgh Magazine* 5, no. 28 (July 1819): 380

72 Ibid.

73 '[T]here is something in the separate styles which is peculiarly adapted to the different emotions they are intended to excite. The light tracery and lofty roof and airy pillars of the gothic seem to accord well with the sublime feelings and spiritual fervour of religion. The massy wall and gloomy character of the castle bespeak the abode of feudal power and the pageantry of barbaric magnificence. The beautiful porticos and columns and rich cornices of the Ionic or Corinthian seem well adapted for the public edifices in a great city for those which are destined for amusement or to serve for the purpose of public ornament. The Palladian style is that of all others best adapted for the magnificence of private dwellings and overwhelms the spectator by a flood of beauty against which the rules of criticism are unable to withstand. If any of these styles of architecture were to be transferred from buildings destined for one purpose to those destined for another the impropriety of the change would appear very conspicuous' (Ibid.: 384).

74 Ibid.: 385.

75 Ibid.

76 Marc Fehlmann, 'As Greek as it Gets: British Attempts to Recreate the Parthenon', *Rethinking History* 11, no. 3 (September 2007): 353–77. This is confirmed in Elliot's accompanying essay to his Pantheon design for Edinburgh, where he states that 'It has been confidently asserted by some writers on the subject that the Parthenon was a National Monument in honour of the glorious conclusion of the Persian war'. Letter from Mr Elliot to National Monument committee. Minutes of the National Monument Committee, 15 June 1821, SL103/4/115, Edinburgh City Archives.

77 Ibid.

78 In Cambridge, the Parthenon was the inspiration for the design of the Fitzwilliam Museum—I say 'successful' in that both it and the Scottish National Monument progressed further than paper proposals, despite the National Monument never being completed.

79 Fehlmann, 'As Greek as it Gets': 371. In David Watkin's book, he notes that Cockerell 'from the start . . .' had 'felt the necessity of setting forth the Parthenon as a free translation of the original'. See David Watkin, *The Life and Work of C. R. Cockerell*, Studies in Architecture (London: Zwemmer, 1974): 152.

80 'I beg leave to submit to consideration a view which as presented to the public in 1817, on a proposal for erecting an exact copy of the Parthenon of Athens with materials and accompaniments worthy of the united efforts of Great

Britain—and as the same effect may be adequately produced by the Freestone of this country . . . I have no doubt that Mr Robertson would cheerfully send his model to the Committee if desired.' Minutes of the National Monument Committee, 23 February 1819, SL103/4/64, Edinburgh City Archives.

81 Ibid., 15 April 1819.

82 For further information on the association between Hellenism and Scottish culture in the eighteenth, nineteenth and early twentieth centuries, see Anuradha S. Naik and Margaret C. H. Stewart, 'The Hellenization of Edinburgh: Cityscape, Architecture, and the Athenian Cast Collection', *Journal of the Society of Architectural Historians* 66, no. 3 (2007): 366–89.

83 Ibid.: 370.

84 Allan Ramsay to Sir William Dick of Prestonfield, 1762. Taken from Lowrey, 'From Caesarea to Athens': fn 1.

85 Cockburn, *Memorials of His Time: The Ordnance Gazetteer of Scotland* of 188(0?) notes that Edinburgh is called 'the Athens of the North' by Stuart of Stuart and Revett, *The Antiquities of Athens*.

86 Edward Daniel Clarke, *Travels in Various Countries of Europe, Asia and Africa, Vol. 6* (London, 1818): 378.

87 Allison, 'On the Proposed National Monument': 385.

88 Ibid.

89 Clarke does not mention Calton Hill at all in his text.

90 Further argument for this can be found in Hamilton's adoption of Greek Revival rhetoric for his Royal High School building on Calton Hill. His earlier 1823 design for a structure situated in the first New Town, adjacent to Register House (Plate 6.6) consisted of 'A broad street . . . to separate the new school from the north side of Adam's Register House, terminating in a triumphal arch leading towards Chamber's Dundas mansion . . . its tall colonnaded dome, resembling that of Gandy's (James Gandon) Four Courts in Dublin [meant that] the effect was Roman, rather than Greek. Apart from the north facing hexastyle portico, little ornament is visible in the drawings, but the upper floor displays a style of massive simplicity, which Hamilton was to use for the side wings of the 1825 High School and for several other buildings. This was marked by pilasters, large windows narrowing towards the top and having recessed panels below the sills and tall, straight topped entablatures' (Fisher, 'Thomas Hamilton': 38–9).

91 Minutes of the National Monument Committee, 19 July 1822, SL103/1/1, Edinburgh City Archives: 76-7.

92 Letter from Lord Elgin to Charles Robert Cockerell, July 1822, MS638, National Library of Scotland, Edinburgh.

93 Minutes of the National Monument Committee, 19 July 1822, SL103/1/1, Edinburgh City Archives: 76.

94 His ability to work in the Greek style had been particularly lauded by Lord Aberdeen. George Hamilton Gordon, Earl of Aberdeen, *An Inquiry into the Principles of Beauty in Grecian Architecture; With an Historical View of the Rise and Progress of the Art in Greece* (London: J. Murray, 1822): 217.

95 Diary of Charles Robert Cockerell, Monday 22 July 1822, COC/9/3 1822. Archives of the Royal Institute of British Architects, Victoria and Albert Museum, London.

96 For further information on the national monument project, and the appointment of Cockerell, Playfair and the aftermath, see Watkin, *The Life and Work of C. R. Cockerell*

and Linning, *Memoranda Publica*.

97 'In Scotland in particular, readers felt their national culture, to say nothing of their national identity, had been validated by Macpherson's "Discoveries".' John Vladimir Price, 'Ossian and the Canon in the Scottish Enlightenment', in Howard Gaskill (ed.), *Ossian Revisited* (Edinburgh: Edinburgh University Press, 1991): 125.

98 Naik and Stewart, 'The Hellenization of Edinburgh'.

99 Isaiah Berlin, *Vico and Herder: Two Studies in the History of Ideas* (London: Hogarth Press, 1980): 172. Taken from Frank Walker, 'National Romanticism and the Architecture of the City', in George Gordon (ed.), *Perspectives of the Scottish City* ([Aberdeen]: Aberdeen University Press, 1985): 129.

100 Watkin, *The Life and Work of C. R. Cockerell*: 151.

101 Ibid.

102 See Walter Scott, *Hints Addressed to the Inhabitants of Edinburgh, and Others, in Prospect of His Majesty's Visit* (Edinburgh: Printed for Bell and Bradfute, Manners and Miller, Archibald Constable and Co., William Blackwood, Waugh and Innes and John Robertson, 1822).

103 'Greek architecture represented the original or primitive source of all classical architecture . . . Scott's image of Scotland as a noble, simple, and primitive land was rather similar to the idea of Greece evoked by the neoclassical interest in Greek architecture. Both were in some senses concerned with a primitive yet Golden Age of their respective cultures, and both had their separate architectural styles that evoked that age' (Lowrey, 'From Caesarea to Athens': 143).

104 Fintain Cullen, 'The Art of Assimilation: Scotland and its Heroes', *Art History* 16, no. 4 (1993): 600–18.

105 See N. T. Phillipson, 'Nationalism and Ideology', in J. N. Wolfe (ed.), *Government and Nationalism in Scotland: An Enquiry by Members of the University of Edinburgh* (Edinburgh: Edinburgh University Press, 1969): iii-vii, and Andrew Noble, 'Versions of the Scottish Pastoral: The Literati and the Tradition 1780–1830', in Thomas A. Markus (ed.), *Order in Space and Society* (Edinburgh: Mainstream, 1982): 263 310.

106 'The extent of the Greek Revival's supremacy can be gauged by its dominance in one particular building type: the public building for legal, administrative, or cultural purposes.' J. Mordaunt Crook, *The Greek Revival: Neo-Classical Attitudes in British Architecture, 1760–1870* (London: J. Murray, 1972): 98.

107 See Phillipson, 'Nationalism and Ideology', Noble, 'Versions of the Scottish Pastoral' and Cullen, 'The Art of Assimilation'.

108 Lowrey, 'From Caesarea to Athens'.

109 Thomas H. Shepherd and John Britton, *Modern Athens! Displayed in a Series of Views: Or Edinburgh in the Nineteenth Century: Exhibiting the Whole of the New Buildings, Modern Improvements, Antiquities, and Picturesque Scenery, of the Scottish Metropolis and its Environs* (London: Jones & Co., 1829): iii, 6.

110 Such as the medieval Old Town. The frontispiece of the book also depicts an image of the Honours of Scotland 'found' by Sir Walter Scott, and a sketch of Abbotsford, Walter Scott's house in the Borders, built in the Scots Baronial style.

111 Gow notes that it was only in the minds of the National Monument Committee that the national monument would be an exact facsimile of the Parthenon; Cockerell never thought it would be so. Ian Gow, 'C. R. Cockerell's Design for the Northern Athenian Parthenon', *Journal of the Architectural Heritage Society of Scotland* 16 (1989): 25.

112 Lowrey, 'From Caesarea to Athens': 150.

113 'While her insular situation, and the union and energy of her people, secure for Great Britain peace and tranquility within her own bounds, the rivalry of the different nations of whom the Empire is composed, promises, if properly directed, to animate her people with the ardour and enterprise which have hitherto been supposed to spring only from the collision of smaller states. Towards the accomplishment of this most desirable object however it is indispensible that each nation should preserve the remembrance of its own distinct origin and look to the glory of its own people with an anxious and peculiar care' (*Blackwood's Edinburgh Magazine* 28 [July 1819]: 379).

114 This was particularly relevant as a relatively high proportion of men involved in the development in overseas colonies came from a Scottish background, which not only emphasises Scots' contribution to the unified imperial goal, but also suggests that Scotland was financially benefiting from imperial expansion. Linda Colley calculates that by the late eighteenth century, 60 per cent of free merchants in Bengal and over 25 per cent of the officers serving in the East India Company were Scottish. Colley, *Britons: Forging the Nation, 1707–1837*: 128.

Chapter 5

1 In the early seventeenth century, the legal rights of the kirk and parish of Restalrig—a parish to the north of Edinburgh, associated with the hamlet of Calton—had been transferred to the parish of South Leith. As a result, residents of Calton began using South Leith kirk and kirkyard for both religious worship and the interment of its dead. This became problematic, not only because it was a mile and a half to the north of the hamlet, but also because the high volume of burials resulted in the residents of Calton only gaining use of the space on specific times and days of the week. A small patch of land on the south side of Calton Hill was therefore granted to the inhabitants of Calton by the landowner, Laird (Lord) Balmerino, so that a burial ground could be formed on an area of land on Calton Hill, adjacent to the hamlet. For further detail, see Paton, 'The Barony of Calton, Part II' and Grant, *Cassell's Old and New Edinburgh*, vol. 5: 131.

2 A society that worked in the interests of the tradesmen or freemen of the hamlet of Calton. Due to the nature of the establishment of the burial ground, and its distance from its associated kirk, the management of (Old) Calton was therefore never directly under the control of a parish kirk, but instead was run as a business by the Incorporated Trades of Calton.

3 Despite the close proximity of Calton burial ground to the Canongate, only those associated with the Calton and the wider parish of north Leith used this site for interment—residents of Canongate and Edinburgh used Canongate and Greyfriars kirkyards. The burial ground was originally defined as a rectilinear area on high ground to the north of

the Canongate, which can be identified on Armstrong's map of 1773 (Plate 4.3), but by the early nineteenth century, the popularity of the burial ground was such that it was extended to the south and the west.

4 See discussion on Nelson monument in Part 1, on its purpose as a tourist 'draw'. The walk around the hill was known as 'Hume's Walk' as David Hume had petitioned the town council in 1775 to provide a public walk on Calton Hill for the benefit of the Edinburgh inhabitants.

5 Designed by William Playfair in 1817. See Plate 5.14.

6 'Proceedings Relative to the ERECTION of a MONUMENT to the Late JOHN PLAYFAIR, Esq., Professor of Natural Philosophy in the University of Edinburgh', 26 December 1820, MYBN 274A Box 4/1–4/29, Ref 4/17, 'Fishsupper', Edinburgh City Archives.

7 This was tucked behind the Hume monument (see Plate 5.1).

8 Proceedings Relative to the ERECTION of a MONUMENT to the Late JOHN PLAYFAIR, Esq.'. The owner, in the end, refused to sell it to the Playfair committee.

9 '[I]t has appeared to them [the committee] to be happily and eminently suited for the monument of a man of Science,—that such a monument would be calculated to bestow, as well as to derive no slight degree of interest or dignity, from its connection with that scientific establishment, of which Mr Playfair was himself so distinguished a member'. 'Proceedings Relative to the Erection of a Monument to the Late John Playfair, Esq. Professor of Natural Philosophy in the University of Edinburgh', 26 December 1820, MYBN 274A Box 4/1-4/29, Ref 4/17, Handlist of Historical Records, Edinburgh City Archives.

10 Letter from Mrs Stewart to Lord Minto, 19 July 1828. MS 11798, f. 176, National Library of Scotland, Edinburgh.

11 Stewart's son, Matthew, erected the tomb. The words above the door are FILIUS ET FILIA LIBERI SUPERSTITES PATRI CARISSIMO MORUM SUPREMUM MOERENTIES HIC SEPULCRUM DEDICAVERUNT ('His son and daughter, his surviving children, have in mourning dedicated here a tomb to a most beloved father of the highest character'). Taken from Gordon Macintyre, *Dugald Stewart: The Pride and Ornament of Scotland* (Eastbourne: Sussex Academic Press, 2003): 231. Latin inscription, 310, fn 18.

12 A comment he had made when referring to the Playfair monument on Calton Hill. Letter from Mrs Stewart to the Marquess of Lothian, 1 January 1830. GD 40/9–321, Lothian Muniments, National Archives of Scotland, Edinburgh.

13 For a fuller description of the debate and those involved in the erection of the Stewart monument, see Macintyre, *Dugald Stewart: The Pride and Ornament of Scotland*.

14 For a more in-depth discussion regarding the instigation of these three monuments and the relationship between the development of these structures and Calton Hill, see K. Carter McKee, *Monument to the Memory of Robert Burns on Calton Hill, Edinburgh*, forthcoming Architectural Heritage Society of Scotland publication.

15 On 8 October 1817, Edinburgh Town Council was presented with a letter from Mitchell, a merchant of the East India Company who had been living and trading in Bombay in the earlier part of the decade. This letter, entitled 'Proceedings respecting a situation for [a] Monument to

the memory of Robert Burns', described the funds donated by a few 'admirers of genius' in India, with the intention that 'a monument could be erected of the Poet in the Capital of his much loved country'. Mitchell requested that the council find a piece of land in the burial ground of Calton Hill or on some part of the summit of the hill for this purpose. Edinburgh Town Council Minutes, 8 October 1817, SL1/1/175.

16 See 'Festival in Commemoration of Robert Burns; And to Promote a Subscription to Erect a National Monument to his Memory at Edinburgh: Held at the Freemasons' Tavern, in London. With an Appendix, Containing the Resolutions of the General Meeting, April 24, 1819, Together with a List of the Subscribers' (London, 5 June 1819): iii–iv. National Library of Scotland.

17 'Mr Flaxman's model for a statue of Burns has been approved by the committee. The poet is represented with a mountain daisy in his right hand, and "the cottar's Saturday night" in his left. It is to be colossal and of bronze and to be erected in the New Town of Edinburgh.' Anon., 'Court of Kings Bench, Westminster, April 30th', *Leeds Mercury*, 4 May 1822. I am indebted to Mr Gordon Astley for drawing my attention to this article.

18 By 1824 John Flaxman was an old man and in poor health. He passed away in the winter of 1826, leaving the statue incomplete. His brother-in-law Thomas Denman finished off the piece, which was reported to be complete by the summer of 1828. Anon., 'Monument in Memory of Burns', *Aberdeen Journal*, 27 August 1828.

19 'The first idea, we understand, was to have the statue executed in Bronze, and to place it in the open air, in a conspicuous situation in Edinburgh. We regret deeply that this design—which, in our opinion was more national, and more suitable to the spirit of the Poet, and the public commemorative end in view—was not carried into effect. But, since it was changed to the less comprehensive and magnanimous determination of having a statue in marble, instead of Bronze, we are not sure that a better site than the college library could have been obtained' (Ibid.).

20 James Cuthbert Hadden, *George Thomson the Friend of Burns. His Life & Correspondence* (London, 1898): 78.

21 'First, it is not to be thought of for a moment that a marble statue can be placed in an open temple in Scotland. It would be at the risk of mischievous boys and drunken blackguards and we might lose our £1400 in the course of a night. The statue of Hygeia in the open temple over St Bernard's mineral well is a warning, with its one arm and its chipped face and figure' (Ibid.: 77).

22 Now known as the Playfair Library. See Fraser, *The Building of Old College: Adam, Playfair & the University of Edinburgh* for further information on Playfair's role in designing Old College.

23 See Robert Burns, 'Epistle to J. Lapraik' (1785), verse 12.

24 Anon., 'Burns' Monument', *Caledonian Mercury*, 26 February 1824.

25 Lord Aberdeen had told Cockerell that he 'thought it might be difficult to apply sculpture to the Church of Scotland. [We thought it] better not at first to bring this matter forward, but let it creep on'; 'It seems that the spirit of the puritan church is diametrically opposed to the Roman Catholic'. Diary of Charles Robert Cockerell, 24 and 25

August 1822, COC/9/3 1822, RIBA Archives, Victoria and Albert Museum, London.

26 Hadden, *George Thomson the Friend of Burns*: 75.

27 '[T]he promotion of this great national object is now unfortunately at a stand in consequence of the funds being exhausted; and the act obtained for making certain improvements in the city of Edinburgh, particularly in the approaches thereto from the south and the west . . . the actual has, as is generally the case, far exceeded the hypothetical or estimated expense; and the fund being exhausted, these works are likewise at a stand . . . There is no apparent mode whatever of completing the first of these undertakings, and scarcely any of completing the other without public aid' (Committee for the National Monument of Scotland and Parliamentary Commissioners for Improvement in the City of Edinburgh to Lords of Treasury, 'Request for Financial Aid'. Committee for the National Monument of Scotland and Parliamentary Commissioners for Improvement in the City of Edinburgh to Lords of Treasury, Memo, February 1831, SL103/2/199, National Monument of Scotland Committee, Edinburgh City Archive).

28 See Part 3 for further detail on the failure of the national monument project.

29 One of the statues depicted in Cockerell's watercolours of the proposed National Monument (Plate 5.4b) looks close to the finished version of the Burns monument (Plate 5.3). This information would have been available at the time of Cockerell's designs, as a maquette of the sculpture had been made up by Flaxman by 1824.

30 See 'Proposed Monument to the Memory of Robert Burns—List of Subscribers'. Pamphlet 1832, GD113/5/114b/4/12, Papers of the Innes family of Stow, Peeblesshire, National Archives of Scotland, Edinburgh.

31 Board of Manufactures—General and Manufacturing Records, NG1/2, National Archives of Scotland, Edinburgh.

32 Public admission was delayed for another four years while George Thomson petitioned unsuccessfully to a (by then) uninterested elite for yet more money to landscape the surrounding gardens and to protect Hamilton's structure by erecting a cast iron fence around it. See Anon., 'Scotland Yet', *Scotsman*, 22 October 1834; Anon., 'Burns Monument, Calton Hill', *Scotsman*, 12 July 1837.

33 Although it was Lord Cockburn who led this, so it is possible that the damage from the gasworks was exaggerated by him, as he had strong feelings against the placement of the statue in the monument at all.

34 'Festival in Commemoration of Robert Burns'.

35 Letter from Thomas Thomson to 2nd Earl of Minto, 5 December 1828, MS 11811, f. 91, National Library of Scotland, Edinburgh.

36 Hadden, *George Thomson the Friend of Burns*: 76.

37 Thomas Hamilton *Design for the Royal High School, Edinburgh*, D2637, National Gallery of Scotland. This building appears to be based on le Roy's 1758 drawings of the Prophylea at Athens. See Julien-David le Roy, *Les Ruines des plus beaux monuments de la Grèce* (Paris: H. L. Guerin & L. F. Delatour, 1758).

38 Stuart and Revett, *The Antiquities of Athens*. This structure had already been associated with the symbolism of death and memorial from the mid eighteenth century.

39 Which by this point was the astronomical observatory, the monument to Prof. John Playfair, and the twelve columns of the national monument.

40 This is in spite of Hamilton having designed another monument to Robert Burns in Alloway (Plate 5.11) which was an (almost) identical copy of Stuart and Revett's drawings of the Greek structure. An early watercolour of the Edinburgh monument suggests that the Alloway monument may well have been influential in the final design, as despite many similarities between the watercolour and the built structure, this image shows that Hamilton's earlier vision for the Edinburgh monument did not replicate the Lysicrates cupola in such intricate detail as is found in the final design. In addition, Hamilton's earlier design for the columns include Ionic, rather than Corinthian capitals, which are found on the Lysicrates and Alloway monuments. See Plate 5.12, Thomas Hamilton, *Design for Burns Monument on Calton Hill*, D2533, National Gallery of Scotland.

41 For a full analysis of the architectural design and imagery found on this structure, see K. Carter McKee, 'Monument to the Memory of Robert Burns on Calton Hill, Edinburgh', *Architectural Heritage* 4 (2013): 21-39.

42 Edinburgh Town Council Minutes, 6 July 1831, SL1/1/210.

43 This preference for a change in site went unheeded and the original site as designated by the town council in 1817 was used for the Edinburgh monument.

44 The view of which is found in numerous late eighteenth- and early nineteenth- century landscapes. For an excellent example, see this late eighteenth-century painting by an unknown French artist in the National Gallery in London. http://www.nationalgallery.org.uk/paintings/french-the-temple-of-the-sibyl-at-tivoli-seen-from-the-gorge. Hamilton recreated the solid drum inside the colonnade of the monument, as is found at Tivoli, which is in comparison to the open colonnade of the Lysicrates monument. In addition, he ensured that the ground underneath the monument was deliberately built up so that it sat on a raised platform, which would give a greater illusion of a 'rocky precipice', as found at Tivoli.

45 This was placed on top of Craig's (uncompleted) octagonal observatory on the summit of Calton Hill.

46 'One such building, placed on Calton-hill might lead to the erection of others, until it should become the acropolis of the Northern Athens, and Edinburgh be called the city of temples and taste.' 'Festival in Commemoration of Robert Burns': iii-iv.

47 G. M. Kemp's view of Calton Hill, showing the completed National Monument, depicts this perfectly. See Plate 36.13.

48 Shepherd and Britton, *Modern Athens*.

49 J. E. Cookson, 'The Edinburgh and Glasgow Duke of Wellington Statues: Early Nineteenth-Century Unionist Nationalism as a Tory Project', *Scottish Historical Review* 83, 1, no. 215 (2004): 23-40.

50 Joseph Noel Paton, *National Memorial of the War of Independence under Wallace and Bruce and of its Results in the Union of England and Scotland, to be Erected in the Scottish Metropolis* (Edinburgh, 1859).

51 These are called this in Walker, 'National Romanticism and the Architecture of the City'.

52 'In other words, by assuming the identity of Athens, the implication was that Edinburgh and Scotland were superior to London and England. Scottish Achievements in the Enlightenment period gave the city the right to claim that it was now the civilizing influence within Great Britain and the empire . . . although Edinburgh was still defining itself in relation to London, it was claiming an identity that in some ways usurped the role of the capital' (Lowrey, 'From Caesarea to Athens': 150).

53 An attempt to rebrand the national monument along this idea of the 'Scottish romantic' can be identified in a souvenir book of Holyrood Abbey of 1849, which displays images of the abbey ruins, Mary, Queen of Scots, John Knox, Robert the Bruce and the Old Town, alongside G. M. Kemp's drawing of the completed national monument from the 1830s.

54 Yarrington also discussed this with reference to the Nelson monuments that were being erected throughout the country during this period. 'Public awareness and appreciation of patriotic heroism was manifested on a local, rather than national level, provincial monuments to national heroes with strong local connections being more successful overall than large national monuments raised in London. Whilst it was possible to stimulate provincial pride with suggestions of rivalry between cities or counties using public monuments as symbols of civic achievement, it was difficult to promote similar feelings nationally. Evidence of this was provided during the war years by Nelson Monuments. Whilst Birmingham, Dublin, Edinburgh, Glasgow, Liverpool and Portsmouth all successfully raised monuments to the hero in public places, no national monument was raised by public subscription in the capital' (Yarrington, 'The Commemoration of the Hero 1800–1864: 327).

55 'Not surprisingly, then, a sequence of highly visible monuments celebrating Dundas, Nelson and Burns, plus the national monument or 'Parthenon' remembering those who had fallen in the Napoleonic campaigns - the cult of the heroic dead—were neo-classical in form, as were sculptures of Pitt and George IV. Hellenic ascendancy dominated architectural design in Edinburgh until the 1840s. However, from the 1830s the unitary British state ceded additional powers to town councils and the local bourgeoisie to such an extent that Westminster was not the prime focus of the 'governing' civil society. The degree of local autonomy exercised by the Edinburgh bourgeoisie over the running of institutions in part explains the resurgence of a national identity in the built environment of the Scottish Capital. Empowered by Westminster and enshrined by statue, a Scottish identity flourished not in opposition to but in association with the British state' (Rodger, *The Transformation of Edinburgh*: 471–2).

56 This is considered in Johnny Rodger's paper on the Burns monument, where he explains this as 'the presentation of Scottish "history" as embodied in a selective series of emotional and sectarian heroes like Robert the Bruce, Mary Queen of Scots, John Knox, William Wallace, Charles Edward Stuart, Robert Burns and . . . Walter Scott'. Johnny Rodger and Gerard Carruthers, *Fickle Man: Robert Burns in the 21st Century* (Dingwall: Sandstone, 2009): 68.

57 Walker, 'National Romanticism and the Architecture of the City'.

58 Mitchell, *Edinburgh Monumental Inscriptions*, Turnbull, *The Edinburgh Graveyard Guide*.

59 The first interments in New Calton were the numerous bodies brought from the displaced part of the Old Calton burial ground and reinterred in new plots in the new burial ground. These are now found in the northern part of the site, near the entrance. Hence there are several stones which pre-date the existence of this site. See Peter McGowan Associates, '064 New Calton Burial Ground', in *Edinburgh: Survey of Gardens and Designed Landscapes* (Edinburgh: City of Edinburgh Council, 2007). A description and photographs of one of those from the eighteenth century can be found in Betty Willsher, 'Midlothian and Edinburgh' in *Survey of Scottish Gravestones* (National Monuments Record for Scotland, c. 1990s?).

60 Minutes of the Incorporated Trades of Calton, 1 February 1816, SL110/1/6, Edinburgh City Archives. Monuments were erected within Old Calton burial ground even after New Calton was opened. This includes the 1844 monument to political martyrs and the emancipation monument of 1893. See Tyrrell and Davis, 'Bearding the Tories' and *The Lincoln Monument in Memory of the Scottish-American Soldiers* (Edinburgh: William Blackwood and Sons, 1893).

61 See Part 1. 'We must look to the extension of the line of Princes Street to the Calton Hill . . . It unfortunately happens, however, that if carried in a direct line it must pass through the Calton Burying Ground. There was time indeed, when, without encroachment upon the Burying Ground, the road could have been made with a curve to the southward of Hume the historian's tomb; but of late years the walls of the burying ground have been extended to the verge of precipitous rocks.' Taken from Stevenson's report to Heriot's Hospital in D. Stevenson, *Life of Robert Stevenson*: 78.

62 Gifford et al., *Edinburgh*: 438

63 Edinburgh Town Council Minutes, 20 August 1817, SL1/1/174.

64 Boyle et al., *Ruins and Remains*: 66, Peter McGowan Associates, '064 New Calton Burial Ground': 4.

65 James Stevens Curl, 'John Claudius Loudon and the Garden Cemetery Movement', *Garden History* 11, no. 2 (1983): 133–56.

66 Ibid.

67 Kirsten Carter McKee, 'The Development of the Monument and the Memorial Landscape in Scotland', conference paper delivered at the 'Death in Scotland' conference, Edinburgh, January 2014.

68 Colvin, *A Biographical Dictionary of British Architects 1600–1840*: 169. This is also shown in both the map-based evidence and from plans currently held in the National Monuments Record of Scotland that date to this period. The graveyard was developed during this period from north to south, and was laid out in a series of vaults that stepped down from the hill in a manner that distorts the size and number of graves when viewed from the entrance. This is due to the steep sloping ground on which the burial ground was created. See Gifford et al., *Edinburgh*: 438 and William Pitcairn Anderson, *Silences that Speak. Records of Edinburgh's Ancient Churches and Burial Grounds, with Biographical Sketches of the Notables who Rest there* (Edinburgh: Alexander Brunton, 1931): 616.

69 See John Claudius Loudon, 'The Principles of Landscape-Gardening and of Landscape-Architecture Applied to the Laying out of Public Cemeteries and the Improvement of Churchyards; Including Observations on the Working and General Management of Cemeteries and Burial-Grounds', *The Gardeners Magazine and Register of Rural and Domestic Improvement*, 1843.

70 It is not well known that Playfair also laid out the area of Princes Street Gardens to the east of the Mound from 1826, including the construction of the banked terraces on which the Scott monument was built in 1844. In 1828 he also laid out the gardens on the other side of the Mound in collaboration with 'William Gilpin' (William Sawrey Gilpin, who was nephew to Rev. William Gilpin, Author of *Observations over the River Wye*), and Thomas Hamilton.

71 'The Highlandization of Scottish culture and the celebration of rural values was largely a middle class response to the demand for nostalgia in an increasingly urbanised and industrialised society.' Richard J. Finlay, 'Caledonia or North Britain?', in Dauvit Broun, Richard J. Finlay and Michael Lynch (eds), *Image and Identity: The Making and Re-Making of Scotland through the Ages* (Edinburgh: John Donald, 1998): 153.

PART 3

Introduction

1 Morris and Morton, 'The Re-Making of Scotland: A Nation within a Nation, 1850–1920': 14.

2 Despite discussions on public architecture in the early nineteenth century setting out the purpose of architecture being for the greater good of society. In particular Wood's literature. See Part 2 for further discussion on this.

Chapter 6

1 'Obituary—Mr Robert Forrest, Sculptor', *The Gentleman's Magazine*, March 1853: 324.

2 Melville was cited by Forrest as 'one of the most illustrious names in Scottish, or any other history'. Joe Rock, 'Robert Forrest (1789–1852) and his Exhibition on the Calton Hill', *Book of the Old Edinburgh Club* 7 (2008): 127–38.

3 These were: the Duke of Wellington, the Duke of Marlborough, Mary, Queen of Scots with Lord Herries, and Robert the Bruce and the Monk of Baston. See Anon., 'Equestrian Statues', *Scotsman*, 28 July 1832: 1.

4 Robert Forrest, 'Descriptive Catalogue of Statuary from the Chisel of Mr Robert Forrest' (Edinburgh: Thomas Allan & Co., 1835): 4.

5 Bruce was depicted in Roman costume and standing next to his horse after the battle of Bannockburn (Plate 6.1). The Duke of Marlborough '[T]he Pillar of our nation in the glorious reign of Queen Anne—the chief support and grand alliance formed to check the formidable power and encroachments of the house of Bourbon' was also depicted in classical dress. The other two statues were clothed with more contemporaneous societal associations. The Duke of Wellington (Plate 6.2) casually leans against his horse in his field-marshal uniform as though he is addressing his troops after the Battle of Waterloo. This statue was to be viewed as part of a pair with the statue of Marlborough, as Wellington was also considered to have 'retrieved . . . the ancient honour and glory of the English nation'. The statue

of Mary, Queen of Scots is noted in at least three contemporaneous texts as being previously paid compliment by Sir Walter Scott—no doubt providing the sculptor with a cultural and national seal of approval. Forrest, 'Catalogue of Statuary' and Anon., 'The Lanarkshire Sculptor', *Chambers Journal* 45, 8 December 1832: 357-8:
http://books.google.co.uk/
books?id=XWAiAQAAMAAJ&lpg=PA358&ots=
VJcAiVh4lQ&dq=robert%20the%20bruce%20and%20
the%20monk%20of%20baston&pg= PA358#v=onepage
&q&f=false
Forrest, 'Descriptive Catalogue of Statuary', Robert Forrest, *Descriptive Account of the Exhibition of Statuary, National Monument, Calton Hill, Edinburgh, by Robert Forrest, Sculptor* ([Edinburgh: s.n.], 1846), Robert Forrest, *Forrest's Statuary, within Area of National Monument, Calton Hill, Edinburgh . . . Catalogue of Statues* ([Edinburgh?, 1850).

6 Forrest, *Descriptive Account of the Exhibition of Statuary*.

7 Anon., 'Forrest's Statuary—Calton Hill', *Scotsman*, 15 September 1832.

8 'Lord Provost of Ed. Suggests Ass should instruct Mr Forrest to discontinue engaging people for the purpose of soliciting persons walking on Calton Hill to visit his exhibition—this system had been a frequent subject of complaint and the Magistrates were determined to suppress it.' Minutes of the National Monument Committee, 20 April 1844, SL103/1/1, Edinburgh City Archives: 502.

9 'At yesterdays meeting of Edinburgh Town Council notice was given of a motion to the effect that, as there was little likelihood of the National Monument on the Calton Hill being soon completed, an effort should be made to get the unseemly wooden erection surrounding it removed, and the ground railed in and laid out in a way becoming to the natural beauty of the town.' Anon., 'The National Monument', *Scotsman*, 18 July 1849.

10 According to Joe Rock, Forrest's statuary was 'loathed by the art critics'. Rock, 'Robert Forrest': 136.

11 'Urban life in Scotland was governed by its own elites, out with central state administration and out with central state created Boards of Control and other Bureaucracies.' Graeme Morton, *Unionist Nationalism: Governing Urban Scotland, 1830–1860* (East Linton: Tuckwell, 1999): 46, 189.

12 Morton uses contemporaneous almanacs and Post Office directories to explore the different groupings of these Edinburgh organisations to get to grips with the role of 'public life' in nineteenth-century Scotland. Ibid.: Ch. 4.

13 Ibid.

14 In particular, the decisions around the development of the third New Town and the docks at Leith made during this period resulted in the city becoming bankrupt. See Thomas Hunter and Robert Porter, 'Report on the Common Good of the City of Edinburgh' (Edinburgh, 1905): 44.

15 The Committee for the National Monument project was set up by the Highland Society of Edinburgh, after the proposals for national monuments in London, Edinburgh and Dublin had been discussed by Parliament in 1816. See Part 2.

16 Stirling was Lord Provost from 1790 to 1800.

17 The Lord Provost quickly withdrew and refused to pay any more money to either the contractors or to James Craig after the university funds for the project had been depleted.

David Myles Gavine, 'Astronomy in Scotland 1745–1900'.

18 'The government confined that grant to the metropolis alone . . . pride and exultation in the very Scottish bosom that the martial spirit of their ancestors has descended untarnished to their posterity . . . rehearsal of Scottish arms . . . It appeared to the Cttee that the most proper plan for a National Monument is to erect within the Metropolis of Scotland, in a situation hereafter to be determined, a splendid edifice, destined for the purposes of Divine Worship and, at the same time, so ornamented as to commemorate the great and prominent events . . . lasting proof of national piety . . . and to serve after ages as the strongest manifestation of our sense of obligation to those whose services this Monument is intended to commemorate' (Speech by the Lord Justice Clerk, addressed to the Duke of Atholl, Minutes of the National Monument Committee, 24 February 1819, SL103/1/1, Edinburgh City Archives: 12-16).

19 John Lowrey, 'The Polis and the Portico: The High School of the Athens of the North', in 'Cast Collection Conference' (Edinburgh College of Art, 2010).

20 The Royal High School has been established in the city since the twelfth century. It has been housed in a number of locations in its 700-year lifespan. This building is now part of the University of Edinburgh and houses the Edinburgh Centre for Carbon Innovatioin (ECCI).

21 This had come about from the expansion of the city in the late eighteenth century.

22 '[T]he extent and population of Edinburgh have of late years increased very much and . . . the present high school is too remote from many parts of the city, particularly the new town . . . The facts stated furnish . . . very strong reasons for removing the present school to a more centrical situation where more ample, and all necessary accommodation, may be afforded for the suitable education of the youth from all quarters of the city': 'A Letter to the Lord Provost on the Mischievous Tendency of a Scheme for Abolishing the High School of Edinburgh', Edinburgh, 1822: 2.

23 Ibid.: 3.

24 Edinburgh Town Council minutes, SL1/1/1.

25 This was later to become Edinburgh Academy, built by William Burn. Lowrey, 'The Polis and the Portico'.

26 Leonard Horner (1785–1864) was a factory inspector, geologist and educationist who played an active part in the city's political and educational reform movements. In 1821 he founded the Edinburgh School of Arts, and in 1823 the Edinburgh Academy. http://www.oxforddnb.com/view/article/13803.

27 Only the higher echelons of Edinburgh society would be able to afford to send their sons there, in fact, the whole set-up of the establishment was geared for this elite, including the curriculum. See Committee of Contributors to the Edinburgh Academy, 'Report by Committee' (Edinburgh, April 1823) and John Campbell, 'Prospectus of an Educational Institution, on Christian Principles, Proposed to be Established in Edinburgh' (Edinburgh, 1825). Also, Lowrey, 'The Polis and the Portico'.

28 Edinburgh Town Council, 'Address from the Town Council of Edinburgh on the Subject of the New Buildings for the High School, of which the Foundation was Laid on 28th July 1825' (Edinburgh, 1825): 2.

29 'The first objection which occurs to the scheme of establish- ing another "Great School", instead of removing the high school, is, that, according to the plan proposed, the ex- pence of education at the proposed Academy will be so great as to exclude all but the very highest and most wealthy classes of community from its instructions'. 'A Let- ter to the Lord Provost on the Mischievous Tendency': 22.

30 Edinburgh Town Council Minutes, 10 July 1822, SL1/1/184.

31 David Walker (ed.), *Scottish Pioneers of the Greek Revival* ([Edinburgh]: Scottish Georgian Society, 1984): 32–3. See Part 2 notes for more information on the style of this structure.

32 'It is most desirable that no class, however humble, should be excluded entirely from the means of attaining the best education'. 'A Letter to the Lord Provost on the Mischievous Tendency': 4.

33 Lowrey, 'The Polis and the Portico'.

34 'It has been suggested . . . that the new High School shall be erected on the earthen mound, or in its vicinity, as the best situation in every point of view for accommodating the whole population of the city . . . It is disposed therefore, not as an indispensable part of any plan for removing the High School to the only open space in the midst of the city, but as a subject for consideration that the great hall or national monument be placed near the north end of the Earthen Mound, opposite to the opening of Hanover Street. In that situation it would be visible from a great many parts, and over a considerable extent of the Old and New Town: it would add another to the very few public buildings which it contains, while it would not interfere with any other view or object, but would give, in the very bosom of the city, a character more truly attic to our metropolis than any other edifice which it contains. Above all it would unite utility with ornament': 'A Letter to the Lord Provost on the Mischievous Tendency': 22, 25.

35 Ibid.: 25.

36 This was proposed to be 'adorned every side with statues and other memorials of Abercromby, of Moore, of Burns, and of other lights in the Land either gone or not yet faded away—would be an arrangement which ought to reconcile the views of all parties, and to secure for this monument the deserved and distinctive epithet of national'. Ibid.: 24.

37 The original school was a long, low building. Lancasterian School, established in 1812 by the 'Society for Promoting the Lancasterian System for the Education of the Poor', was placed on the summit of Calton Hill where it was 'the fashion to stow away anything that was too abominable to be tolerated elsewhere'. Cockburn, *Memorials of his Time*: 256–8.

38 These niches follow the wall along Regent Road, creating a walk of contemplation similar to that established by the arches of George Heriot's School on the south side of the city. For further information on the arches of George Heriot's, and their significance to students attending the school, please see Giovanna Guidicini, 'A Scottish Triumphal Path of Learning at George Heriot's Hospital, Edinburgh', *International Review of Scottish Studies* 35 (2010): 65-96.

39 Edinburgh Town Council, 'Address from the Town Council of Edinburgh on the Subject of the New Buildings for the High School': 2.

40 William Ross, in his monograph of the High School, notes that it was the salubrious air, and space available for the building and its grounds at Calton Hill in general that determined the site of the new school. William C. A. Ross, *The Royal High School* (Edinburgh, 1934): 31–2.

41 'There is in bending alignment of streets much beauty. Public buildings break upon the eye the most favourable point of view, showing at once a front and a flank.' Quoted in Fisher, 'Thomas Hamilton': 39, taken from Stark, *Report to the Right Honourable the Lord Provost*: 8.

42 Stark, *Report to the Right Honourable the Lord Provost*: 17.

43 See David Rhind, 'Documents and Correspondence Relative to Trinity College Church' (Edinburgh: Thomas Constable, 1848).

44 Alternative sites were considered within Edinburgh Castle, Holyrood Palace, Greyfriars, Princes Street Gardens, Market Street and Leith Wynd.

45 The area originally proposed for the relocation of the church at Ireland's Woodyard, located in the Waverley Val- ley close to the original site on the south side of the railway. However, once the railway company had settled the sum of £16,000 by means of compensation, the council considered such substantial investment in a development that would solely benefit the poor to be a waste of civic opportunity. Report by the Lord Provosts Committee regarding Trinity College Church, minutes of the Trinity Hospital Commit- tee, 25 January 1853, SL152, Edinburgh City Archives.

46 (1803–1876), the architect of Fettes College: http://www.scottisharchitects.org.uk/architect_full. php?id=100014.

47 According to the town council minutes, this was placed at the back of Calton Convening Rooms, at the steps leading up to Calton Hill. See Edinburgh Town Council Minutes, 25 March 1852, SL1/1/257.

48 Lord Provosts Committee, 'Report by the Lord Provosts Committee Regarding Trinity College Church', 25 January 1853, SL152.

49 The Burns' monument's removal and resurrection would have cost £1,800. Hugh Miller, 'Trinity College Church versus the Burns Monument', *The Witness*, 5 March 1856: 6.

50 Robert William Billings, *The Baronial and Ecclesiastical Antiquities of Scotland*, vol. 2 (Edinburgh: Blackwood, 1852): 170–1.

51 The same trust that incidentally owned a large proportion of the area proposed for development as the third New Town. See Part 1.

52 Billings, *The Baronial and Ecclesiastical Antiquities of Scotland*, vol. 2: 170–1.

53 Hugh Miller, 'Trinity College Church versus the Burns Monument': 10.

54 1802–1856. Geologist and writer.

55 Miller, 'Trinity College Church versus the Burns Monument'.

56 This is further supported when it is considered that the church was built to serve the parish of Greenside in 1851. Greenside parish included the affluent community living in Royal, Regent and Carlton Terraces, and their environs. This church was built by James Gillespie Graham on the north side of the hill in a much less prominent position. I am indebted to John Lowrey for bringing this to my attention.

57 This was done by Bryce, and was apparently his first foray into photography. From the date of the kirk's destruction, and the evidence found in the Hill and Adamson archive in Glasgow, it is possible that he may have been advised and assisted in this venture by Hill and Adamson: http://www.gla.ac.uk/services/specialcollections/ collectionsa-z/hilladamson/

58 The stones were carefully numbered and placed on the slope to the south of Regent Road, where they lay for twenty-five years.

59 The suitability of grandstructures for working-class neighbourhoods was considered during this period elsewhere. See Lucy MacClintock, 'Monumentality versus Suitability: Viollet-le-Duc's Saint Gimer at Carcassonne', *Journal of the Society of Architectural Historians* 40, no. 3 (1981): 218–35. In order to provide a church for the new residents of the terraces, Greenside Church was built near the foot of Royal Terrace, on the north side of the hill.

60 Shepherd and Britton, *Modern Athens!*

61 It is thought by some that the style of the building showed the renewed emphasis on the teaching of Greek in the school's curriculum. See Fisher, *Thomas Hamilton*.

62 The industrialisation of the city and the destitute air of the barefoot woman who has evidently just buried her children's father are suggestive of this.

63 'True, they have a public walk round Calton Hill, but that is merely a thing of yesterday; and though they have placed upon the top of it a monument to Lord Nelson, modelled exactly after a dutch skipper's spy-glass, or a butter-churn; an astronomical observatory, tasteful enough in its design, but not much bigger than a decent rat trap, or a twelfth cake at the Mansion House; and are to build "the national monument"; yet they have never thought of planting so much as a thistle, but have left the summit of the hill in all its native bleakness, and allowed it to be so much infested by lazy blackguards and barefooted washerwomen, as to be unsafe for respectable females even at noon day;—while after dusk this, the most fashionable promenade of the Athens, is habitually the scene of so much and so wanton vice, that instead of an ornament to the city, as it might easily be made, it is a nuisance and a disgrace.' Robert Mudie, *The Modern Athens: A Dissection and Demonstration of Men and Things in the Scotch Capital*, 2nd edn [London: Printed for Knight and Lacey, 1825]: 153.

64 Capital Collections, no. 14700. http://www.capitalcollections.org.uk/index. php?WINID=1390135469444.

65 Maria Short was granddaughter to Thomas Short (see Part 1), who had been the instigator of the original observatory on the Calton Hill in the late 1770s. This had been set up after Maria returned to Edinburgh claiming that the council had taken advantage of her grandfather's ill health and they had used 'legal trickery' that had denied her what was legally hers. Edinburgh Town Council Minutes, 8 January 1828, SL1/1/202. See also Gavine, 'Astronomy in Scotland 1745–1900'.

66 Denoted by the number of wooden huts erected adjacent to the monument (Plate 6.3).

67 This was the second camera obscura cited on Calton Hill, the first housed in the gothic tower, until 1839. For further information on the history of astronomy on the hill, see Gavine, 'Astronomy in Scotland 1745–1900'.

68 Henry Cockburn, *Journal of Henry Cockburn; Being a Continuation of the Memorials of His Time. 1831–1854* (Edinburgh: Edmonston and Douglas, 1874): 61–2.

69 Cockburn 'assailed the council, and excited the press, and agitated in all quarters', until Short's grant was rescinded. But this was reversed shortly after, and the camera obscura was placed adjacent to Forrest's exhibition in a 'less offensive position'. The Astronomical Institution, alarmed that 'a person' had been allowed to erect a kind of observatory of boards within sight of their own, had suggested to the provost an alternative site, a piece of waste ground originally intended for a debtors jail' (Edinburgh Astronomical Institution, Minute Book 1, Royal Observatory, Edinburgh).

70 In 1792, James Douglas Short failed to negotiate terms with the council that would have resulted in the octagonal observatory being available for use in academic teaching (as had originally been envisioned,) after the council intimated that they wanted nothing more to do with the building, despite the majority of the funds for the structure coming from the university, and the council's initial sanctioning of the project as a public work. James Douglas was therefore left with no choice but to go to sea to recoup some of the costs of completing the structure, in addition to providing a popular observatory for public viewings in order to pay for its upkeep. For more detail on this, see David Myles Gavine, 'Astronomy in Scotland 1745–1900', Bryden, 'The Edinburgh Observatory 1736–1811' and Bryden, 'James Craig's Original Design for the Observatory'.

71 David Gavine, 'The Calton Hill Observatories', *Journal of the Astronomical Society of Edinburgh* 3 (October 1981): v.

72 In 1822, the building was awarded the title of Royal Observatory by George IV during his visit to Edinburgh.

73 Gavine, 'Astronomy in Scotland 1745–1900': 344. This was sold in 1848 by auction. Royal Observatory (Herstmonceux) Airy Ms Class L Shelf 4: Printed sale catalogue of Tait and Nisbet, 19 June 1848, Edinburgh.

74 'the inscriptionless Stewart monument, the purpose of which is now made known only by tradition . . . is learnt by a stranger only by the inquiry of the first ragged urchin he meets with on the Calton' (Letter from Lord Palmerston to Lord Rutherford, 3rd Viscount Palmerston, 12 December 1853, MS 9717, f. 153. National Library of Scotland, Edinburgh). Henry Cockburn, who was an ardent supporter of placing the statue of Burns in one of the purpose-built halls of learning already found in Edinburgh, instead suggested that the monies could be put towards a similar project, but for a different aim: '[d]isposing of the statue by placing it in some 'worthy large place' such as the college library, the new library begun for the faculty of advocates, in the exhibition room of the royal institution, in the circular dome of register house . . . Disposing of the statue in this way leaves you, I understand some hundred pounds over—a strong additional recommendation; for, besides the statue, sacred to the rich, it enables you to erect some architectural edifice, sacred to his memory with the poor.' Hadden, *George Thomson the Friend of Burns*: 77–8.

75 Short's observatory was also forcibly removed from Calton Hill by the council in the 1850s. In 1854 Short announced

that she would erect another public observatory on Castle Hill. This continued as Short's Observatory for a number of years and was bought by Patrick Geddes in 1892 for conversion to an outlook tower. Edinburgh Town Council Minutes, 8 January SL1/1/253, 19 February SL1/1/253, 11 June SL1/1/254, 30 July SL1/1/254, 27 September 1850 SL1/1/254 and 25 March 1851 SL1/1/255.

76 This was set up in 1850 by the Dean of Guild in Edinburgh. See Edinburgh City Archives for further information on the records of the Dean of Guild.

77 Capital Collections, no. 11677: http://www.capitalcollections.org.uk/index. php?WINID=1390135469444.

78 Completed in 1866: http://www.gla.ac.uk/services/specialcollections/ collectionsa-z/hilladamson/disruptionpicture/.

79 Dana MacFarlane, 'The Fishwives of Newhaven', 'The National Galleries of Scotland Research Conference' (Edinburgh, 2013), Sara Stevenson et al., *Hill and Adamson's the Fishermen and Women of the Firth of Forth* (Edinburgh: Scottish National Portrait Gallery, 1991).

80 http://www.gla.ac.uk/services/specialcollections/ collectionsa-z/hilladamson/.

81 Stevenson et al., *Hill and Adamson's the Fishermen and Women of the Firth of Forth.*

Chapter 7

1 I. Levitt, 'Scottish Sentiment, Administrative Devolution and Westminster, 1885–1964', in Michael Lynch (ed.), *Scotland, 1850–1979: Society, Politics and the Union* (London: The Historical Association, 1993): 35–42. Henry J. Littlejohn, 'Report on the Sanitary Condition of the City of Edinburgh' (Edinburgh, 1863). The reports by Littlejohn were commissioned as a result of the concerns risen by these boards. See also Henry J. Littlejohn, 'Report on the City Cemeteries' (Edinburgh, 1883).

2 R. J. Finlay, 'Scottish Nationalism and Scottish Politics 1900–1979', in Michael Lynch (ed.), *Scotland, 1850–1979: Society, Politics and the Union* (London: The Historical Association, 1993): 20.

3 'Letter and Sketch by Mr Fairholm for the Completion of the National Monument, included in Letter from Mr Skene of Rubislaw to Mr Linning', Minutes of the National Monument Committee, 25 November 1837, SL103/2/403.

4 'We have seen a very imposing drawing by Mr James Raeburn, architect of this city, illustrating a plan for placing the Wellington Testimonial on the Calton Hill . . . The expense of the plan, according to Mr Raeburn's estimate, would be about £7000—independent of the statue, and whatever differences may exist with regard to his idea as a matter of taste, the expedience of completing in some shape or form a building which was intended to commemorate the final victory of the great Duke will not be disputed. The unfinished state of the National Monument has long been a subject of regret and the prospect of its completion according to the original design appears to be exceedingly remote . . . the beautiful columns are at once an ornament and a reproach to our city' (Anon., *Edinburgh Advertiser*, 8 December 1840).

5 Forrest, 'Descriptive Catalogue of Statuary from the Chisel of Mr Robert Forrest' (Edinburgh: Thomas Allan & Co.): 5

and Anon., *Chambers Journal* 45, 8 December 1832: 358 fn. http://books.google.co.uk/books?id= XWAiAQAAMAAJ&lpg= PA358&ots=VJcAi Vh4lQ&dq=robert%20the%20bruce%20and%20the%20 monk%20of%20baston&pg=PA358 #v=onepage&q&f=false.

6 It is notable that in proposing a porch to 'finish the west end of the National Monument', Raeburn leaves open the possibility of the rest of the structure being erected in the future.

7 In fact, the Scott memorial itself perpetuated the idea of the author as Shakespeare's 'wee brother' in its inscription. See Morris and Morton, 'The Re-Making of Scotland': 17.

8 One key example of this is the Scottish National Portrait Gallery by Sir Robert Rowand Anderson, opened in 1889.

9 See the previous section covering 'imperial development' in the early nineteenth -century, which had, by mid century, become more concerned with transport and communication networks within the British Isles. Personal communication, Dr Alex Bremner, Department of Architectural History, University of Edinburgh.

10 Minutes of the National Monument Committee, 6 April 1844, SL103/1/, Edinburgh City Archives: 499–500.

11 Anno 3 George IV c.100, 'An Act to Incorporate the Contributors for the Erection of a National Monument in Scotland to Commemorate the Naval and Military Victories Obtained during the Late War' (1822).

12 Secretary to the National Monument Committee after Michael Linning.

13 'But besides giving a powerful impulse to architecture and the sister arts of sculpture and painting, its completion, by commemorating the great men and warlike achievements of Scotland, will effect another national and most important object,—it will resuscitate and keep alive that patriotic independence and martial spirit for which our countrymen were so distinguished, when Scotland was an independent kingdom, but which is apt to die away when united to a larger and richer Kingdom like England'. George Cleghorn and Architectural Institute of Scotland, 'Essay on the National Monument of Scotland' ([Edinburgh?]: Architectural Institute of Scotland, 1852): 112.

14 The obelisk to the Scottish political martyrs of 1794 (Plate 6.20), designed by Thomas Hamilton and placed in the Old Calton burial ground, was proposed in late 1837 by Joseph Hume and William Tait. This was considered to have been sited on the hill particularly to loom over the skyline of 'tyrrany and corruption' identified in the monuments to Pitt, Melville and George IV. For further discussion on this in this context, see Tyrrell and Davis, 'Bearding the Tories: The Commemoration of the Scottish Political Martyrs of 1793–94'.

15 The Tory-focused *Blackwood's Magazine* had encouraged support for the development of Calton Hill as a national 'Valhalla' during the 1820s.

16 This was actually designed in 1892 by Walter Wood Robertson, then architect for HM Office of Works, Edinburgh. http://www.scottisharchitects.org.uk/architect_full. php?id=201227.

17 The proposed new North British Hotel has some elements of French architecture in the Renaissance style, with

mansard roofs on each corner. John Dick Peddie *Suggestions for the Improvement of Edinburgh* (ink and watercolour, c. 1870) Royal Scottish Academy collection.

18 A civic association set up in memory of Lord Cockburn's critique of the city. See Cockburn Association and William Mitchell, *The Cockburn Association: A Short Account of its Objects and its Work, 1875 to 1897* (Edinburgh, 1897).

19 William Mitchell, *The National Monument to be Completed for the Scottish National Gallery on the Model of the Parthenon at Athens: An Appeal to the Scottish People* (London: Adam and Charles Black, 1906).

20 'The idea of the Monument being at last completed . . . evoked an enthusiastic response by many men of taste in the sister country. One of them . . . predicted that the reproduction of the Parthenon might make the school of sculpture'. William Mitchell, *The National Monument to be Completed for the Scottish National Gallery on the Model of the Parthenon at Athens: An Appeal to the Scottish People* (London: A. and C. Black, 1907): 36.

21 http://www.legislation.gov.uk/ukpga/Edw7/6/50/contents.

22 Mitchell, *The National Monument*, 1907.

23 This is depicted in the perspective in drawing VII of Mitchell's revised 1907 proposals.

24 William Mitchell and C. I. Lacock, *A New National Patriotic Poem or Song Entitled 'The Royal Standard of Our Queen'* (London, 1900). William Mitchell, *Queen Victoria and the Scottish Monument* (London, 1911).

25 Graeme Morton, 'Scotland's Missing Nationalism', in Dauvit Broun, Richard J. Finlay, and Michael Lynch (eds), *Image and Identity: The Making and Re-Making of Scotland Through the Ages* (Edinburgh: John Donald, 1998): 160.

26 Ibid.: 163.

27 'The key components of British identity in Scotland had a distinctive tartan complexion. Monarchism was associated with the tartan clad George IV or the Balmoralised Queen Victoria'. Finlay, 'Caledonia or North Britain?': 153.

28 Frank Mears and Ramsay Traquair, 'Public Monuments, Edinburgh', *The Blue Blanket* 1 (January 1912): 68-80.

29 Ibid.: 69.

30 Graeme A. S. Purves, 'The Life and Work of Sir Frank Mears: Planning with a Cultural Perspective' (Edinburgh: Heriot-Watt University, 1987): 268–70.

31 Architects who were invited to submit proposals were: Sir Robert Lorimer, A.N. Paterson, A. Marshall Mackenzie, John Kinross, G.W. Browne and Robert Rowand Anderson. Duncan Macmillan and Antonia Reeve, 'Scotland's Shrine: The Scottish National War Memorial' (Lund Humphries, 2014) 25.

32 Ibid. 25

33 This was exhibited at the RSA in 1918. Anon, 'The Royal Scottish Academy', *Builder*, 5 July 1918.

34 Ann Petrie, 'Scottish Culture and the First World War, 1914–1939' (Dundee: University of Dundee, 2006).

35 'A dinner was held to discuss the matter at the invitation of Ewart in 1917.' Katharine Marjory Murray, *Working Partnership. Being the Lives of John George, 8th Duke of Atholl . . . and of his Wife Katharine Marjory Ramsay* (London: A. Barker, 1958): 106–7.

36 For example, the Duke of Atholl, on hearing that a war memorial to be erected in London could house Highland and other Scottish regiments' trophies he 'wrote to Sir Alfred Mond that he could talk about his own nation, but that he had no right to speak for the Scottish nation, and that if the Scottish nation wanted their own memorial, they would put it up with their own hands, in their own country, and with their own money'. *Scotsman,* 19 January 1934.

37 By the early twentieth century, '[Lorimer] . . . had established his reputation as an imaginative interpreter of Scottish styles'. Duncan Macmillan and Antonia Reeve, 'Scotland's Shrine: The Scottish National War Memorial' (London: Lund Humphries): 25.

38 'Lorimer's original designs . . . proposed in 1918 . . . involved the demolition of the "Billings Building". This was heavily critiqued after the Ancient Monuments Board requested a temporary full sized model at the castle of wooden poles and canvas, which was bombasted in the *Scotsman*. Lorimer redesigned the building four times, but it was his second design that was adopted.' Petrie, 'Scottish Culture': 176 fn.

39 Macmillan and Reeve, 'Scotland's Shrine': 66.

40 Petrie, 'Scottish Culture': 219.

41 This is carved around the entranceway to the shrine, and represents the contribution to the British Empire by the Scottish diaspora. See Jenny Macleod, 'By Scottish Hands, with Scottish Money, on Scottish Soil: The Scottish National War Memorial and National Identity', *Journal of British Studies* 49, no. 1, Scotland special issue (2010): 89.

42 Petrie, 'Scottish Culture': 220.

43 Ian Hay, *Their Name Liveth: The Book of the Scottish National War Memorial* (London: J. Lane, The Bodley Head, 1931): 13.

44 'The Glasgow and Edinburgh difficulty is fully appreciated by me, but I think if they will meet on any common ground, it will be that Edinburgh Castle is National property, and not Edinburgh property. Glasgow will never give a penny to help on a thing like the Calton Hill. With all due respect, I think, and hope, that I am not over sanguine in this matter, and I am not altogether without having made some careful enquiries.' Letter from the Duke of Atholl to Lord Rosebery, 16 August 1917, 980, Bundle 162, Blair Castle Archive, National Archives, Kew, London. See also Murray, *Working Partnership*: 106–7.

45 There had been some interest in Scotland about the First Irish Home Rule Bill in the mid-1880s, but that had been to do with the economic implications to the Clyde as an imperial port. See William Miller, 'Politics in the Scottish City', in George Gordon (ed.), *Perspectives of the Scottish City* ([Aberdeen]: Aberdeen University Press, 1985): 187.

46 Levitt, 'Scottish Sentiment'. The parochial boards were set up to focus on the administration of local services related to the Poor Law reform of 1845. This allowed local taxes to be raised to cover the costs of Poor Relief, rather than the poor being placed in the workhouse. In Edinburgh, the boards also commissioned reports on issues that directly affected those in poverty, such as overcrowding. See fn 543.

47 'Scotland's [cultural] nationalism was sustained primarily through civil society, it was not state created - therefore, as long as civil society was sustained and managed the everyday affairs, then no demand for a Scottish parliament was made'. Morton, 'Scotland's Missing Nationalism': 167.

48 A post which had been abolished in the British government after the Jacobite rebellion in 1746.

49 Finlay, 'Scottish Nationalism': 20.

50 Levitt, 'Scottish Sentiment'.
51 Brad Beaven, *Visions of Empire: Patriotism, Popular Culture and the City, 1870–1939* (Manchester: Manchester University Press, 2012).
52 Hay, *Their Name Liveth*: 5–6.
53 'The first war was scarcely over before the first of nine Nationalist bills or motions to be placed before the commons within the next eight years was presented. Inspired by the notion of National Independence within a wider British Empire, such as was being discussed for Ireland and India, the proposal reflected the status of Scotland at the time, which, with its own partial administration and legal system, was that of a Crown colony. Of the early bills, all but one of the Scots MPs voting were in favour, and the concept of "Scottish national self-determination" was supported by Lords Alness, and Shelbourne, Austen Chamberlain and the Duke of Montrose' (McKean, *The Scottish Thirties*: 15).
54 Finlay, 'Scottish Nationalism and Scottish Politics 1900–1979': 20.
55 http://hansard.millbanksystems.com/bills/government-of-scotland-bill.
56 http://hansard.millbanksystems.com/commons/1913/may/30/government-of-scotland-bill.
57 1st Baron Tweedsmuir (1875–1940), Scottish novelist, historian and unionist-nationalist politician.
58 I. Levitt (ed.), *The Scottish Office: Depression and Reconstruction, 1919–1959*, vol. 5, Scottish History Society (Edinburgh: Pillans & Wilson, 1992): 6.
59 Charles McKean, *Edinburgh: Portrait of a City* (London: Century, 1991): 214.
60 David Walker, *St Andrew's House: An Edinburgh Controversy, 1912–1939* (Edinburgh: Historic Buildings and Monuments, Development Department for the Secretary of State for Scotland, 1989).
61 First published in the *Scotsman,* 24 July 1930. Image taken from McKean, *The Scottish Thirties*: 16.
62 'The issue welded together disparate people who would never have supported the Scottish Renaissance, nationalism, or even the revivification of Edinburgh. A Scottish National Committee, led by the Moderator of the General Assembly of the Church of Scotland, with the Dukes of Atholl and Montrose, Lord Elphinstone, the Marquess of Aberdeen, and half of the Scottish nobility and gentry with industrial magnates, institutions, associations, Provosts and writers in tow, raised the fiery cross. Driven by invisible forces, the natives of Edinburgh disdained to accept the desecration of Calton Hill by bureaucratic offices' (McKean, *Edinburgh: Portrait of a City*: 214).
63 Personal communication, Charles McKean.
64 Walker, *St Andrew's House*: 52.
65 This may have also been influenced by Francis Lorne, who was in the Burnet, Tait and Lorne practice and was American.
66 http://www.scottisharchitects.org.uk/architect_full.php?id=200729
67 Darney sandstone is favoured in Edinburgh because of its pale colour, quartz-rich nature and fine-grained texture, as it is considered a good match for the Craigleith stone from which much of Edinburgh was built, but which is no longer available. Darney stone was used in the construction of the Usher Hall (1910–14) and the City Chambers extension (1930–4) in Cockburn Street. http://geoscenic.bgs.ac.uk/asset-bank/action/viewAsset;jsessionid=D17C45A3BA940B19D10FD6E7071624A4?id=97034&index=365&total=64262&collection=Unsorted%20Images&categoryId=2&categoryTypeId=1&filterId=0&sortAttributeId=1025&sortDescending=true&movedBr=null
68 Such as the thistle decoration flanking the bronze relief doors by Walter Gilbert; the royal arms on top of the doors by Alexander Carrick; the lion and unicorn reliefs by Phyllis Bone. Gifford et al., *Edinburgh*: 441.
69 The association of the structure with Calton Hill and government administration has also been discussed in Dawn Caswell, 'The Economy of Style: Thomas S. Tait and the Interior of St Andrews House', *Architectural History* 10, no. 1 (1999): 74–89.
70 McKean, *Edinburgh: Portrait of a City*: 214.
71 Gifford et al., *Edinburgh*.
72 McKean, *Edinburgh: Portrait of a City*: 214–15.
73 The Bridewell had been demolished in 1881.

Chapter 8

1   Roger G. Kennedy and John M. Hall, *Greek Revival America* (New York: Stewart, Tabori & Chang, 1989): 5.
2   This explained that the twelve pillars should be swept away and a completely new establishment housing a Scottish national military and naval museum and library should be placed on the site instead. Anon., *Scotsman,* 26 December 1944.
3   The 1949 Festival of Britain proposals, although keeping the twelve columns of the national monument, described an area for leisure and pleasure, to be created with modern materials and to a simple yet modern design.
4   Finlay, 'Scottish Nationalism and Scottish Politics 1900–1979': 23.
5   Whiteford's artworks rendered the neoclassical British structures 'redundant', as their over-scaled size dominated the site. Brettle's adaptation of the national monument took focus away from the neoclassical elements and instead emphasised the space in between the dominant masculine columns.
6   Jane Brettle's work also considered the relationship between the classical structures on Calton Hill and gender, which could be considered as similar to the influence that the hill had on Hill and Adamson, and their subsequent work with the Newhaven fishwives discussed in Chapter 6. See David Ward, 'Jane Brettle's Allegorical Blueprint', *Untitled: A Review of Contemporary Art,* no. 10 (1996): 7–8.
7   House of Commons Debates, 27 April 1977 http://www.theyworkforyou.com/debates/?id=1977-04-27a.1204.3#g1205.2.
8   Further information on this can be found at http://www.scottishpoliticalarchive.org.uk/wb/pages/exhibition.php.
9   http://www.holyroodinquiry.org/FINAL_report/chapter%2003.pdf: 45.
10 Alan Balfour, *Creating a Scottish Parliament* (Edinburgh, StudioLR, 2004): 7.

Bibliography

ARCHIVAL

Bodleian Library Archives,
University of Oxford
Gough Collection: Mss. Gough, Scotland: 182.

Centre for Special Collections,
University of Edinburgh
Playfair Drawings Collection.
Robert Barker, *Edinburgh from the Calton Hill*, 1792.

Edinburgh City Archives
Edinburgh Town Council Minutes, SL1.
Subject Lists (SL).
Handlist of Historical Records.
Macleod Bundles.
Minutes of the Committee 16 July 1814 to 31 Aug 1820—Discussion regarding the new gaol to go in King George IV Act to alter and amend 53, 54, 56 Geo.3., December 1814, Shelf 32u 9/41, Historical Hand List.
Minutes of the Committee for Feuing Calton Hill Grounds & Co., Shelf 32 9/41, Historical Hand List.
Minutes of the Incorporated Trades of Calton, SL110.
Minutes of the National Monument Committee, SL103.
Minutes of the Nelson Pillar Committee, 9.41 62u, Historical Hand List.
Minutes of the Trinity Hospital Committee, SL152.
'Petition of Thomas Short, Optician of Edinburgh for a Feu of Half an Acre of Ground on Top of Calton Hill to Build an Observatory. With Plan of the Ground Etc.', 1 January 1776, D015R, Macleod Bundles. Plan of half the acre of ground at the top of Calton Hill. Site of the Observatory. John Laurie, 20 April 1776, Miscellaneous Items and Deposits, SL12.
'Proceedings relative to the Erection of a Monument to the Late John Playfair, Esq., Professor of Natural Philosophy in the University of Edinburgh', 26 December 1820, MYBN 274A Box 4/1-4/29, Ref 4/17, Handlist of Historical Records.
Plan of half the acre of ground at the top of Calton Hill—site of the Observatory—John Laurie, 20 April 1776, D0105R, Macleod Bundles, 'Moses'.

Articles and Conditions of Roup [Auction/Sale] for a Tack [Lease] of the Lands of Calton Hill and of Green Gate Site, Belonging to the Town. 29 October 1756, 'Moses'.

National Archives, Kew, London
Letter from the Duke of Atholl to Lord Rosebery, 16 August 1917, 980, Bundle 162, Blair Castle Archive.

National Archives of Scotland, Edinburgh
Board of Manufactures. General and Manufacturing Records, NG1/2.
Letter from Mrs Stewart to the Marquess of Lothian, 1 January 1830, GD 40/9-321, Lothian Muniments.

National Library of Scotland, Edinburgh
Letter from Lord Elgin to Charles Robert Cockerell, July 1822, MS 638.
Letter from Lord Palmerston to Lord Rutherford, 3rd Viscount Palmerston, 12 December 1853, MS 9717, f. 153.
Letter from Mrs Stewart to Lord Minto, 19 July 1828, MS 11798, f. 176.
Letter from Thomas Thomson to 2nd Earl of Minto, 5 December 1828, MS 11811, f. 91.

Private Collection
Paterson Papers, courtesy of Dr Allen Simpson.

Royal Institute of British Architects Archives, Victoria and Albert Museum, London
Diary of Charles Robert Cockerell, Monday 22 July 1822, COC/9/3 1822.

Royal Observatory, Edinburgh
Edinburgh Astronomical Institution, Minute Book 1.

Sir John Soane's Museum, London
Robert Adam, *Bridge over (?) from Princes Street at (?) Calton Hill Edinburgh*, undated, c. 1791, vol. 2, Soane Museum Archives.

PRIMARY AND SECONDARY SOURCES

'A Letter to the Lord Provost on the Mischevous Tendency of a Scheme for Abolishing the High School of Edinburgh'. Edinburgh, 1822.
Ainslie, John. *Old and New Town of Edinburgh and Leith with the Proposed Docks*, Edinburgh, 1804.
Allison, Sir Archibald. 'On the Proposed National Monument at Edinburgh'. *Blackwood's Edinburgh Magazine 5,* no. 28 (July 1819): 377–87.

'An Act for Enlarging and Improving the Harbour at Leith; for Making a New Bason, Quays, Wharfs or Docks; for Building Warehouses; for Making New Roads and Widening Others; Leading to and from the Said Harbour; and for Empowering the Lord Provost, Magistrates and Council of the City of Edinburgh to Purchase Lands, Houses and Areas; and to Borrow Money for these Purposes'. Edinburgh, 1788.

'An Act for Building and Maintaining a Bridewell and Correction-House, in and for the City and County of Edinburgh'. Item 16 D0021 Macleod Bundles, Edinburgh City Archives. Edinburgh, 1791.

Anderson, William Pitcairn. *Silences that Speak. Records of Edinburgh's Ancient Churches and Burial Grounds, with Biographical Sketches of the Notables who Rest there*. Edinburgh: Alexander Brunton, 1931.

Andrews, Malcolm. *The Search for the Picturesque: Landscape Aesthetics and Tourism in Britain 1760–1800*. Stanford, CA: Stanford University Press, 1989.

Anno 3 George IV c.100. 'An Act to Incorporate the Contributors for the Erection of a National Monument in Scotland to Commemorate the Naval and Military Victories Obtained during the Late War'. 1822.

Anno 53 George III c.77. 'An Act for Erecting and Maintaining a New Gaol and Other Buildings for the County and City of Edinburgh'. 21 May 1813.

Anno 54 George III c.53. 'An Act for Erecting and Maintaining a New Gaol and Other Buildings for the County and City of Edinburgh'. 1814.

Anon. 'Edinburgh Observatory', *Caledonian Mercury* 8517 (3 June 1776): 4.

Anon. 'New Jail', *Scots Magazine and Edinburgh Literary Miscellany* 76 (May 1814): 393–4.

Anon. 'The Panorama, with Memoirs of its Inventor, Robert Barker, and his Late Son, Henry Aston Barker', *The Art-Journal* 3 (1857): 46-7.

APC Archaeology Group. 'Appendix 5—Archaeological Analysis', in LDN Architects for City of Edinburgh Council (eds), *Calton Hill Conservation Plan*. Edinburgh, 1998.

Armstrong, Mostyn John, Andrew Armstrong and Thomas Kitchin. 'To the Nobility, Gentry & Clergy of the Counties of Haddington, Edinburgh and Linlithgow this Map of the Three Lothians'. [Edinburgh], 1773.

Arnold, Dana. *The Metropolis and its Image: Constructing Identities for London, c. 1750–1950*. Oxford: Blackwell, 1999.

Arnold, Dana. *Re-Presenting the Metropolis: Architecture, Urban Experience and Social Life in London 1800–1840*. Aldershot: Ashgate, 2000.

Arnold, Dana (ed.). *Cultural Identities and the Aesthetics of Britishness*. Studies in Imperialism. Manchester and New York: Manchester University Press, 2004.

Arnold, Dana. *Rural Urbanism: London Landscapes in the Early Nineteenth Century*. Manchester: Manchester University Press, 2005.

Arnot, Hugo. *The History of Edinburgh, by Hugo Arnot, Esq; Advocate*. Edinburgh, 1779.

Astley, Stephen. *Robert Adam's Castles*. [London]: Soane Gallery, 2000.

Balfour, Alan. *Creating a Scottish Parliament*. Edinburgh: StudioLR, 2005.

Beaven, Brad. *Visions of Empire: Patriotism, Popular Culture and the City, 1870–1939*. Manchester: Manchester University Press, 2012.

Bentham, Jeremy. *Panopticon: Or, the Inspection-House. Containing the Idea of a New Principle of Construction Applicable to Any Sort of Establishment, in which Persons . . . Are to Be Kept . . . and in Particular to Penitentiary-Houses, Prisons . . . in a Series of Letters, Written in . . . 1787 . . . by Jeremy* Bentham. Dublin: Thomas Byrne, 1791.

Berlin, Isaiah. *Vico and Herder: Two Studies in the History of Ideas*. London: Hogarth Press, 1980.

Billings, Robert William. *The Baronial and Ecclesiastical Antiquities of Scotland*. Edinburgh: Blackwood, 1852.

Black, Charles. *Black's Picturesque Tourist Guide of Scotland. With . . . Map; Engraved Charts and Views . . . Plans of Edinburgh and Glasgow and a Copious Intinerary*. Edinburgh: A. & C. Black, 1840.

Blondel, Jacques François. *Cours d'architecture; ou, traité de la décoration, distribution & construction des bâtiments*. 2 vols. Paris, 1771.

Boyle, Anne, Colin Dickson, Alasdair McEwan and Colin MacLean. *Ruins and Remains: Edinburgh's Neglected Heritage*. Edinburgh: Scotland's Cultural Heritage, 1985.

Brodie, Allan, Jane Croom, James O. Davies and English Heritage. *English Prisons: An Architectural History*. Swindon: English Heritage, 2002.

Brown, Alice, David McCrone and Lindsay Paterson. *Politics and Society in Scotland*, 2nd edn. Basingstoke: Macmillan, 1998.

Brown, Iain Gordon. 'David Hume's Tomb: A Roman Mausoleum by Robert Adam', *Proceedings of the Society of Antiquaries of Scotland* 121 (1991): 321–422.

Brown, James. *The Epitaphs and Monumental Inscriptions in Greyfriars Churchyard, Edinburgh*. Edinburgh: J. Moodie Miller, 1867.

Browne, George Washington. *Proposal for the Scottish National War Memorial*, 1918.

Bryden, D. J. 'The Edinburgh Observatory 1736–1811: A Story of Failure', *Annals of Science* 47, no. 5 (1 Sept. 1990): 445–74.

Bryden, D. J. 'James Craig's Original Design for the Observatory on Calton Hill, May 1776', *Book of the Old Edinburgh Club* 7 (new edn). Edinburgh: self-published, 2008: 161-6.

Buchan, James. *Capital of the Mind: How Edinburgh Changed the World*. London: John Murray, 2003.

Buckham, Susan (ed.), *The Edinburgh Graveyards Project, 2013*. Edinburgh: World Monuments Fund, Edinburgh World Heritage, 2011.

Burke, Edmund. *A Philosophical Enquiry into the Origin of Our Ideas of the Sublime and Beautiful.* London: printed for R. and J. Dodsley, 1757.

Burns, Robert. 'Epistle to J. Lapraik', 1785.

Byrom, Connie. *The Edinburgh New Town Gardens: 'Blessings as Well as Beauties'.* Edinburgh: Birlinn, 2005.

Campbell, Ian and Margaret Stewart. 'The Evolution of the Medieval and Renaissance City', in *Edinburgh: The Making of a Capital City*, ed. Brian Edwards and Paul Jenkins. Edinburgh: Edinburgh University Press, 2005.

Campbell, John. *Prospectus of an Educational Institution, on Christian Principles, Proposed to be Established in Edinburgh.* Edinburgh, 1825.

Caswell, Dawn. 'The Economy of Style: Thomas S. Tait and the Interior of St Andrews House', *Architectural History* 10, no. 1 (1999): 74–89.

Clarke, Edward Daniel. *Travels in Various Countries of Europe, Asia and Africa, Vol. 6.* London, 1818.

Cleghorn, George and Architectural Institute of Scotland. *Essay on the National Monument of Scotland.* [Edinburgh] Architectural Institute of Scotland, 1852.

Cockburn Association and William Mitchell. *The Cockburn Association: A Short Account of its Objects and its Work, 1875 to 1897.* Edinburgh, 1897.

Cockburn, Henry. *A Letter to the Lord Provost on the Best Ways of Spoiling the Beauty of Edinburgh.* Edinburgh: Adam & Charles Black, 1849.

Cockburn, Henry. *Memorials of His Time.* Edinburgh: Adam and Charles Black, 1856.

Cockburn, Henry. *Journal of Henry Cockburn; Being a Continuation of the Memorials of his Time. 1831–1854.* Edinburgh: Edmonston and Douglas, 1874.

Colley, Linda. *Britons: Forging the Nation, 1707–1837*, 2nd edn. New Haven, CT and London: Yale University Press, 2005.

Colvin, Howard. *A Biographical Dictionary of British Architects 1600–1840*, New Haven, CT: Yale University Press, 1995.

Committee of Contributors to the Edinburgh Academy. 'Report by Committee', Edinburgh, April 1823.

Committee of Subscribers for the Erection of a Monument to Professor Playfair. *Proceedings Relative to the Erection of a Monument to the Late John Playfair, Esq., Professor of Natural Philosophy in the University of Edinburgh. Printed for the Information of the Subscribers*, Edinburgh, 1820–2.

Cookson, J. E. 'The Edinburgh and Glasgow Duke of Wellington Statues: Early Nineteenth-Century Unionist Nationalism as a Tory Project', *The Scottish Historical Review* 83, 1, no. 215 (2004): 23–40.

Cosh, Mary. *Edinburgh: The Golden Age.* Edinburgh: John Donald, 2003.

Craig, James. 'Plan for a General Bridewell'. [Edinburgh?], 1780.

Craske, Matthew. 'Westminster Abbey 1720–1770: A Public Pantheon Built upon Private Interest', in Richard Wrigley and Matthew Craske (eds), *Pantheons: Transformations of a Monumental Idea.* Aldershot: Routledge, 2004: 57–79.

Craske, Matthew. *The Silent Rhetoric of the Body: A History of Monumental Sculpture and Contemporary Art in England, 1720–1770.* New Haven, CT and London: Published for the Paul Mellon Centre for Studies in British Art by Yale University Press, 2007.

Crook, J. Mordaunt. *The Greek Revival: Neo-Classical Attitudes in British Architecture, 1760–1870.* London: J. Murray, 1972.

Cruft, Kitty and Andrew G. Fraser. 'The Ingenious Architect of the New Town of Edinburgh': *James Craig 1744–1795.* Edinburgh: Mercat Press, 1995.

Cullen, Fintain. 'The Art of Assimilation: Scotland and its Heroes', *Art History* 16, no. 4 (1993): 600–18.

Cullen, Fintain. 'Union and Display in Nineteenth Century Ireland', in Dana Arnnold (ed.), *Cultural Identities and the Aesthetics of Britishness.* Manchester: Manchester University Press, 2004): 111-33.

Curl, James Stevens. 'John Claudius Loudon and the Garden Cemetery Movement', *Garden History* 11, no. 2 (1983): 133–56.

Curl, James Stevens. *Death and Architecture: An Introduction to Funerary and Commemorative Buildings in the Western European Tradition, with Some Consideration of their Setting*, revd edn. Stroud: Sutton, 2002.

Davis, Terence. *John Nash. The Prince Regent's Architect.* London: Country Life 1966.

Dennison, E. Patricia. *Holyrood and Canongate: A Thousand Years of History.* Edinburgh: Birlinn, 2005.

Edinburgh Town Council. 'Edinburgh Town Council Minutes'. Vol. 175. Edinburgh, 1817.

Edinburgh Town Council. 'Address from the Town Council of Edinburgh on the Subject of the New Buildings for the High School, of which the Foundation was Laid on 28th July 1825', Edinburgh, 1825.

Fehlmann, Marc. 'A Building from which Derived "All that is Good": Observations on the Intended Reconstruction of the Parthenon on Calton Hill', *Nineteenth Century Art Worldwide* 4, no. 3 (Autumn 2005): http://www.19thc-artworldwide.org/autumn05/207-a-building-from-which-derived-qall-that-is-goodq-observations-on-the-intended- reconstruction-of-the-parthenon-on-calton-hill

Fehlmann, Marc. 'As Greek as it Gets: British Attempts to Recreate the Parthenon', *Rethinking History* 11, no. 3 (September 2007): 353–77.

'Festival in Commemoration of Robert Burns; And to Promote a Subscription to Erect a National Monument to his Memory at Edinburgh: Held at the Freemasons' Tavern, in London. With an Appendix, Containing the Resolutions of the General Meeting, April 24, 1819, Together with a List of the Subscribers', London, 5 June 1819.

Finlay, R. J. 'Scottish Nationalism and Scottish Politics 1900–1979', in Michael Lynch (ed.), *Scotland, 1850–1979: Society, Politics and the Union.* London: The Historical Association, 1993: 19-25.

Finlay, R. J. 'Caledonia or North Britain?', in Dauvit Broun, Richard J. Finlay and Michael Lynch (eds), *Image and Identity: The Making and Re-Making of Scotland through the Ages*. Edinburgh: John Donald, 1998.

Fisher, Ian. 'Thomas Hamilton', in *Scottish Pioneers of the Greek Revival*, ed. David Walker and Scottish Georgian Society. [Edinburgh]: Scottish Georgian Society, 1984: 37-42.

Forrest, Robert. *Descriptive Catalogue of Statuary from the Chisel of Mr Robert Forrest*. Edinburgh: Thomas Allan & Co., 1835.

Forrest, Robert. *Descriptive Account of the Exhibition of Statuary, National Monument, Calton Hill, Edinburgh, by Robert Forrest, Sculptor*. [Edinburgh: s.n.], 1846.

Forrest, Robert. *Forrest's Statuary, within Area of National Monument, Calton Hill, Edinburgh . . . Catalogue of Statues*. [Edinburgh?], 1850.

Fraser, Andrew G. *The Building of Old College: Adam, Playfair & the University of Edinburgh*. Edinburgh: Edinburgh University Press, 1989.

Fry, Michael. *The Scottish Empire*. East Linton: Tuckwell Press, 2001.

Gavine, David. 'The Calton Hill Observatories', *Journal of the Astronomical Society of Edinburgh,* 3 (October 1981): v.

Gavine, David. 'Astronomy in Scotland 1745–1900', PhD thesis, Open University, 1982.

Gavine, David and Laurence Hunter. *A Caledonian Acropolis: The Story of Calton Hill*. Edinburgh: Scotland's Cultural Heritage, 1982.

Gifford, John, Colin McWilliam, David Walker and Christopher Wilson. *Edinburgh*. The Buildings of Scotland: Pevsner Architectural Guides. London: Penguin, 1991.

Gifford, John. 'The National Monument of Scotland', *Architectural Heritage* 25 (2014): 43–83.

Gilpin, William. *Observations on the River Wye, and Several Parts of South Wales . . . Relative Chiefly to Picturesque Beauty; Made in the Summer of . . . 1770*. London, 1782.

Gilpin, William. 'Three Essays on Picturesque Beauty; on Picturesque Travel; and on Sketching Landscape: To which is Added a Poem, on Landscape Painting. By William Gilpin'. London: printed for R. Blamire, 1792.

Godwin, William. *Essay on Sepulchres: Or, a Proposal for Erecting some Memorial of the Illustrious Dead in All Ages on the Spot where their Remains have been Interred*. London, 1809.

Gordon, George Hamilton, Earl of Aberdeen. *An Inquiry into the Principles of Beauty in Grecian Architecture; With an Historical View of the Rise and Progress of the Art in Greece*. London: J. Murray, 1822.

Gordon, James. 'Edinodunensis Tabulam'. Amsterdam?: National Library of Scotland, 1647.

Government of Great Britain. *Journal of the House of Commons*, 'An Act for Erecting and Maintaining a New Gaol and Other Buildings for the County and City of Edinburgh' (4 November 1813–1 November 1814) Anno 54 George III c.53.

Gow, Ian. 'C. R. Cockerell's Design for the Northern

Athenian Parthenon', *Journal of the Architectural Heritage Society of Scotland* 16 (1989): 20–5.

Grant, James. *Cassell's Old and New Edinburgh: Its History, its People, and its Places*. London and New York: Cassell, Petter, Galpin & Co., 1881.

Groseclose, Barbara S. *British Sculpture and the Company Raj: Church Monuments and Public Statuary in Madras, Calcutta, and Bombay to 1858*. Newark/London: University of Delaware Press; Associated University Presses, 1995.

Guidicini, Giovanna. 'A Scottish Triumphal Path of Learning at George Heriot's Hospital, Edinburgh', *International Review of Scottish Studies* 35 (2010): 65-96.

Hadden, James Cuthbert. *George Thomson the Friend of Burns. His Life & Correspondence*. London, 1898.

Hansard, T. C. 'Parliamentary Debates'.

Hay, Ian. *Their Name Liveth: The Book of the Scottish National War Memorial*. London: J. Lane, The Bodley Head, 1931.

Holloway, James, Lindsay Errington and National Gallery of Scotland. *The Discovery of Scotland: The Appreciation of Scottish Scenery through Two Centuries of Painting*. Edinburgh: National Gallery of Scotland, 1978.

Hoock, Holger. 'The British Military Pantheon in St Paul's Cathedral: The State, Cultural Patriotism, and the Politics of National Monuments, c. 1790–1820', in *Pantheons: Transformations of a Monumental Idea*, ed. Richard Wrigley and Matthew Craske. Aldershot: Ashgate, 2004: 81–105.

Howard, John. *The State of the Prisons in England and Wales, with Preliminary Observations, and on Account of Some Foreign Prisons*. Warrington, 1777.

Howard, John. *The State of the Prisons in England and Wales, with Preliminary Observations, and an Account of Some Foreign Prisons*. (Appendix). Warrington, 1777.

Hunter, Thomas and Robert Porter. 'Report on the Common Good of the City of Edinburgh'. Edinburgh, 1905.

Irvine, Malcolm Sinclair. *The Calton of Caldtoun of Edinburgh 1631–1887*. [Edinburgh: s.n.], 1887.

Jackson, Gordon. *The History and Archaeology of Ports*. Tadworth: World's Work, 1983.

Jenkyns, Richard. *Westminster Abbey*, Wonders of the World. London: Profile Books, 2004.

Johnson, Jim and Louis Stanley Rosenburg. *Renewing Old Edinburgh: The Enduring Legacy of Patrick Geddes*. Glendaruel [Edinburgh]: Argyll Publishing; Scottish Centre for Conservation Studies, 2011.

Kay, William. 'Robert Adam: Some Responses to a Scottish Background', *Architectural Heritage* 4 (1993): 23–38.

Kennedy, Roger G. and John M. Hall. *Greek Revival America*. New York: Stewart, Tabori & Chang, 1989.

Kerr, Charles H. *Plan and Estimate for Enlarging and Improving the Town and Harbour of Leith*. [Edinburgh], 1787.

Kerr, Henry F. *Proposed Development of Calton Hill as an Open Air Valhalla or Park of Memories and Hall of Recreation*, 1909.

Knight, Richard Payne. *The Landscape: A Didactic Poem, Addressed to Uvedale Price*. London, 1794.

Kornmeier, Uta. 'Madame Tussaud's as a Popular Pantheon', in Richard Wrigley and Matthew Craske (eds), *Pantheons: Transformations of a Monumental Idea*. Aldershot: Routledge, 2004: 81–105.

Lamont, Stewart. *When Scotland Ruled the World: The Story of the Golden Age of Genius, Creativity and Exploration*. London: HarperCollins, 2001.

Law-Dunbar and Naismith (LDN) Architects. 'Calton Hill Conservation Plan', Edinburgh, 1999.

Leith Walk Research Group. *Leith Walk and Greenside: A Social History*. [Edinburgh]: [The Group], 1979.

le Roy, Julien-David. *Les Ruines des plus beaux monuments de la Grèce*. Paris: H. L. Guerin & L. F. Delatour, 1758.

Levitt, I. (ed.), *The Scottish Office: Depression and Reconstruction, 1919–1959*. Vol. 5, Scottish History Society. Edinburgh: Pillans & Wilson, 1992.

Levitt, I. 'Scottish Sentiment, Administrative Devolution and Westminster, 1885–1964', in Michael Lynch (ed.), *Scotland, 1850–1979: Society, Politics and the Union*. London: The Historical Association, 1993: 35-42.

Lewis, A. R. 'The Builders of Edinburgh's New Town 1767–1795', PhD thesis. University of Edinburgh, 2006.

Lincoln Monument in Memory of the Scottish-American Soldiers. Edinburgh: William Blackwood and Sons, 1893.

Linning, M. *Memoranda Publica*. [Edinburgh: s.n.], 1834.

Littlejohn, Henry J. 'Report on the Sanitary Condition of the City of Edinburgh'. Edinburgh, 1863.

Littlejohn, Henry J. 'Report on the City Cemeteries'. Edinburgh, 1883.

Llewellyn, Nigel and Victoria and Albert Museum. *The Art of Death: Visual Culture in the English Death Ritual c.1500-c.1800*. London: Reaktion, 1991.

Lord Provosts Committee. 'Report by the Lord Provosts Committee Regarding Trinity College Church', 25 January 1853. SL152, Edinburgh City Archive.

Loudon, John Claudius. 'The Principles of Landscape-Gardening and of Landscape-Architecture Applied to the Laying out of Public Cemeteries and the Improvement of Churchyards; Including Observations on the Working and General Management of Cemeteries and Burial-Grounds', *The Gardeners Magazine and Register of Rural and Domestic Improvement*, 1843.

Lowrey, John. 'Robert Adam and Edinburgh', *Rassegna* 64 (1995): 26-33.

Lowrey, John. 'The Urban Design of Edinburgh's Calton Hill'. Paper presented at the St Andrews 'Studies in the History of Scottish Architecture and Design. The New Town Phenomenon: The Second Generation'. [St Andrews], 2000.

Lowrey, John. 'From Caesarea to Athens: Greek Revival Edinburgh and the Question of Scottish Identity within the

Unionist State'. *Journal of the Society of Architectural Historians* 60, no. 2 (2001): 136-57.

Lowrey, John. 'Architect's Monuments at Greyfriars'. Paper presented at the Death, Commemoration and Memory Conference. University of Edinburgh, 2010.

Lowrey, John. 'The Polis and the Portico: The High School of the Athens of the North'. Paper given at Cast Collection Conference. Edinburgh College of Art, 2011.

Lowrey, John and Anthony Lewis. 'James Craig: Architect of the First New Town of Edinburgh', *Architectural Heritage: The journal of the Architectural Heritage Society of Scotland* 5 (1994): 39–50.

MacClintock, Lucy. 'Monumentality versus Suitability: Viollet-le-Duc's Saint Gimer at Carcassonne', *Journal of the Society of Architectural Historians* 40, no. 3 (1981): 218–35.

MacFarlane, Dana 'The Fishwives of Newhaven'. The National Galleries of Scotland Research Conference. Edinburgh, 2013.

MacInnes, Ranald. 'Robert Adam's Public Buildings', *Architectural Heritage: The Journal of the Architectural Heritage Society of Scotland* 4 (1994): 10–22.

Macintyre, Gordon. *Dugald Stewart: The Pride and Ornament of Scotland*. Eastbourne: Sussex Academic Press, 2003.

MacKenzie, John M. 'Empire and National Identities: The Case of Scotland', *Transactions of the Royal Historical Society* 8 (1998): 215–31.

Macleod, Jenny. 'By Scottish Hands, with Scottish Money, on Scottish Soil: The Scottish National War Memorial and National Identity', *Journal of British Studies* 49, no. 1, Scotland special issue (2010): 73–96.

Macmillan, Duncan and Antonia Reeve. *Scotland's Shrine: The Scottish National War Memorial*. London: Lund Humphries, 2014.

Markus, Thomas A. 'Buildings for the Sad, the Bad and the Mad in Urban Scotland 1780–1830', in *Order in Space and Society*, ed. Thomas A. Markus. Edinburgh: Mainstream, 1982: 25–114.

Markus, Thomas A., ed. *Order in Space and Society*: Mainstream, 1982.

Markus, Thomas A. *Buildings & Power: Freedom and Control in the Origin of Modern Building Types*. London: Routledge, 1993.

McKean, Charles. *The Scottish Thirties: An Architectural Introduction*. Edinburgh: Scottish Academic Press, 1987.

McKean, Charles. *Edinburgh: Portrait of a City*. London: Century, 1991.

McKean, Charles. 'The Incivility of Edinburgh's New Town', in *The Neo-Classical Town: Scottish Contributions to Urban Design since 1750*, ed. W. A. Brogden. Edinburgh: Rutland, 1996: 36-45.

McKean, Charles. 'Twinning Cities: Modernisation Versus Improvement', in Brian Edwards and Paul Jenkins (eds), *Edinburgh: The Making of a Capital City*. Edinburgh: Edinburgh University Press, 2005: 42-63.

McKean, Charles. 'Improvement and Modernisation in

Everyday Enlightenment Scotland', in Elizabeth A. Foyster and Christopher A. Whatley (eds), *A History of Everyday Life in Scotland*. Edinburgh: Edinburgh University Press, 2010.

McKee, K. Carter, 'Monument to the Memory of Robert Burns on Calton Hill, Edinburgh', *Architectural Heritage* 4 (2013): 21–39.

McLaren, Martha. *British India & British Scotland, 1780–1830: Career Building, Empire Building, and a Scottish School of Thought on Indian Governance*. Series on International, Political, and Economic History. Akron, OH: University of Akron Press, 2001.

McQueen, B. 'Appendix 1—Archival and Documentary Research', in LDN Architects for City of Edinburgh Council, *Calton Hill Conservation Plan*.Edinburgh, 1999.

Mears, Frank and Ramsay Traquair. 'Proposals for the National Monument, Edinburgh'. *The Blue Blanket* 1 (January 1912): 68-80.

Mein, Robert. *The City Cleaned, and Country Improven. By Following out this Proposed Method, for Paying only One Penny per Week, for an 8l. Rent, and so Proportionally by the Possessors of each Bounds, Consisting of 800l. Of Yearly Rent, which is 50 Houses, at 16l. Rent*. Edinburgh, 1760.

Mein, Robert. *The Edinburgh Paradise Regain'd, on the City Set at Liberty, to Propagate and Improve her Trade and Commerce . . . By a Merchant-Citizen . . .* Edinburgh, 1764.

Miller, Hugh. 'Trinity College Church versus the Burns Monument', *The Witness*, 5 March 1856: 6.

Miller, William. 'Politics in the Scottish City', in George Gordon (ed.), *Perspectives of the Scottish City*. [Aberdeen]: Aberdeen University Press, 1985: 180–211.

Minto, Sir Gilbert Elliot. 'Proposals for Carrying on Certain Public Works in the City of Edinburgh'. Edinburgh, 1752.

Mitchell, Ann K. *The People of Calton Hill*. Edinburgh: Mercat Press, 1993.

Mitchell, J. F. *Some Edinburgh Monumental Inscriptions*. [Edinburgh]: self-published, 1961.

Mitchell, John F. *Edinburgh Monumental Inscriptions (pre-1855). Vol. 1, Old Calton Burial Ground, New Calton Burial Ground*. Ed. Stuart E. Fleming. Edinburgh: Scottish Genealogy Society, 2003.

Mitchell, William. *The National Monument to be Completed for the Scottish National Gallery on the Model of the Parthenon at Athens: An Appeal to the Scottish People*. London: Adam and Charles Black, 1906.

Mitchell, William. *The National Monument to be Completed for the Scottish National Gallery on the Model of the Parthenon at Athens: An Appeal to the Scottish People*. London: A. and C. Black, April 1907.

Mitchell, William. *Queen Victoria and the Scottish People*. London, 1911.

Mitchell, William and C. I. Lacock. *A New National Patriotic Poem or Song Entitled* 'The Royal Standard of Our Queen'. London, 1900.

Monteith, Robert. *An Theatre of Mortality: Or, the Illustrious Inscriptions Extant Upon the Several Monuments Erected over Dead Bodies (of the Sometime Honourable Persons) Buried within the Greyfriars Church-Yard; and Other Churches within the City of Edinburgh and Suburbs*. Edinburgh, 1704.

Morris, Richard J. 'Civil Society and the Nature of Urbanism: Britain 1750–1850', *Urban History* 25, no. 3 (1998): 289–301.

Morris, Richard J. and Graeme Morton. 'The Re-Making of Scotland: A Nation within a Nation, 1850–1920', in *Scotland, 1850–1979: Society, Politics and the Union*, ed. Michael Lynch, London: The Historical Association, 1993: 13-18.

Morton, Graeme. 'Civil Society, Municipal Government and the State: Enshrinement, Empowerment and Legitimacy, Scotland 1800–1929', *Urban History* 25, no. 3 (1998): 348–67.

Morton, Graeme. 'What If?: The Significance of Scotland's Missing Nationalism in the 19th Century', in Dauvit Broun, Richard J. Finlay and Michael Lynch (eds), *Image and Identity: The Making and Re-Making of Scotland Through the Ages*. Edinburgh: John Donald, 1998: 157–76.

Morton, Graeme. *Unionist Nationalism: Governing Urban Scotland, 1830–1860*. East Linton: Tuckwell, 1999.

Mudie, Robert. *The Modern Athens: A Dissection and Demonstration of Men and Things in the Scotch Capital*. 2nd edn. London: Printed for Knight and Lacey, 1825.

Murray, Katharine Marjory. *Working Partnership. Being the Lives of John George, 8th Duke of Atholl . . . and of his Wife Katharine Marjory Ramsay*. London: A. Barker, 1958.

Naik, Anuradha S. and Margaret C. H. Stewart. 'The Hellenization of Edinburgh: Cityscape, Architecture, and the Athenian Cast Collection '. *Journal of the Society of Architectural Historians* 66, no. 3 (2007): 366–89.

Nash, John. '1st Report to HM Commissioners of Woods, Forests and Land Revenues'. {Edinburgh?}, 1809.

Nasmyth, James and Samuel Smiles. *James Nasmyth, Engineer. An Autobiography*. Popular edn. London: John Murray, 1897.

Noble, Andrew. 'Versions of the Scottish Pastoral: The Literati and the Tradition 1780–1830', in Thomas A. Markus (ed.), *Order in Space and Society*. Edinburgh: Mainstream, 1982: 263–310.

'Obituary—Mr Robert Forrest, Sculptor', *The Gentleman's Magazine*, March 1853.

P.A.R. & O.D.E.. 'Account of the Observatory on Calton Hill', *Scots Magazine* 50, (December 1788): 605–6 and 33–4.

Paton, Henry M. 'The Barony of Calton, Part I', *Book of the Old Edinburgh Club* XVIII (1932): 33–78.

Paton, Henry M. 'The Barony of Calton, Part II', *Book of the Old Edinburgh Club* XIX (1933): 92–141.

Paton, Joseph Noel. *National Memorial of the War of Independence under Wallace and Bruce and of its Results in the Union of England and Scotland, to be Erected in the Scottish Metropolis*. Edinburgh, 1859.

Paxton, Roland, J. Shipway and Royal Commission on the Ancient and Historical Monuments and Constructions of

Scotland. *Scotland—Lowlands and Borders*, Civil Engineering Heritage. London: Thomas Telford, 2007.

Peter McGowan Associates. '064 New Calton Burial Ground', in *Edinburgh: Survey of Gardens and Designed Landscapes*: Edinburgh: City of Edinburgh Council, 2007.

Petrie, Ann. 'Scottish Culture and the First World War, 1914–1939'. Dundee: University of Dundee, 2006.

Phillipson, N. T. 'Nationalism and Ideology', in J. N. Wolfe (ed.), *Government and Nationalism in Scotland: An Enquiry by Members of the University of Edinburgh*. Edinburgh: Edinburgh University Press, 1969: iii-vii.

Playfair, William. *Report to the Right Honourable the Lord Provost, Magistrates, and Council of the City of Edinburgh . . . On a Plan for Laying out the New Town between Edinburgh and Leith, Etc.*. Edinburgh, 1819.

Port, M. H. *600 New Churches: The Church Building Commission, 1818–1856*. New edn. Reading: Spire Books, 2006.

'Proposed Monument to the Memory of Robert Burns—List of Subscribers'. Pamphlet 1832, GD113/5/114b/4/12, Papers of the Innes family of Stow, Peeblesshire, National Archives of Scotland, Edinburgh.

Poulot, Dominique. 'Pantheons in Eighteenth-Century France: Temple, Museum, Pyramid', in Richard Wrigley and Matthew Craske (eds) *Pantheons: Transformations of a Monumental Idea*. Abingdon: Routledge, 2004: 123–45.

Price, John Vladimir. 'Ossian and the Canon in the Scottish Enlightenment', in Howard Gaskill (ed.), *Ossian Revisited*. Edinburgh: Edinburgh University Press, 1991: 109-28.

Price, Sir Uvedale. *An Essay on the Picturesque as Compared with the Sublime and the Beautiful: And on the Use of Studying Pictures for the Purpose of Improving Real Landscape*. 2 vols. London, 1794.

Purves, Graeme A. S. *The Life and Work of Sir Frank Mears: Planning with a Cultural Perspective*. Edinburgh: Heriot-Watt University, 1987.

Reed, Peter. 'Form and Context: A Study of Georgian Edinburgh', in *Order in Space and Society*, ed. Thomas A. Markus: Mainstream, 1982: 115-53.

Reed, Peter. 'Georgian Edinburgh', in Thomas A. Markus (ed.), *Order in Space and Society*. Edinburgh: Mainstream, 1982: 115-54.

Repton, Humphry. *A Letter to Uvedale Price, Esq. [Commenting on his 'Essay on the Picturesque', Etc.]*. London, 1794.

Rhind, David. *Documents and Correspondence Relative to Trinity College Church*. Edinburgh: Thomas Constable, 1848.

Richardson, Harriet and Ian H. Goodall. *English Hospitals 1660–1948: A Survey of their Architecture and Design*. Swindon: Royal Commission on the Historical Monuments of England, 1998.

Robertson, Andrew. *The Parthenon Adapted to the Purpose of a National Monument to Commemorate the Victories of the Late War; Proposed to be Erected in Trafalgar Square or Hyde Park [with Plans]*. London, 1838.

Rock, Joe. *Thomas Hamilton Architect 1784–1858*. [Edinburgh?]: J. Rock, 1984.

Rock, Joe. 'Robert Forrest (1789–1852) and his Exhibition on the Calton Hill', *Book of the Old Edinburgh Club* 7 (New Series) (2008): 127–38.

Rodger, Johnny. *The Hero Building: An Architecture of Scottish National Identity*. Surrey: Ashgate, 2015.

Rodger, Johnny and Gerard Carruthers. *Fickle Man: Robert Burns in the 21st Century*. Dingwall: Sandstone, 2009.

Rodger, Richard. *The Transformation of Edinburgh: Land, Property and Trust in the Nineteenth Century*. Cambridge: Cambridge University Press, 2001.

Ross, William C. A. *The Royal High School*. Edinburgh, 1934.

Rowan, Alistair John. *Vaulting Ambition: The Adam Brothers. Contractors to the Metropolis in the Reign of George III*. London: Sir John Soane's Museum, 2007.

Rowan, Alistair and Soane Gallery. 'Bob the Roman': *Heroic Antiquity & the Architecture of Robert Adam*. London: The Soane Gallery, 2003.

Royal Commission on the Ancient and Historical Monuments and Constructions of Scotland. *An Inventory of the Ancient and Historical Monuments of the City of Edinburgh, with the Thirteenth Report of the Commission*. Edinburgh: HM Stationery Office, 1951.

Scott, Walter. *Hints Addressed to the Inhabitants of Edinburgh, and Others, in Prospect of His Majesty's Visit*. Edinburgh: Printed for Bell and Bradfute, Manners and Miller, Archibald Constable and Co., William Blackwood, Waugh and Innes and John Robertson, 1822.

Shepherd, Thomas H. and John Britton. *Modern Athens! Displayed in a Series of Views: Or Edinburgh in the 19th Century: Exhibiting the Whole of the New Buildings, Modern Improvements, Antiquities, and Picturesque Scenery, of the Scottish Metropolis and its Environs*. London: Jones & Co., 1829.

Slezer, John. *The North Prospect of the City of Edenburgh*. Edinburgh: National Library of Scotland, 1693.

Smith, John. *Epitaphs and Monumental Inscriptions in Old Calton Burying Ground, Edinburgh*. Handwritten and self-published, 1907.

Smith, John. *The Calton Hill, Edinburgh and its Monuments*, Edinburgh: n.d.

Spanou, Sorina. 'Edinburgh Trams Project: South Leith Parish Church Graveyard, Constitution Street', in *Discovery and Excavation in Scotland*, Volume 11. Wiltshire: Cathedral Communications Limited, 2010.

Stark, William. *Report to the Right Honourable the Lord Provost, Magistrates, and Council of the City of Edinburgh, and the Governors of George Heriot's Hospital . . . On the Plans for Laying out the Grounds for Buildings between Edinburgh and Leith*. Edinburgh: Printed by A. Smellie, 1814.

Stechow, Wolfgang. *Dutch Landscape Painting of the Seventeenth Century*. [London]: Phaidon, 1966.

Steuart, D. and A. Cockburn. *General Heads of a Plan for*

Erecting a New Prison and Bridewell in the City of Edinburgh. Edinburgh, 1782.

Steven, W. *The History of the High School of Edinburgh.* Edinburgh: Maclachlan & Stewart, 1849.

Stevenson, David. *Life of Robert Stevenson, Civil Engineer.* Edinburgh, 1878.

Stevenson, Sara, David Octavius Hill, Robert Adamson and Scottish National Portrait Gallery. *Hill and Adamson's the Fishermen and Women of the Firth of Forth.* Edinburgh: Scottish National Portrait Gallery, 1991.

Stuart, James and Nicholas Revett. *The Antiquities of Athens Measured and Delineated by James Stuart F.R.S. and F.S.A. and Nicholas Revett Painters and Architects.* 4 vols. London: John Haberkorn, 1762.

Summerson, John. *The Life and Work of John Nash, Architect.* London: George Allen & Unwin, 1980.

Summerson, John. *Architecture in Britain, 1530 to 1830.* 9th edn. New Haven, CT and London: Yale University Press, 1993.Summerson, John and John Nash. *John Nash. Architect to King George Iv.* London: George Allen & Unwin, 1949.

Turnbull, Michael T. R .B. *The Edinburgh Graveyard Guide*, Edinburgh: Scottish Cultural Press, 2006.

Tyrrell, Alex and Michael T. Davis. 'Bearding the Tories: The Commemoration of the Scottish Political Martyrs of 1793–94', in *Contested Sites: Commemoration, Memorial and Popular Politics in Nineteenth Century Britain*, ed. Paul A. Pickering and Alex Tyrrell. Aldershot: Ashgate, 2004; 25-56

University of Edinburgh, Department of Extra-Mural Studies; Edinburgh New Town Conservation Committee. *The Calton Conference: National Shrine, City Park and Outstanding Vantage Point: Does Edinburgh Make the Most of This National Asset?* Edinburgh: Edinburgh New Town Conservation Committee, 1983.

Walker, David (ed.), *Scottish Pioneers of the Greek Revival.* [Edinburgh]: Scottish Georgian Society, 1984.

Walker, David. *St Andrew's House: An Edinburgh Controversy, 1912–1939.* Edinburgh: Historic Buildings and Monuments, Development Department for the Secretary of State for Scotland, 1989.

Walker, Frank. 'National Romanticism and the Architecture of the City', in George Gordon (ed.), *Perspectives of the Scottish City.* [Aberdeen]: Aberdeen University Press, 1985: 125-59.

Ward, David. 'Jane Brettle's Allegorical Blueprint', *Untitled: A Review of Contemporary Art*, no. 10 (1996): 7–8.

Watkin, David. *The Life and Work of C. R. Cockerell.* Studies in Architecture. London: Zwemmer, 1974.

Whinney, Margaret Dickens. *Sculpture in Britain, 1530–1830.* Harmondsworth: Penguin, 1964.

Wilcox, Scott Barnes. 'The Panorama and Related Exhibitions in London', MLitt thesis. Edinburgh: University of Edinburgh, 1976.

Willsher, Betty. 'Midlothian and Edinburgh', in *Survey of Scottish Gravestones*. National Monuments Record for Scotland, c. 1985.

Willsher, Betty. 'Midlothian and Edinburgh', in *Survey of Scottish Gravestones*: National Monuments Record for Scotland, c. 1990s? Folder of notes.

Wood, William. *An Essay on National and Sepulchral Monuments.* London: William Miller, 1808.

Yarrington, Alison. *The Commemoration of the Hero 1800–1864: Monuments to the British Victors of the Napoleonic Wars*, Oxford: Garland, 1988.

Youngson, A. J. *The Making of Classical Edinburgh, 1750–1840.* Edinburgh: Edinburgh University Press, 1988.

NEWSPAPER ARTICLES

Alison, Sir Archibald, 'On the Proposed National Monument at Edinburgh', *Blackwood's Edinburgh Magazine,* 28 July 1819.

Anon, 'Burns' Monument', *Caledonian Mercury*, 26 February 1824.

Anon, 'Burns Monument, Calton Hill', *Scotsman*, 12 July 1837.

Anon, *Caledonian Gazetteer*, 1, 31 May 1776.

Anon, *Caledonian Mercury*, 8517, 3 June 1776.

Anon, *Caledonian Mercury,* 10, 27 August 1787.

Anon, *Chambers Journal*, 45, 8 December 1832.

Anon, 'Court of Kings Bench, Westminster, April 30th', *Leeds Mercury*, 4 May 1822.

Anon, *Edinburgh Advertiser,* 8 December 1840.

Anon, *Edinburgh Evening Courant*, 1 June 1776.

Anon, 'Equestrian Statues', *Scotsman,* 28 July 1832.

Anon, 'Forrest's Statuary—Calton Hill', *Scotsman*, 15 September 1832.

Anon, 'Monument in Memory of Burns', *Aberdeen Journal*, 27 August 1828.

Anon, 'The National Monument', *Scotsman,* 18 July 1849.

Anon, 'New Jail', *Scots Magazine and Edinburgh Literary Miscellany*, 76, May 1814, 393-4.

Anon, 'The Royal Scottish Academy', *Builder*, 5 July 1918.

Anon, 'Scotland Yet', *Scotsman,* 22 October 1834.

Anon, *Scotsman,* 26 December 1944.

Miller, Hugh, 'Trinity College Church Versus the Burns Monument', *The Witness*, 5 March 1856.

O.D.E. & P.A.R., 'Account of the Observatory on Calton Hill', *Scots Magazine*, 50, December 1788, 606.

Scots Magazine, 38, July 1776, 393-394.

Scotsman, 19 January 1834.

Timon, 'View of Different Proposals for the Situation of the New Jail, with the Plan of a Bridge and Road across the Calton Hill', *Scots Magazine and Edinburgh Literary Miscellany*, 76, January 1814, 4–5.

Index

Entries in *italic* denote illustrations. Entries with an 'n' suffix, e.g. '185n', refer to the Notes at the end of the book.